M000281721

Communication and the Globalization of Culture

Communication and the Globalization of Culture

Beyond Tradition and Borders

Shaheed Nick Mohammed

LEXINGTON BOOKS
A division of
ROWMAN & LITTLEFIELD PUBLISHERS, INC.
Lanham • Boulder • New York • Toronto • Plymouth, UK

Published by Lexington Books
A division of Rowman & Littlefield Publishers, Inc.
A wholly owned subsidiary of The Rowman & Littlefield Publishing Group, Inc.
4501 Forbes Boulevard, Suite 200, Lanham, Maryland 20706
http://www.lexingtonbooks.com

Estover Road, Plymouth PL6 7PY, United Kingdom

British Library Cataloguing in Publication Information Available

Library of Congress Cataloging-in-Publication Data

Mohammed, Shaheed Nick, 1968–
Communication and the globalization of culture : beyond tradition and borders / Shaheed Nick
Mohammed.
p. cm.
Includes bibliographical references and index.
ISBN 978-0-7391-6651-2 (cloth : alk. paper) — ISBN 978-0-7391-6652-9 (ebook)
1. Culture and globalization. 2. Communication. 3. Mass media. I. Title.
HM621.M65 2011
303.48'209—dc23
2011021136

Printed in the United States of America

To my dearest Wendie
and for Sarah

For my parents,
Shaffie and Hassina,
and for
Salima, Nabeel, and Shana

Contents

Preface

This work began with a simple observation. A brilliant young scholar had just joined our faculty at the American University of Kuwait where I was heading up the Communications program. I was in the process of giving her a quick tour of the surrounding town, Salmiya, when we stopped at a shopping mall for lunch. It was there that we reflected on the remarkable similarity of the food court to any other in the world despite the fact that we were in the Middle East. She was originally from Hungary and I am originally from the small Caribbean nation of Trinidad and Tobago. We both had lived and studied in the United States as well. Yet, the amazing sameness of this scene to almost any other in the world struck us both. There was a McDonald's, a Pizza Hut, a KFC, with a few local counters thrown in for good measure (but that is also true of other places). Except for the duplicate Arabic menus, we could have been almost anywhere else on the planet.

When I first approached the issue from a cultural/communications point of view and with reference to most of the material coming from those fields, it seemed pretty straightforward. It was clear that the multinational corporations were in a process of leveling the cultural landscape and erecting in its place a homogenized McCulture. It was clear that local cultures were in danger from this steamroller process.

However, in the years of research that would follow, which involved interviews and literature searches as well as much personal reflection, I would come to question many of those ideas. In fact, I would come to question, as well, the very foundations upon which I had been trained in intercultural communication. I heard Kuwaitis speak, for example, of breaking their religious fasts at Burger King. I realized that the Burger King franchise is owned by a Kuwaiti and that Kuwaitis eat American food and watch American movies (as do the Egyptians, Lebanese, and so many others that I would encounter) not because they are poor hapless brainwashed creatures, but because they choose to do these things.

So yet I argued that their choices were conditioned by extra-cultural forces dominated by multinational corporate interests. But as I reflected on even that position, I became more and more aware that these people I would encounter, and I myself, and my Hungarian friend, were all ourselves part of a global environment. In examining my own various and multiple identities, I came to the realization that it was not the state of global culture that needed investigating, but rather, our assumptions about culture itself. It was at this point that the fragility of our notions of culture became apparent. From this perspective it became possible to interrogate many of the basic notions of culture as somehow organic and as tradition in some sacrosanct sense. I began to focus more of my attention on some of the less popular ideas in cultural analysis—to some of the cynics who have the gall to contend that much of what we consider culture is either arbitrary or just plain made up. This was a personally harrowing phase for me. After all, I was trained in intercultural communications. Cultural differences, respect for them, and their importance—these were my stock in trade—the things in which I was an expert.

Yet, when I gave up my insistence on the primacy of culture and was willing to engage in a dispassionate analysis of the roots of our cultural imaginings, I was also able to give up my old friend (culture—not the Hungarian).

The food court is still there in Salmiya. It is still like so many others in Poughkeepsie, New York, London, Paris, and Addis Ababa, a mixture of the global and the local. Like its patrons, it expresses culture not only as a set of traditions, but also as a new set of inherited norms and practices, easily woven into the strictures of traditional culture but at the same time subversive of it. This dynamic relationship is not a new one, but one which has arguably become more intense and rapid with the global scope of media and information flows, including not only mass media messages, but also interpersonal contacts and transnational family ties. Globalized culture is at once what Kraidy (2005) has called *hybridity*, and what Varan (1998) called *erosion*. Yet it is also protects persistent divisions, prejudices, and exclusions.

I argue in the following pages that the very idea of the existence of culture is in serious need of revision. This of course, requires some qualification and some explanation—if for no other reason than the fact that you are reading this now and you are probably awash in cultural symbols all around you. It is this contradiction that eventually took up most of my attention. With any luck, it will also occupy some of yours.

Introduction

Ideas about the subversion of culture are not new. Huxley ([1932] 1998) and Orwell (1949) both envisioned the death of culture at the hands of technology and politics, respectively. In both cases "natural" human culture is replaced by the social creations of powerful classes. A culture of sorts still exists in each case, but implicit in both works is the notion that real human culture has been sacrificed.

In Huxley's ([1932] 1998) *Brave New World*, society is reordered along the lines of efficient production and humans become soulless cogs in the technological production process. This theme is echoed in numerous popular culture expressions including Charlie Chaplin's (1936) *Modern Times* and George Lucas's ([1971] 2004) *THX 1138*. George Orwell's (1949) masterpiece *Nineteen Eighty-Four* envisioned a world where all aspects of culture, including the production of newspapers, books, magazines, and films, were part of the process of political domination being imposed on the population.

Common to both Huxley and Orwell's visions was the notion of a powerful central authority imposing structural and social changes necessary for the death of culture. Today, it is increasingly apparent that neither technology nor politics alone, nor even the power of totalitarianism in its many traditional forms has been enough to eradicate human culture on any significant global scale.

The globalization of the ironically termed "culture industries" (Adorno, 2007) and their multinational parent and cousin corporations have been portrayed as posing the most important threats to culture yet faced by humankind. Mattelart (1979) drew attention to the impact of global corporations on culture and their role as the "ideological apparatuses of imperialism." Clinard (1990, 1) called the power of large corporations "awesome," noting that today "transnational corporations dominate the Western world in much the same manner in which the Roman Catholic Church dominated medieval society."

According to Rantanen (2005) serious academic studies of globalization began in the early 1990s but although most analysts agree on the pivotal role of media and communications, scholars of communications were lacking in their contribution. Rantanen noted that despite the central role of media in the process, communications scholars have tended to miss the boat, writing that

> most theorists agree that there is practically no globalization without media and communications, as many of the definitions of globalization at least indirectly acknowledge. Yet ironically it was not media and communications scholars who either started the debate or actively contributed to it. The role of media and communications is, of course, obvious in globalization theories, but it is not necessarily visible. (4)

Wheeler (2000, 432) also argued for a role of media in identity formation and maintenance when she asserted that

> communication is the cement of identity. It is through communication that cultures define themselves. In modern societies, much of this sense of shared identity is communicated through media technologies. These technologies help to transmit shared symbolic forms, a sense of group culture.

This notion of the shared symbolic form becomes somewhat more contentious and the shared identities can demonstrate a greater level of fluidity than previously encountered in human history if considered in the context of distance-reducing technologies. The sense of group culture that Wheeler referenced can mean the traditional groups and cultures to which we are accustomed; it can also relate to the development of identities that are more rooted in virtual than real relationships. The sharing of symbolic forms and meanings are no longer necessarily limited by the boundaries of space and time and communities can be defined in much larger terms. Thus, nonresident Indian–themed websites help overseas Indians to remain culturally connected (Goswami 2010) and Cameroonians in Oslo can keep up with developments in the homeland (Mainsah 2009).

Mass mediated communication aside, material culture in the form of goods and services exchanged worldwide is another key driver of culture and identity. In terms of resources, influence and information, multinational corporations are more powerful than many governments. Critics such as Clinard (1990) have argued that, with the support of their own powerful governments, transnational corporations are engaged in a process of cultural change that simultaneously conditions their domestic societies to accept their actions as infallible and prepares the international markets for their domination.

This focus on changing local cultures to be more accepting to the overtures of the multinational corporations is evident in the literature of international commerce and marketing. Take, for example, Strizhakova, Coulter, and Prince's (2008, 78–79) recommendation in the *Journal of International Marketing* that

> multinational corporations and local firms investing in emerging markets need to be aware of consumers' limited understanding of branding and to determine appropriate local mechanisms to develop consumer culture. Practices such as cobranding and joint ventures may be necessary to facilitate a greater prominence of brands in people's lives and, ultimately, to build stronger loyalty and equity in these markets.

This dual pronged attack of domestic support and foreign preparation builds support for MNCs actions in their home countries while seeking to condition markets abroad—at both points using corporate power and its relationship with military and political power to overturn cultural resistance—or so the argument goes (Marín 2008).

The argument further posits that this steamroller process of market development suppresses native cultures, replacing them with not only an imported consumer culture but also a set of values aimed at establishing and keeping the corporation as a primary organizing focus of society. Menninger (1985, 212), for example, argued that

> whether regarded with a mistrustful eye or a tolerant one, the corporation reveals itself inevitably as part of the essential core of modern society. It stands next to the state as an institutional anchor of industrial political economy, and shares with the state, for better or worse, the rule and direction of social development.

Bakan (2004, 5) called the corporation "the world's dominant economic institution." What is less obvious is that modern corporations also constitute the most important influences on modern culture—however we may define this elusive concept. It is easy to conceptualize (and observe) the corporations' sphere of influence in all things economic. It is also easy to imagine culture as an independent phenomenon, emerging from the misty depths of history and shrouded in the sanctity of tradition and emotion of identity. However, many argue that the multinational corporations, in addition to dominating commercial life internationally, have also usurped human culture. In Bakan's words: "Today, corporations govern our lives. They determine what we eat, what we watch, what we wear, where we work, and what we do." In the pursuit of profit and markets, corporations are well-known exploiters and destroyers of the physical environment. Commentators such as Bakan argue that the same is true of the cultural environment; that like so many eco-systems and environments, the cultural environment has been overtaken, ravaged, and perhaps irretrievably destroyed by the corporate manipulation of culture and society for profit.

Through international media, the culture of corporate exploitation is spread in international labor, capital, and management markets, demonstrating an increasingly pervasive symbiosis with political power. This particular evolution of corporate capitalism, unchecked and largely blessed by governments, academics, and economists, paves the way for what some analysts see as the rule of the corporations by the corporations for the corporations. It is a process that, for many critical observers, has already begun—a process in which democratically elected governments yield to the economic force of multinational corporations. It is a process in which corporate interests determine decisions about war and peace, and a process in which multinational corporations are thought to dictate the foreign policies, internal laws, and even political (mis)fortunes of their home and host nations (Hertz 2001).

Bhagwati (2004, 167–168) argued that "perhaps the critics' greatest fear has been that multinationals intruding dramatically into the political space of the host countries in nefarious ways." He cited Chile's election of Salvador Allende, after which, he noted, "Leading multinationals operating in Chile drew a line in the sand with the active assistance of the CIA and Henry Kissinger." He added that "ITT and Pepsi are now known to have played a role in the coup against this elected president of Chile." He similarly cited the assassination of an elected leader and installation of a puppet regime in the Congo in 1961 with the complicity of a Belgian multinational corporation, arguing that

> the elected Iranian Prime Minister Mohammed Mossadegh was overthrown by the CIA, partly if not principally because of the giant oil companies' interests, and . . . the CIA intervened in Central and South America to protect the commercial interests of multinationals such as the United Fruit Company. (168)

Bhagwati (2004, 182) also argued that the corporate interests of the multinationals are sometimes injurious to the most vulnerable in the global context, suggesting, for example, that

> we must consider the possibility that the multinationals have, through interest-driven lobbying, helped set the rules in the world trading, intellectual property, aid and other regimes that are occasionally hostile to the interest of the poor countries.

In the face of this emerging reality and myriad examples of the overwhelming influence of international media, multinational corporations and their associated business culture, there are inevitable questions about how this expansion has been possible and its implications for human culture systems. In light of the (real and perceived) power of multinational global corporations and their media arms, activists and commentators are quick to condemn the current process of global corporate cultural expansion as the death knell of indigenous cultures worldwide. Using an argument closely aligned with ideas from ecology (Lieber and Weisberg 2002) and environmental science (Varan 1998), their suggestion is that the loss of cultural and linguistic diversity will affect the global cultural system in negative ways—as the loss of species and biodiversity threatens the global ecosystem (Marín 2008).

Despite the popularity of the notion that modern corporate globalization is the primary driver of cultural change and erosion, it is possible to identify numerous examples of cultural change over the centuries that occurred in the absence of the modern transnational corporation. The piecemeal process of cultural change through history has been consolidated with the dominance of the modern corporate structure but it certainly did not begin with corporations or corporate media.

There is also need to question the implicit assumption that culture, as we understand it, is incompatible with (and diametrically opposed to) the spread of corporate interests and activities. To do so we must first question our insistence on culture as some kind of pure and sacred set of rules and realities. Once over that hurdle, we can begin to approach a more rational conception of what has been called culture, and address the dynamic creation and re-creation of cultural ideas and artifacts. I propose here at least three processes with which we can understand the dynamic creation of culture over the ages and in the present day; they are cultural (re)invention, cultural retroconstruction, and fictional osmosis. This triple logic of cultural processes, taken all at once, suggests that culture is not necessarily only a set of rigid handed-down rules, but also a fluid, negotiated, very current manifestation of group aspirations and ideals. In a globalized environment where mediated realities supplement real ones, those aspirations and ideals can, today, be influenced by images and ideas from almost anywhere.

That major multinational corporations are intertwined with the spread of ideas is part and parcel of the modern global reality, indeed, part of the modern culture. Far from killing culture, the multinational corporation and international advertising have in fact supported cultural development in the sense of the creation of artifacts and systems in various countries. What rubs against our instincts about culture is the extent to which these artifacts and systems seem to be homogenized. It is here that we can begin to see that our assumptions about culture were comfortable enough when relative isolation justified them. However, as the global scope of reference becomes wider, it becomes easier to see just how specious those assumptions were.

The globalization of culture, then, has less to do with the destruction of something called culture by evil multinationals, and more to do with our increasing ability to discard the strictures and prejudices of traditional, parochial culture. Indeed, it is not so much that culture is dead, and not about who killed it, but rather about asking the question whether culture is a valid concept anymore (and was it ever as good an idea as we made it out to be).

The globalization of culture also raises the question of whether culture can be a debilitating influence—a set of strictures quite out of step with the ethos of increasing possibilities in the modern world. Decrepit ideas from ancient cultures often creep into the modern world in the guise of religion. Not only are they unscientific, but they are often anti-scientific. Yet, in the same way that some churches are granted tax exemptions, religious beliefs are granted intellectual exemptions. With little scrutiny or interrogation, they are allowed to pass into public policy and even scientific arguments where they should have ceased to exert influence centuries ago. In many parts of the world this is one aspect of cultural belief structures that is still protected, both officially and in common discourse, and we will consider the extent to which such protections are relevant today. Such religious ideas, normally off-limits for whatever reason, may actually be the best argument for questioning and changing perspectives on traditional concepts of culture as their anachronistic nature becomes more evident in the globalized environment.

To be sure, we will meet the evil multinationals along the way (we have met some already), and the brutal colonizers, and the self-serving religious authorities. They are all part of the story. In fact, they are often a greater part of the story of culture than we choose to admit. The purity of our culture can never be tainted by the suggestion that we believe, do, or aspire in a certain way only because of the arbitrary outcome of some conquest or the result of some war. To us, our beliefs and traditions are natural, right and fixed. They are not artificial, arbitrary and fluid. Yet, today's global frame of reference, and an examination of the globalizing forces of the past suggest a different perspective. It is a perspective in which we can no longer rely on the ailing paradigms of culture that have comforted us in the past—but which have also led us to conflicts, wars, and worse.

In fact, one of the accepted elements of our traditional cultural discourse is the heavy focus on the discourse of wars and battles, with many of our histories setting these as the major milestones and checkpoints of civilization. This is ironic, because wars are particularly uncivilized affairs. While the mortal tolls of battles obviously render them memorable to historians, we must ask if the defining moments of culture are not often found at greater junctures than the violent death of many over land, religion, or imagined codes of honor.

At a much more personal level, the globalization of culture and re-conceptualization of the very idea of culture have implications for each of our lives. Can we really continue to hold prejudices of the past in the name of culture? Are old ideas about others valid when we can disprove them everyday not only in the images we consume from all over the world, but also in our mediated and direct personal experiences with "the other." The protective shield of xenophobia that served us so well in the past has suddenly become unnecessarily heavy. Self-examination and the evidence of our own experiences will demonstrate that the globalized environment, even with the agency of corporate interests, creates conditions of greater understanding (or at least the potential for them). The globalization of culture is, then, not just a global event or the experience of specific cultures. It is also a personal experience—wrenching and dislocating as any culture shock, in which the familiar is yanked out from under us and we can, finally, shaken and hesitant, enter a brave new world.

Chapter One

Culture, Humankind, and Society

A number of reservations have been expressed and a variety of questions raised about the growing impact of business on culture. Is the morality of business and the market economy, for example, a sufficient code of conduct for human behavior in the modern world? Should the engineering principles and management ideologies developed in complex technological systems be used in the design of educational programs? Does the concentration of ownership and control in the media foreshadow a new Orwellian manipulation of mass consciousness? Are there viable alternatives to the dominance of business practices, business values, business symbols, and business languages in the shaping of modern culture and society?
—Deeks (1993, 213)

CULTURE—AN INTRODUCTION

Grainy pictures and film footage of people in brightly colored costumes doing a ritual dance to drums of some sort have been offered to the popular imagination as culture. The words "exotic," "quaint," and "savage" have all been associated with the culture of "the other." Even modern travelogues tend to focus on the strange, the visible, and the spectacular in other cultures—and understandably so. It is easier to convey the sights and sounds of a ritual than to express the subtle and often imperceptible variations in attitudes and aspirations among people who are "different" from the viewer. The differences make for good television these days and the exotic makes for good travel packages.

In developing modern ideas about culture shock, Oberg (1960) noted the great variety and tremendous subtlety of the everyday and mundane cues that are replaced or changed when one experiences a new culture. From a practi-

1

cal point of view it is easy to dismiss the fancy headdress as quaint or exotic. Variations in ideas about duty, respect, God, good, evil, cleanliness, and fate are much less obvious but much more powerful in terms of the actual cultural makeup of the wearer. These are, however, seldom in play when the "cultural experience" is either vicarious (e.g., when experienced through television) or contrived (as is often the case with tourist events).

ORIGINS OF THE TERM "CULTURE"

Thompson (1990) traced the term "culture" back to the Latin *cultura* that was used in reference to the care and cultivation of crops and livestock. He suggested that this term evolved the meaning of cultivation of other things such as the mind and that by the late eighteenth to early nineteenth centuries, the term "culture" had acquired a meaning similar to the idea of "civilization" connoting a movement from savagery to enlightenment. Wagner (1981, 24) similarly traced the term "culture" back to the Latin verb *colere* (meaning "to cultivate") suggesting that it draws at least some of its meaning from associations with agriculture, arguing that

> in later times "culture" took on a more specific sense, indicating a process of progressive refinement and breeding in the domestication of some particular crop, or even the result or increment of such a process. Thus we speak of agriculture, apiculture, the "culture of the vine," or of a bacterial culture.

Thompson (1990, 129) gave one description of the culture of a group or society as "the array of beliefs, customs, ideas and values, as well as the material artifacts, objects and instruments, which are acquired by individuals as members of the group or society." Tylor ([1871] 1903) described culture as follows:

> Culture or Civilization, taken in its wide ethnographic sense, is that complex whole which includes knowledge, belief, art, morals, law, custom, and any other capabilities and habits acquired by man as a member of society. The condition of culture among the various societies of mankind, in so far as it is capable of being investigated on general principles, is a subject apt for the study of laws of human thought and action. (1)

Others, such as Clifford Geertz and Stuart Hall would perhaps argue that culture is in fact in the meanings that people make. In such conceptualizations, culture is the product of symbolic forms and conventions, negotiated over time and imbued with conventional meaning. Culture is, of course, all of these and more.

Hanson (2007, 11) pointed to one of the primary difficulties in conceptualizing culture while he described his experience at Disney's "It's a Small World" exhibit:

> We piled into small boats and were ferried through a series of artificial landscapes ranging from Alpine pastures to Asian rice paddies to central African villages. Animated dolls peopled each location, of a color and costumes ethnically appropriate to it, all smiling and singing 'It's a small world, after all.' The experience was annoying, partly because I could not get the tune out of my head and partly because it trivialized cultural differences. Of course we enjoy the cultural diversity of costume and cuisine, folklore, and music and dance in restaurants and concert halls and at street fairs and community festivals. But culture more fundamentally concerns convictions about the texture of reality, the shape of the divine, the nature of truth, and the morality of behavior.

Hanson was correct in noting that the manifest, ritual, expressive, and outward trappings of social life are easier to observe and more commonly presented as culture (which is not to say that there is any excuse for the annoying music and creepy displays at the particular exhibit). Outrage at the Disney display's concession to the evident should be tempered with the understanding that, as Hanson noted, we are more likely to perceive music and ritual as culture than to perceive attitudes and beliefs as culture. In an interview on Canadian television Marshall McLuhan once said, "I don't know who discovered water but I am sure it wasn't the fish." Within our own cultural environment—whether native or acquired, we exist within an enveloping set of ideas, beliefs, and propensities that are often so well accepted as to become invisible. Often, these ideas and norms are only visible when they are challenged or broken—such as when we travel abroad to another cultural context, or in our home environments when we encounter someone with different cultural assumptions.

The term "culture" has also had to contend with a variety of new uses. Wagner (1981) pointed to a certain ambiguity surrounding the term, and manifest in the tensions between conceptions such as what he termed "operahouse" interpretations and anthropological interpretations. Terms such as "Popular Culture" and "Culture War" have been made popular by television news analysts and conservative radio talk show hosts reporting on gay marriage and similar debates in the United States in recent years. These terms have served to focus attention on the most obvious and the most saleable issues within a larger cultural picture. At the same time, media-centered attempts at cultural change in the interest of marketing have also served to distort everyday culture. Sherrow (2006, 356) provided an example of such distortion from the turn-of-the-twentieth-century writing that the makers of razors and blades realized that they would sell far more products if women shaved their armpits and legs regularly. One major force in this campaign was the Wilkinson Sword Company, a British company that produces razor blades. Fashion editors took up the cause of shaving by labeling underarm hair as un-feminine and a sign of poor hygiene. They pointed out that underarm odors tended to cling to these hairs. Sleeveless dresses featured models with neatly shaved armpits, and smooth, shaved legs appeared beneath the short skirts that emerged during the Roaring Twenties.

It would be expedient here to be able to argue that observances such as Mother's Day are also merely the product of commercial marketing. However, despite the popular rumor that Mother's Day was invented by Hallmark or some other card company, the formal observance of this event was recognized by an act of Congress on May 8, 1914, in the United States and followed by a proclamation on May 9, 1914, by President Woodrow Wilson. However, within a few years of the formal declaration, there were already protests against the commercialization of the event.

The term "culture" has also been over-extended. You will find references, for example, to academic culture, athletic culture, and youth culture. Some scientists studying animal groups even refer to the "cultures" among those groups. Trouillot (2003, 98) noted what he called a "massive diffusion" of the world "culture," pointing to its spread outside of the fields such as anthropology and ethnography:

> One Internet search engine produced more than five million pages on "culture," even after exclusion of most references to cultivation and agriculture. When culture was coupled with anthropology or ethnography, the total went down to 61,000 pages. While the search engine of a major Internet bookseller produced more than 20,000 titles with the word culture, the list went down to 1,350 titles when culture was coupled with anthropology or ethnography in the subject index.

The wide popular application of the term "culture," sometimes with the most tenuous relevance, makes it difficult to pin down the specifics of the term "culture" that we need to wrestle with. In some senses, it might be useful to suggest that the larger concept we are after—the one that defines who you are and the things that you see in yourself when you land in a foreign country—might be designated as "culture." It is like moving to a new place and realizing for the first time that you have an accent (either that or everyone else does). Well, you also have a culture.

Within the last hundred years, fascinating accounts of the spectacular and the foreign have been supplemented by a much broader understanding of culture as involving much more of human existence. The development of cultural anthropology and related fields (including intercultural communications) have contributed to a somewhat greater academic understanding of the concept of culture overall. Indeed, definitions of culture now tend to be couched in terms of the totality of human existence, both material and conceptual.

CULTURAL RELATIVISM

Wagner (1981, 13) described cultural relativism as emerging out of a lack of objective measures or criteria for cultural evaluation, writing that

> because every culture can be understood as a specific manifestation, or example, of the phenomenon of man, and because no infallible method has ever been discovered for "grading" different cultures and sorting them into their natural types, we assume that every culture, as such, is equivalent to every other one.

Cultural relativism is, simply put, the recognition that culture, taken at its global scale, has no universal standard. It is common, normal, and perhaps inevitable for each culture to judge other cultures in relation to their own norms and expectations. It may be an innate and defensive tendency to judge the other as both inferior and dangerous. Such an approach would guarantee at some basic level the avoidance of threats and infiltration.

Cultural relativism either as a tool of analysis or a political reality is not universally accepted. Conservative elements in many communities hold fast to the idea that their way of life is inherently superior to others. Even academic communities are guilty of a kind of flat-earth philosophy in their analysis of other cultures, often implicitly making judgments about other cultures in terms of their own parochial expectations.

ETHNOCENTRISM (US, THEM, AND WHO IS BETTER)

The tendency to judge "the other" in terms of our own experiences and expectations is called "ethnocentrism" in cultural analysis. In some ways it embodies the antithesis of cultural relativism. You might call ethnocentrism "cultural absolutism"—the notion that there are absolute standards of culture and that your own culture is superior to others. Someone adopting such a stance would point out the most obvious failings of other cultures—to make the point that their own culture is superior. So an American might claim that US culture is superior to Saudi Arabian culture because American culture allows women equality and freedom under the law. A Saudi might claim that Saudi culture is superior because it advocates a religious respect for women that protects them in ways that US laws could not. Regardless of the merits of the arguments and the respective realities, in the eyes of both, their own arguments are stronger than the other's and their own culture is superior.

THE LIMITS OF RELATIVISM

Despite the negative-sounding notions of ethnocentrism and the allure of relativism, it is useful to note that like many things in the study of culture, the matter is not that simple. Relativism, strangely enough, has its limits. Even the most liberal analyst will often come to a point in the study of culture where particular practices of other cultures become abhorrent. For each analyst or each person experiencing another culture, that point may be different. For a Western observer, for example, it may be the ritual slaughter and eating of dogs in Benin. For some Eastern analysts the acceptance of secularism in everyday life may be equally abhorrent.

There are a few cultural practices that receive almost universal condemnation, even in their own contexts. Many of these today have to do with traditional practices that are commonly viewed as barbaric among most people in the modern world. Among these are the various forms of female genital mutilation and the existence of slavery in some areas. It is difficult to maintain the notion of relativism in the face of practices that blatantly dehumanize and exploit. The cultural absolutist may point to this as the fatal flaw in the relativist position. Yet, that does not end the debate.

For the relativist, cultural flux within societies with such practices offers something of an explanation. Thus the gradual but persistent and widespread outlawing of the practices associated with suttee (ritual wife suicide) in parts of India has resulted in an almost de facto elimination of the practice and to widespread condemnation even among members of the home culture. This evolutionary view of culture would suggest that in some instances, practices clearly out of step with the broadest modern standards of human conduct are simply a throwback to ancient times and are to be understood in that context. It does not, however, relieve the cultural relativist of the realization that value judgments are a necessary and unavoidable factor in cultural analysis.

Chapter Two

The Birth of Culture

Throughout the world, media have become a part of the rhythm of human life.
As means of communication, as symbols for modernity and transformation,
and as resources for cultural action, they have become part of human culture.
—Peterson (2004, 2)

MCLUHAN'S FISH

To speak of the birth of culture, we must look not to the beginnings of human
social groups or the development of language. Even though the things that
we identify as culture were probably mostly developed quite early in human
history, the idea of culture is a somewhat different one than the practice of
human civilization. As noted earlier, the term culture in the sense of civilization is of relatively recent coinage.

In most "cultures" (as we now think of them) there is little account of "the
other" and little internal realization of the cultural qualities of the home
group. One of the very markers of what we have traditionally imagined to be
culture is the notion that one's home group or culture acts in ways that are
natural or obvious.

Early Spanish colonialists of the Americas were in the habit of appending
names to the people that they encountered. One such group was the Navajo
of the southwest United States. The so-called Navajo of (what is today)
Arizona, refer to themselves as *Diné*. This term can best be translated as "the
people." This means that outsiders (*billigana*) are, technically speaking, not
"the people" or, by extension, not even "people." It is very common to find
that social groups have historically considered themselves to be people but
others to be something else. In fact, Al-Biruni, a Muslim scholar who lived

7

between 973 and AD 1050 described the inhabitants of eleventh-century India as extremely xenophobic and treating all foreigners as impure. However he pointed out that not only his own (Arab) people, but all others as well, could be accused of the same predisposition against outsiders.

With this in mind, we can also view our own "Western" creation myths (and for the moment we will accept this inaccuracy). A common logical issue with our dominant creation tradition arises when Genesis 4:16–17 tells us that Cain's wife was an outsider to Eden from a land called Nod. The seeming paradox of a creation myth that allows for outsiders to the creation process is most plausible when the creation myth is understood as specifically referring only to the in-group that generated the myth. In this (fairly common) casting of a creation myth, "others" are either not human or somehow sub-human in the scope of the story.

A similar explanation applies to the Old Testament story of the great flood. Today, it is well understood by most rational investigators that this is a borrowed tradition from earlier regional mythology. For example, in the Sumerian epic of Gilgamesh (a king who may have lived as early as twenty-seven centuries before Christ), the character Utnapisthim is warned of a great flood to be sent by the great gods and survives by building a boat and loading it with, among other things, male and female animals from every country; the boat comes to rest atop a mountain after the flood. Frazer (1916) recounted the Babylonian tradition of the Great Flood which took place during the rule of the King Xisuthrus. He is also told to provision a boat in preparation for a great flood and to include animals. He sent birds out to check for the end of the flood and ended up running aground on a mountain. There are several other versions of such flood stories, including a Greek one in which Zeus does the warning.

The corresponding Biblical story suggests that the entire world was destroyed by a flood except for the few members of Noah's party and the animals they brought aboard the ark. Despite the obvious logical and logistic problems presented by the flood myth, serious anthropological and scientific investigations have been conducted into the nature and extent of the literal truth of this story. However, it is simply (and quite reasonably) explained by this tendency of preglobalized societies to conceive of as themselves as all of humanity (or at least the only part that mattered) and their environment as the whole of the world. Even with the knowledge of other peoples or other lands, the frame of reference of myth generally did not need to account for the non-people outsiders in their non-world lands. The scope of even the definition of god in the Hebrew tradition is characterized in exactly this manner by Al Faruqi (1963, 284) who argued that the "God" of the Hebrews is a deity which belonged to the Hebrews alone. They worshipped it as "their God," always calling it by its own proper names, of which it had many. To be sure that it is not confused with any other gods— the possibility and existence of which was never denied, though they were always denigrated. . . . This deity could not even conceive of itself as capable of being worshipped outside the limits of their geographic domain. . . . True, at a late stage of their history and only at that stage, they did regard their god as lord of the universe, but their doing so was always an attempt at extending its jurisdiction so as to requite their own national enemies.

It is important to note that the same argument can be made of almost any deity in common fashion. When parochial mythologies are reinterpreted as universal stories, localized notions of creation and cultural development can be mistaken for global realities when that was never their purport. Of course, much of the unfortunate debates and wasted energies also stem from the fallacy of taking such mythic and legendary material literally (as some sort of historical record) rather than a figurative telling of cautionary and moral tales—whether that be the problem of murder/fratricide or the consequences of displeasing a divine figure who is at once vengeful and merciful.

To return to the notion of McLuhan's fish, the notion of culture cannot generally emerge from a group's introspection due to its very pervasiveness. If we are immersed in our own culture it is difficult for us to remove ourselves enough to see our own culture around us. Certainly, we can enjoy brief moments of clarity where we catch a glimpse of ourselves but in general our every attempt at analysis will be conditioned by who we are—or were trained to be. As with the ancients who saw only their culture as valid, we often only see other cultures in relation to our own.

What, then, makes our modern study of culture any better informed than the ancient who saw his way as sacred and the way of the other as profane? Despite our modern techniques of social science investigation and the emergence of theoretical positions, we could argue that very little has in fact changed in the basic approach to culture. It can be argued that the analysis of culture is still subject to the same rules today as in the past. The notion of "otherness" that has been so integral in developing ideas about culture persists despite our best analysis.

Central to the present analysis is the idea that our very approaches to culture are in need of revision—to such an extent, that we might consider our prior notions of culture to be effectively obsolete. The present work does not constitute the first such call. In *The Invention of Culture*, Wagner (1981) argued that culture is not a set of received absolutes, but rather the product of active creation by its participants. A little like actors in an improvised play, we tend to create culture as we go. For Wagner, who is most directly concerned with anthropological practice, "the study of culture *is* culture" (21,

emphasis in original), a process in which we develop ideas about other cultures based on our perceptions of our own cultures and couched in terms of
differences and generalities that can be gleaned from comparisons.

The present analysis argues that we need to begin with this position of
culture as other than absolute, but to move further to examine the active
creation and constitutive interpretation of culture on an increasingly global
scale. It is not only that we are creating culture as we go, but we are also
inheriting this sort of creation from the past, re-interpreting it and re-imagin-
ing ourselves. Hobsbawm and Ranger (1992) in *The Invention of Tradition*
provide us with a link between the processes of cultural invention and those
of globalization. They argued that while traditions have been invented
throughout history, the phenomenon accelerates in times of rapid social
transformation when old traditions become displaced by emerging new realities.

Our creation and constitutive interpretations of culture are not necessarily
the stuff of grand theory or design either, but rather, the stuff of everyday
discourse. Consider that the Virgin Mary on someone's toast is a cultural
experience of today (which might be experienced via mass media). Yet it is
based on someone's recognition of a likeness of painted representations from
renaissance Europe (we don't really know what Mary looked like). The
representations are of an idealized (by Western European standards mostly)
image of a Hebrew peasant living under Roman occupation. That person
would later be vested with quasi-divinity through the vagaries of the politics
of a Church which she probably could not have imagined in her day. It takes
all of this baggage to understand how Mary ends up on toast. But the glib
acceptance of the phenomenon whether as meaningful or not, masks several
powerful levels of cultural remaking and re-fashioning which lead to the
conclusion that God (or something like her) is making an appearance on a
breakfast food. How did we get to this acceptance of cultural baggage as
though it is an absolute to be respected rather than a set of accidental codes to
be deciphered?

In the traditional discourse of culture the origins of culture are sought in
the evolution of human language, environmental adaptation, settlements, and
economic systems. Adam Smith (1776) and others of his time, for example,
conceived of human culture as advancing through four stages including hunt-
ing, pasturage, farming, and commerce. However, modern and post-modern
views of culture are the result of more than the evolution of social systems.
Our modern views of culture also represent the evolution of a particular kind
of social science inquiry predicated on particular ideas.

SOCIAL SCIENCE

The phenomenon of social science involves the use of scientific methods to understand human behavior. There is little that is absolute about social science methods, demonstrated amply by the lack of fundamental laws and principles such as we find in the natural sciences. Yet, even the physical sciences are not themselves absolute as Thomas Kuhn (1962) has ably pointed out in *The Structure of Scientific Revolutions*. So, as with any science, modern social science is part of a transitory system of scientific paradigms that are always in flux and emerging into new views of the world. This is simply to say that when we speak of today's social science (or equally of today's natural science) we refer only to the state of such a science at a point in time.

Precursors to social science were known early in recorded human history. Certain recorders of historical events such as the Greek Herodotus of Halicarnassus (480–425 BC) and the Hebrew soldier (turned Roman writer) Titus Flavius Josephus (37–ca. 100) are often considered early historians. Additionally the Persian scientist Al-Biruni (973–1048) is considered to be one of the pioneers of anthropology for his studies of foreign cultures while Ibn Khaldun's (1332–1406) *Muqaddimah* is often cited as one of the first great works of sociology.

Modern social science owes its present form to several currents in late nineteenth-century and early-twentieth-century thought. Many historians point to development and sophistication of the natural sciences in the nineteenth century as one force driving the use of scientific methods to understand and explain social behavior. In this regard, the influence of Darwin and other evolutionists cannot be discounted. Later, movements such as the so-called Frankfurt School and Robert E. Park's Chicago School would be credited with the widespread development of ideas related to the investigation and critique of society. According to McLaughlin (1999) the Frankfurt School provides us with a useful example of how a (once) relatively insignificant school of thought became important in the evolution of social science, eventually spanning academic and scientific boundaries as well as different cultural traditions.

The influences of the empirical approach of the physical sciences, established more firmly and earlier in history, and the participation in social investigation of persons themselves trained in the physical sciences went some way in influencing a social science approach that brought empiricism (in the sense of observation-based analysis) to the study of social phenomena.

Hall did not accept certain important aspects of an anthropological perspective, however. Anthropologists generally focus on macro-level, single culture studies, investigating the economic, government, kinship, and religious systems of a single culture. Hall's approach at FSI focused on the micro-level behaviors of interactions between people of different cultures.

Rogers et al. (2002) also noted that Hall was influenced by his colleague George L. Trager, a disciple of Edward Sapir and Benjamin Lee Whorf, and that he had an interest in ethology (the study of animal behavior)—also connecting him to the natural sciences—as with others we have noted before. Hall is important to the current discussion particularly because he spread a number of relatively new conceptions of culture to popular audiences with a series of books on specific aspects of cultural differences in perceptions.

Hall's books, including the *The Silent Language* (1959), *The Hidden Dimension* (1966), and *Beyond Culture* (1976), bridged an important divide. While investigations into culture were well known in academic circles, Hall's work brought them squarely into the popular imagination. In fact, Hall is reported to have suggested that the very popularity of his work brought him into conflict with his own field of anthropology. Not for the first time, but certainly on the largest scale for that time, Hall's books explored in simple everyday language, ideas about the differences among various peoples and the existence of cultural patterns both obvious and hidden.

Geert Hofstede

Geert Hofstede (1980, 1986, 1998) analyzed differences in management and working styles in different cultures and identified several dimensions of variation from one culture to another. Some of these dimensions have proven to be useful tools of analysis in cultural analysis, while others are doubtful in value at best. His dimensions are variously presented as:

- Power distance
- Male/female orientation
- Long-term/short-term orientation
- Individualism/collectivism
- Uncertainty avoidance

Apart from some strikingly elitist implications of his findings, Hofstede's work has been well accepted in management and business circles. Reid (2004) noted that Hofstede's approach was designed specifically to serve the interests of international business. Given the great influence of these areas in modern society and the drive toward globalization of commerce, it is hardly surprising, then, that his ideas have become socially dominant as well, despite several strong critiques of the dimensions, their existence, and utility (McSweeny 2002).

Hofstede, while speaking of "national cultures" has, like many others, tended to perpetuate national stereotypes though his particular focus involves tendencies and behaviors encountered in corporate contexts. He defends this "national culture" focus as relating to some dominant set of ideas among middle classes in various nations—still a weak rationale. Hofstede (1998) himself acknowledged the particular weakness of at least the nomenclature of the masculine/feminine dimension, for example. More troubling, perhaps, is the reduction of diversity both within and among national environments into simplistic dimensions. Something is a little suspicious when these "dimensions," construed from surveys of people working at the local offices of a single large multinational company in a particular niche of manufacturing during the 1960s are then taken as evidence of the nature of complete societies. As we shall argue presently, the increasing convergence of international media and commercial influences draws such a paradigm into question. Today, in the well-insulated corporate boardrooms of multinational enterprise, the participants are increasingly of a unified set of understandings of the objectives of international business regardless of their national origins and increasingly homogenized in their lives outside of the multinational company as well.

Kalervo Oberg

Kalervo Oberg (1901–1973) popularized one concept that would become a powerful influence on the popular imagination and which also strongly conditions the view of culture as contrast. The notion of "culture shock" has become something larger than it originally was intended. Oberg himself noted that he owed the term to another scholar named Cora DuBois who used the term in 1951. Oberg then developed the ideas further over a number of years with later scholars further refining the concept. Michael Winkelman (1994) and others, for example, have developed this idea into a system of adjustments, sometimes described as the U-curve of cultural adjustment. This U shape represents a tracking of the traveler's levels of happiness from high at the start of the encounter through lows in times of difficulties in adjustment and excitement about return. Other models of this process include further refinements to show a W-shaped curve accounting for various stages of preparation, adjustment as well as reentry and readjustment back to the traveler's home culture.

Perhaps the major weakness of Oberg's model and its various progeny is the fact that they generally underestimate or fail to account for the potential for permanent change in the sojourner after the return. Additionally, the term

"culture shock" has been widely misinterpreted and misused in general par-
lance to include such things as minor cultural encounters with immigrants
while in one's home environment or difficulties adjusting to spicy food in an
"ethnic" restaurant. Unfortunately, time and space dictate that the present
analysis forego discussion of the useless term "ethnic" (a euphemism for
non-white) in common US usage.

GENERAL APPROACHES TO THE POPULAR DESCRIPTION OF CULTURE

Culture as Contrast

These influences have all contributed to the modern popular view of culture.
The implicit assumptions of the popular view include the idea that culture is
somehow about differences or contrasts among peoples. The early popularization of cultural literature featured an emphasis on the sensational and
visible differences that could be demonstrated in the "other." From tales of
cannibalism and ritual sacrifice to stories of harems and eunuchs, the more
salacious the view of other cultures, the more books could be sold and the
more illustrated lectures presented. The opportunity for contrast often involved specific examples that were particularly shocking to the Western
mind and resulted in the impression that these were the most important
cultural elements of the other. Wood (2002, 46) traced this tradition further
back to early writers about foreign lands, suggesting that it was somewhat
universal to hold the idea that foreign lands abound with the wild and fanciful monsters of various types:

> There is the wakwak tree, full of talking heads, which appears in a romance of
> Alexander the Great and is illustrated in a Chinese encyclopedia with the
> caption: "There are trees in the mountains on whose branches grow flowers
> which are in the shape of men's heads. They do not speak but merely laugh
> when questioned. If they laugh too often they fall to the ground"; and there are
> the one-eyed people in both Herodotus and Chinese sources (living somewhere
> in Scythia or India), and the long-eared people also from India.

Allen Palmer (2007, 3) elaborated the myth of the fictitious Christian King
named Prester John (who supposedly lived near the Tower of Babel) whose
fame was widely publicized in the twelfth century, saying he "was believed
to rule over a land inhabited by men with horns, along with giants and
curious creatures, like Cyclops." He was also thought to be a direct threat to
Europe, capable of marshalling armies of various monsters to launch attacks.

Culture as Generality

In addition to drawing extreme contrasts with specific others, the discourse of popular culture (and to some extent, its academic counterpart) also involved attempts at grand generalizations about and across cultures. Take, for example, the assertion that

> some cultures restrain or restrict their body language, and other cultures are more openly and grandly expressive. . . . Those with restricted body language are typically countries with a very strong military history, countries such as Japan, Germany and England. (Morris 2005, para. 3)

In practice we may find these generalizations to be tenuous at best. One of the best examples of the search for cultural generalities is the much-vaunted work of Geert Hofstede described above. Even with the very broad generalities about cultures claimed by Hofstede, it is difficult to substantiate these characteristics with any certainty especially in the light of individual variations within members of each culture and the existence of complex groups and interrelationships that may or may not influence behavior. Hall is sometimes similarly guilty of this type of generalization, though much more tenuously. The reason for doing this generalization is the same as with any sort of stereotype, it is to create simplicity out of complexity. Particularly in relation to the popular audience, these generalizations help to communicate broad characteristics that could not otherwise be effectively described.

Culture as Spectacle

The second most popular type of picture postcard in the late nineteenth and early twentieth century was the scenic or travel postcard that featured an exotic locale, often with appropriately exotic people in exotic attire (Desmond 1999; Sigel 2000). This visual emphasis was understandable given that newly mass-produced realistic images were the driving force behind this medium—which also explains why the most popular type of these postcards was the genre featuring nudity or sexual content (see Sigel, 2000). Patterson (2006, 142) argued for an even more severe cultural role of the postcard during the late-nineteenth and early-twentieth centuries, arguing that they were

> integrally linked to the justification of the Raj, since they emphasize the civilizing mission of empire and the "backwards" nature of India. Nearly all aspects of imperial life, whether running the bungalow, dispensing justice or even travelling by train, required the British to maintain an imperial façade of control and an aura of invincibility. Part of this process required the British to

depict Indians as incapable of self-rule, and the postcards depict the British as
natural overlords of India, born "booted and spurred" to rule, while Indians are
portrayed "saddled and bridled."

These postcards presented stylized and often eccentric views of the exotic
"other" to ready audiences in Western nations, preconditioned by prior colonial experiences and attitudes. Sigel (2000, 861–862) pointed out that in the
content of the mass-produced postcard:

"Natives" came from a variety of colonized and exoticized places over which
Europeans and Americans exerted dominion. . . . Postcards featuring "natives"
displayed then in their "natural habitat" by showing harem scenes, landscapes
and huts. . . . The exoticized "natives" in the cards appear naked or partially
naked, but theirs is a staged nakedness designed for perusal by a Western
audience.

The otherness of the subjects in these postcards is also evident in the fact that
their nudity was considered acceptable to the public censors in that "pubic
hair, genitalia, and nipples could pass by the censors if the card portrayed a
colonial or foreign subject" (861). The deliberate and artificial spectacle in
such postcards is clearly evident in Sigel's observation that

in some of the locales, nakedness was clearly a creation of the photographer.
Algerian women appeared naked on postcards even though in Algerian culture
nakedness was never public. Algerian women in public appeared fully dressed
and often veiled. Photographers, however, portrayed Algerian women as half-
naked, veiled but naked, or fully naked with head coverings. (862)

Soon after the scenic postcard made it big, the age of the film brought so-
called travelogues or scenics to audiences in Europe and North America.
Notable examples of these include "In the Land of the Head-Hunters" (1914)
by Edward Curis, Robert Flaherty's "Nanook of the North" (1922), "Nionga"
(1925) by the Stoll production company, and "Stampede" (1929) by Major
and Stella Court Treatt. In this genre, Benelli (2002, 3) noted that the producers of such films demonstrated a

surprising willingness to give up the priority of narrative for the advantage of
providing audiences with digressive documentary interludes devoted to the
spectacle of exotic cultures, landscapes and wildlife.

Sandon (2000, 118–119) described the general tone of one of these films
which reinforced colonial stereotypes and focused on the visible to establish
derogatory otherness:

The viewer is encouraged to compare the everyday activities of the primitive with those of the modern and often through the titles the film implies that the viewer is superior. . . . Furthermore the audience is appealed to through the exoticism of difference. The furniture and costumes, through the use of leopard skins, carved seats and drums, all lend an air that the portrayal is of authentic Africa. . . . The viewer is presented with displays of spectacle and performance.

Benelli (2002, 7) noted one pertinent example of the primacy of visuals over the accuracy of content or portrayals as well as the worldview that informed such portrayals:

In 1930, for example, the film *Ingagi* successfully and notoriously presented itself as the record of an expedition which had inadvertently stumbled across the solution to the age-old riddle of the missing link, this purported solution being a group of bare-breasted black women living contentedly in the jungle with gorillas.

Such spectacularly erroneous impressions of the other formed part of the idea of culture in the popular Western imagination and centered the focus of attention on the visible, the sensational, and the tangible.

Nor were these encounters limited only to those who traveled abroad or joined the ranks of the colonists. Levine (2007, 152) told how the sensationalization of foreign cultures also came to European shores at times:

In the summer of 1810 in London those who could afford the steep 2*s*. 6*d*. entrance fee could view in the flesh the woman the papers were calling the "Hottentot Venus," shipped for display from the Cape of Good Hope. Sara (or Saartje as she was known in South Africa) Baartman was a Khosian woman who had made the long and perilous journey from South Africa to London by ship. Displayed by white entrepreneurs in fashionable Piccadilly on account of her allegedly vast buttocks, breasts and labia, Baartman has come to symbolize the early nineteenth-century European obsession with an abundant and exotic colonial sexuality.

It has been against this backdrop that academics involved in the study of culture have had to engage the fluid and often elusive concept. Those who have lived in foreign cultures realize that the reality of this thing called culture is a far more insidious phenomenon—or range of phenomena. Much scholarly work has been done on the subtle and powerful elements of culture that drive social behavior. Anthropologists and others involved in the scientific investigation of culture have considered everything from differing conceptions of social space to variations in ideas about justice and clashing ideas about what is clean and what is dirty. Such invisible elements of culture feature heavily in the work of pioneers such as Hall and Oberg and do form part of the modern popular view of culture. However, the legacy of culture as contrast, generality, and spectacle continues to dominate the popular imagination.

Thus, the concept of culture has emerged into one that encompasses both strict academic terminology and broad popular interest. Add to this, the broad and increasing influence of mass mediated culture and its particular manifestations in what is sometimes termed the culture industries. Kellner (1995, 16) described this relatively recent phenomenon thusly:

> While the new forms of culture industries described by Horkheimer and Adorno (1972) in the 1940s of film, radio, magazines, comics, advertising, and the press began to colonize leisure and stand at the center of the system of culture and communication in the United States and other capitalist democracies, it was not until the advent of television in the post World War II period that media culture became a dominant force within culture, socialization, politics, and social life. . . . Since then, cable and satellite television, video recorders and other multimedia home entertainment technologies, and more recently home computers have all accelerated the dissemination and increased the power of media culture.

At each stage along the spectrum of analysis and understanding lie tremendous variations and controversies about the specific meanings of the term culture and its related concepts. It is within this complex situation that we must address the claims and implications of the modern culture industries embodied particularly in the various forms of electronic media from traditional mass communication to computer mediated interpersonal communication and so-called new media.

As Kuhn tells us about science as a whole, paradigms come and go through a process of examination and questioning. The current paradigm, owing much as it does to the work and insights of great social scientists of the past is also deserving of scrutiny. In this regard it is important to note that much of the investigation into culture that still happens today recognizes the importance of investigating beyond the visible or observable (which is what empiricism really means) into the interpretative and intuitive. Anthropologists and interculturalists in general operate within the confines of a social science paradigm that is, today, often opposed to their emic methods and the universe of interpretation. The predominance of numerative empirical methods and conventions serves to marginalize and repress to a certain extent, the discourse of the cultural scholar.

Yet, the modern social science paradigm ultimately fails to account for the cultural changes being experienced globally both as a result of geopolitics and the spread of the technologies of modern media for these very reasons. Measurements are indeed useful and often necessary, but empirical investigation alone often fails to account for the deeply seated issues of cultural change. Here, critical scholars attempt to fill the void in areas such as cultural studies and political economy of media when traditional analyses fail to answer the new questions posed by new realities—a situation typical of the need for paradigmatic change in the field. New approaches are needed; approaches that are aware of the interconnectedness of world cultures.

INTERCULTURALITY

Julia Kristeva (1986) contends that no text exists in isolation and that all texts are the product of every other text. She calls this concept intertextuality. This contention itself raises the question of cultural context. If all texts are related then we must assume that the writers of all texts have some connection with writers of other texts. In a hypothetical isolated culture, could their texts be unique and isolated from all others thereby breaking the intertextuality rule? To follow this idea through, our hypothetical society would not only have to be isolated, but they would also have had to always be isolated. Even if they were isolated and always were isolated, it is conceivable that they would also have developed multiple texts as multiple persons spoke or multiple experiences were narrated.

This notion of intertextuality is important to a discussion of global culture and its supposed demise because, if we hold that all cultures are the product of all other cultures then the notion of a pure culture becomes very difficult to maintain. There is evidence of what we may call interculturality both within and prior to the mediated or globalized world structures. Despite a lack of global communications media (at least as we know it today) the Nabateans at Petra, for example, were a starkly globalized population, reflecting interculturality and a global perspective.

More recently, consider the spread of specific festivals and observances between and among cultures partly because of media but also because of trade, migration, and economics. Two incarnations of Caribbean pre-Lenten celebrations are celebrated annually outside of the Caribbean. The observances, featuring costumed street parades, are strongly associated with the Anglophone Caribbean islands of Trinidad and Tobago as well as smaller counterparts in places like Barbados (where it is known as "Cropover"). Although the carnival (or carnevale) was originally a pre-Lenten observance, the transplanted festivals take place in July and September in Notting Hill, London, and Brooklyn in New York (Harrison 1999).

The transplantation of this festival has occurred in part because Caribbean islanders have migrated in large numbers to these urban centers. However, it is unlikely that the observance would have survived unless it satisfied a set of other criteria. As much as the cultural purists may resist the notion, economics plays a tremendous role in the transplantation of these festivals. Consider that cultural exchange on the Silk Route was a secondary achievement to the real business of trading and consider that the mixing of European and Indian cuisines was a secondary event to the business of colonial exploitation and political expansion. In these and in the examples of the Caribbean (also called West Indian) carnivals, there is no reason to expect that some sort of pure cultural determinism drives the final form or expression of transplanted festivals. In as much as commerce and trade are the driving forces of the modern economy, they are also driving forces of modern culture. However, they always have been driving forces of what we know to be culture. Without the need to trade and exchange, there is no need to interact. Thus interculturality has economic roots and the role of businesses in modern cultural expression is simply a continuation of the tradition.

What has changed is the primacy of the economic force as cultural device. Whereas in earlier times the exchange of culture was secondary to the exchange of goods, the modern globalized media environment also exchanges culture in preparation for the exchange of goods. Thus advertising for a product may begin well before the product is launched in a particular market—or the traditions of consumerism may be imparted to a target audience before goods are sold to them. It is extremely naive to expect that this is not an exchange of culture and that the advertised product as well as the advertisement become part of the receiving audience's culture.

When a British person vacuums his living room, he "Hoovers" it. For many Americans a carbonated beverage is a Coke regardless of its brand. In such subtle ways the business of corporations has influenced culture. Not only have they added to the lexicon, but commerce and industry have also introduced material elements, artifacts, and practices that both influence and form modern culture. Watson (2004, 156) argued that even McDonald's and similar fast-food chains can introduce social and cultural changes

> in Japan, for example, using one's hands to hold and simultaneously eat prepared foods was considered a gross breach of etiquette before the popularization of McDonald's hamburgers. The company had such a dramatic impact on popular attitudes that it is not uncommon to see Tokyo commuters eating in public, without chopsticks or spoons.

What is more useful for the present analysis is his argument that some of these changes are not only beneficial but also come to be defining features of culture in the host societies. He argued, for example, that another innovation that has had a revolutionary effect on local cultures in Asia, Latin America, Europe, and Asia is the provision of clean toilets and washrooms. McDonald's was instrumental in setting new standards, and thereby raising consumer expectations, in cities that had never had public facilities. (157)

He further claimed that

when McDonald's opened in 1975, customers clumped around the cash registers, shouting orders and waving money over the heads of people in front of them. The company responded by introducing queue monitors (young women) who channeled everyone into orderly lines. (156)

This, he went on to say, led to queuing becoming a "hallmark of Hong Kong's cosmopolitan, middle class culture." Thus stereotypes or generalizations about particular cultures can be of relatively recent vintage, and can be the result of global and multinational trade and commercial forces including not only marketing and advertising but also the specific forms of business practices and conduct. These are important ideas that we will return to in greater detail.

Chapter Three

Conquest, Imperialism, and Culture

Bhagwati (2004) recounted a news item from France in 1999 that might have been easily missed but for its reflections of globalization concerns. On the surface it was a single act of resistance to a perceived threat to livelihood:

> On August 12, 1999, José Bové, an obscure Frenchman, and a group of other farmers enter the town of Millau in southwestern France and flattened a McDonald's that was still under construction. The rubble was driven, in a celebratory fashion and much like a corpse in a hearse, through the town on trucks and tractors and dumped on its outskirts. (106)

Yet, the action of these farmers, perhaps motivated more by fear than ideology, was couched in ideological and cultural terms by the media. According to Bhagwati (2004, 106), the French media commented that McDonald's "commercial hegemony threatens our agriculture and its cultural hegemony insidiously ruins alimentary behavior—both sacred reflections of the French identity." We shall return to this idea of the sacredness of identity in later discussions, but for now, we take note of the British Broadcasting Corporation's (BBC) reporting of the incident that compared Bové to the fictional French hero Astérix the Gaul. It is worth noting here too, since we are discussing global influences, that Lieber and Weisberg (2002, 286) described Bové not as an obscure farmer or as a folk hero but rather as "an antiglobalization activist who learned his tactics while a foreign student at the University of California at Berkeley."

ASTERIX AND THE GAULS

In Goscinny and Uderzo's series of illustrated (comic) books, their hero Asterix repeatedly and successfully leads their Gaulish village in defense of their way of life and culture against the onslaught of Roman armies. The portrayal of life under the pressures of cultural domination is quite idyllic and full of optimism and pride. In Asterix and Obelix's adventures, thanks to their magic potion and lots of dumb luck, the Gaulish village always prevails. Its culture is shown to be intact at the end of each adventure with a lavish celebration featuring meals of wild boar and traditional music (though someone invariably figures a way to tie up and silence the famously untalented bard—Cacaphonix is his name in the English versions).

We know that the history of human culture is less rosy. Humankind's history has included numerous instances of (often violent) conquest and domination of others and significant cultural influences have been spread by these means. The term "conquest" is a contested one on cultural grounds as well since we may argue that a group or people invaded and subjugated may not necessarily be conquered—particularly if their culture survives the ordeal. Here let us hold that conquest refers simply to a condition in which one group is subject to the rule of a culturally alien other group by force.

The culture of "conquered" peoples has often been destroyed along with their populations. Despite humankind's long history of barbaric conquests, Godsen (2004, 25) singled out modern colonialism for its barbarity and destruction:

> In a comparative survey of colonialism modern modes stand out as unique. These led to the creation of settler societies in north America, south Africa, Siberia, Australia and New Zealand, the mass killing and dispossession of the indigenous inhabitants and the active deployment of domination and resistance. Few other colonial forms operated in this manner or had such negative effects.

For just one example, consider that between the late fifteenth and early sixteenth centuries Spanish conquistadores wiped out entire populations of Arawak natives in the Caribbean and the Arawak culture died with the conquered (Lopez 1990; Stannard 1992). Much of what we know of these people comes from the accounts of early European arrivals to their lands. Many of the people giving the accounts were extremely biased, having had little contact with alien people and cultures and unable in most part to understand the language of the people they subjugated.

Bartolome de las Casas was one of the few among early Spanish arrivals to the Caribbean who viewed the natives with some measure of humanity and also recorded the activities of his fellow colonizers. Lopez (1990, 4) summarized some of Las Casas observations this way:

> One day, in front of Las Casas, the Spanish dismembered, beheaded, or raped 3000 people. "Such inhumanities and barbarisms were committed in my sight," he says, "as no age can parallel. . . ." The Spanish cut off the legs of children who ran from them. They poured people full of boiling soap. They made bets as to who, with one sweep of his sword, could cut a person in half. They loosed dogs that "devoured an Indian like a hog, at first sight, in less than a moment." They used nursing infants for dog food. (see also de las Casas 1992)

The native Caribs (from whom the region derives its name) fared only slightly better in terms of physical and cultural survival. A small number of this genetic and cultural grouping survived and vestigial remains of their culture may still be found today on the islands of Dominica, St. Vincent, and Trinidad. However, most of the surviving members of this culture do not speak their native language. Ironically, scholars from outside are currently working to reconstruct the language from the little that is still known of it.

ROMAN INFLUENCES AND COUNTERINFLUENCES

Empires could scarcely be built if the natives of conquered land were always destroyed. Conquered peoples have themselves often come to constitute the empires of the conquering forces. Despite the often significant and forced imposition of outside values, ideas, and material goods, native cultures persist to varying degrees in its surviving members. Many successful empires spread their influence and consolidated their rule precisely because of their ability to tolerate, engage, and even assimilate the cultures of the conquered. Under Roman rule, for example, despite strict and sometimes brutal regimes, many different cultures were not only allowed but also encouraged as long as they did not interfere with the rule of the Empire. McKay, Hill, and Buckler (2006, 125) argued that

> Rome's achievement lay in the ability of the Romans not only to conquer peoples but to incorporate them into the Roman system. Rome succeeded where the Greek *polis* had failed. Unlike the Greeks, who refused to share citizenship, the Romans extended their citizenship first to the Italians and later to the peoples of the provinces. With that citizenship went Roman government and law.

Scarre and Fagan (2003, 301) noted, however, that even the powerful (and more insular) Greek cultural and linguistic imperial influence in the Mediterranean and beyond to Africa, followed this pattern of cultural retention and hybridity:

> In Egypt, for example, royal instructions were written in hieroglyphic even though the ruling family, the Ptolemies, were Macedonians, did not intermarry with the local population, and habitually spoke Greek. In other regions of the Hellenistic world, a curious hybrid culture developed, combining Greek elements with local styles.

Scarre and Fagan emphasized this retention of cultural identity in their description of an empire as "an amalgam of several states that are allowed to retain a measure of cultural identity, and even political autonomy, provided they deliver tribute to the imperial heartland and not deviate from their allegiance" (230).

This frequently meant that cross influences or mutual influence were not out of the question. To return to our fictional heroes Asterix and Obelix, the reality of their situation in the first century BC included mutual influences and what Woolf (1997, 349) called the "persistence of cultural diversity in the course of the extension of Roman power over Gaul." According to Woolf,

> It is evident that, as a result of the extension of Roman power over Gaul, local societies there were drawn into a much more complex imperial world. Romans were more differentiated from one another in terms of wealth, occupation, experience and status than were Gauls who mostly lived in locally circumscribed societies ruled by warrior and religious elites and were mostly full-time agriculturalists. Yet the effects of Roman expansion were not limited to recruiting new members to a more complex society. Roman expansion also resulted in a complexification of Roman society itself. (345–346)

JESUS AND THE SPIES

This particular dynamic is evident in the Gospel story of Jesus being asked whether he condoned paying taxes to the Romans. The repressive force of Roman rule is evident in the loaded nature of the question to Jesus. The question itself was a trap since we are told in Matthew 22:15 that the Pharisees and the Herodians plotted as to "how they might entangle him in his talk." According to Luke 20:20 "They watched him, and sent forth spies, which should feign themselves just men." These "spies" posing as "just men" knew that an open challenge to Roman taxation would have dire consequences should Jesus be caught in such an utterance. Jesus's response at

Matthew 22:21 "Render therefore unto Caesar the things which are Caesar's; and unto God the things that are God's" reflected that the matters of the Empire, though serious, were also quite removed from issues in the local culture. Godsen (2004, 104–106) addressed the relationship between the imperial and the local, suggesting that

> Roman culture was spread not solely, or mainly, by Romans, but in some considerable measure through local people in the western provinces of the empire adopting Roman ways in their own manner. . . . The empire as a whole formed a giant circulation system which connected flows of people, religious practices and material culture throughout the empire, so that influences came from everywhere and flowed to everywhere. . . . The influence of the empire as a whole was felt on each of the parts and vice versa.

He also suggested that the conquered subjects of the Roman Empire had quite some measure of choice as to how much of the Roman culture they wished to adopt. Yet, it would be another cultural force that would be the most important influence on the Roman Empire, that of the nascent cult surrounding a carpenter's son turned religious and moral teacher, Jesus of Nazareth, which was eventually to become what we know as Christianity (Godsen 2004; Scarre and Fagan 2003). We shall examine this particular cultural influence in more detail in later chapters, including the several influences upon its adoption and evolution over the millennia.

ISLAMIC EMPIRE

A somewhat less recognized but nevertheless culturally important factor is the notion that similar colonial influences were exercised by the Islamic Empire in the period from the mid-seventh century. Nagel (2006, 408–409) described the rise of the Islamic Empire in the following terms:

> The Muslim conquests of the seventh and early eighth centuries were among the largest, most rapid, and most permanent in history. Syria, Mesopotamia, and Egypt fell by mid-seventh century and Arab armies moved across north Africa to Spain. . . . Rome was sacked, Sicily occupied, and raids conducted regularly throughout Italy.
>
> The Persian kingdom of Iran was destroyed by 644 and the conquerors moved on into what is today Pakistan. By 715, some 80 years after the death of Muhammad, the Islamic world stretched from the Atlantic to the Chinese frontier.

Karsh (2007, 23) echoed this assessment, saying,

few events have transformed the course of human history as swiftly and profoundly as the expansion of early Islam and its conquest of much of the ancient
world. Within twelve years of Muhammad's death in June 632, Iran's long-
reigning Sasanid Empire had been reduced to a tributary, and Egypt and Syria
had been wrested from Byzantine rule. By the early eighth century, the Muslims had extended their domination over Central Asia and much of the Indian
subcontinent all the way to the Chinese frontier, had laid siege to Constantinople, the capital of the Byzantines, and had overrun North Africa and Spain.

The Islamic Empire was also marked by a duality of purpose as it attempted
to balance its imperial and religious goals with the demands of local and
native populations. Despite the essentially religious nature of the expansion,
political and cultural goals were also pursued and the level of integration of
other cultures was always problematic for the empire. Curtin (1984, 104)
argued that this empire, which he marked as starting with the capture of Syria
in 636 and the establishment of a capital in Damascus, was an Arab state but
was also influenced by the world around it, saying that

> the resulting state was Arab, and it was to spread the use of Arabic in much the
> same way the Roman Empire spread and left a heritage of Latin as a written
> language for a large part of Europe, lasting for centuries after the Roman
> Empire had disappeared. But, in most important aspects of culture, it also
> picked up the heritage of the two civilizations combined under the new empire,
> namely the Byzantine heritage in the West and the Sassanian heritage of Iraq
> and Persia in the East.

In a similar vein, Toy (1912, 509–510) noted that

> there was often a social fusion of conquerors and conquered, and this was
> accompanied by mutual religious influence. The conquered peoples, while
> adopting Islam, retained every one its native intellectual and religious color-
> ing, and contact with ancient culture (mainly through translations of Greek
> works) brought new points of view and new constructions of religious thought
> and life. These conditions produced certain modifications of the Koranic
> scheme in various parts of the Moslem world.

Despite these early mutual counter-influences, it may yet be argued that
Islam, until this day, and despite its widespread diffusion, has never successfully divested itself of its connections to the Arab land, people and language.
The paradox of this is that the initial promulgators of this faith were themselves a diverse (and somewhat ragtag) group including women, an African
slave, and others who were not part of the Arab power hierarchy. According
to Karsh (2007, 19),

it is true that Muhammad's community was predominantly Arab in composition, but this was merely an historical accident attending Muhammad's Arabian descent and the environment in which he operated. Even before the establishment of the umma, some of the first converts to Islam had been of foreign extraction, notably Byzantine and Ethiopian, and in creating his community the prophet took great care to ensure its universal nature by substituting religion for tribal kinship as the basis of social and political affinity.

Unable or unwilling to divest themselves of their highly Arab-centered ideas, the Muslim conquerors exercised a modicum of tolerance in keeping with their religious tenets—which essentially prescribed some level of special treatment for Jews and Christians (*ahl al-Kitab*, or people of the book). This in itself was probably more due to religious edicts that were previously handed down by the Prophet Muhammad or contained in their holy scriptures than to any sense of either cultural engagement or compassion on the part of the conquerors.

According to Nagel (2006, 408),

> the heartland of Christianity fell to the Arab invaders without a struggle. The inhabitants of these regions did not immediately convert to Islam but remained, as did the peasants of Mesopotamia, as a separate category of subordinate taxpayers.

The non-Muslim inhabitants of the Islamic Empire (known as the *dhimmi*) were always doomed to be second-class citizens unless they converted to Islam. In the case of conquered groups, they forfeited their lands to the invaders but were allowed to work that land in return for a tribute (called the *kharaj*—a sort of protection money) to be paid to the Empire. In parts of the Empire the dhimmi were reduced to serfdom and their children emerged into the same state of bondage. In addition to the kharaj, another tax called the *jizya* was also imposed on able-bodied adult male dhimmis. To add insult to economic injury, some such as Bat Ye'or (1985) suggest that the payees were publicly beaten during the payment ceremony and also made to wear the receipt for the tax around their necks or on their wrists—without which they were not free to move around.

Given these social and economic discrepancies, one might imagine that many of the dhimmi tried to convert to improve their conditions. However, despite the religious underpinnings of the Islamic Empire, its rulers often discouraged conversion. Karsh (2007) gave the example of Hajjaj ibn Yusuf who ruled the Iraqi region for twenty years (694–714) and who actively discouraged conversion in order to preserve revenues from taxes and tributes. According to Karsh,

> Hajjaj took draconian measures to discourage conversion and to drive the new
> converts back to their villages, including having the names of their villages
> branded on people's hands to prevent them from returning to the towns. One of
> his favorite modes of torture was to apply hot wax to his victims' naked
> bodies. This was then pulled off till the flesh was all lacerated, following
> which vinegar and salt were poured on the wounds until death ensued. (39)

Thus even after conversion, the dhimmi were still victimized by the largely
Arab and completely Muslim ruling classes. Noting that many of the Emper-
ors paid little more than lip service to religion, Karsh characterized the Islamic Empire as an Arab military autocracy run by Arabs for Arabs. He concludes that

> it dissuaded non-Arabs from converting to Islam so as to keep them subjugated
> and in a position of inferiority, and treated those who nevertheless converted
> (not to mention non-Muslim subjects) as second-class citizens. Non-Arabs
> played no role in the making of imperial policies and had to endure numerous
> encroachments on their social and cultural identities. (43)

The remnants of these policies and attitudes are still evident in vestigial form
in some Islamic countries today long after the demise of the Islamic Empire.
Freedom of religion in several Gulf countries involves a tacit acknowledge-
ment that Christian observances may be privately held without any outward
preaching. People of other religions such as Hindus are often denied religious
privileges (such as renting or building public places of worship) because
their religions are not mentioned in the Muslim scriptures (US Department of
State 2008). Rampant suspicion and political influences make Jewish observances quite rare as well.

Fast-forward a few hundred years and European colonization of the so-
called new world (new to whom?) if arbitrarily marked at the start of Columbus's voyages in 1492, began in the context of a flourishing printing industry
in Europe. It would take another few hundred years until printing evolved
into a form of mass mediated communication and exerted its role in the
Empire. Though Harold Innis ([1950] 2007) has amply demonstrated the
importance of various forms of communication and communicative developments in the spread and maintenance of empires throughout history, it is at
the pinnacle of the British Empire that we begin to see the connection between what we might recognize today as mass media and the imperial agen-
da.

MEDIA, CULTURE, AND THE BRITISH EMPIRE

Hannerz (1992, 182) noted the cultural influences of British Colonialism in India. He calls Calcutta, for example, a "product of Western colonialism" and claims that the Bengal Renaissance was in large part a matter of an encounter between Bengali and European cultures. Bearing in mind that many communications scholars and others have noted the communicative and propagandistic power of buildings and other edifices, the extent of the British cultural influences could even be felt in the homes of the Indians themselves, as Hannerz noted: "By the beginning of the nineteenth century. . . . A British visitor would describe the houses of the established Bengali families, with Corinthian pillars in front and English furniture inside" (183).

Plunkett (2003) characterized Queen Victoria as the first "media monarch." While primarily concerned with the effects of press coverage on the image of the monarchy in Victorian England, he also noted the impact of this and other media on the British empire of the time. He pointed to Queen Victoria's Diamond Jubilee in 1897 being one of the first major public events ever to be filmed, saying that "the Diamond Jubilee pictures proved highly successful and were a standard feature of many variety programs in both London and the provinces" (240). The clear role of mediated communications in promoting and consolidating the empire is also evident in the British Crown's use of the telegraph:

> By the end of her reign, Victoria was the Great White Empress, the symbolic hub of the British Empire. Demonstrations of Victoria's personal concern for her multitudinous subjects continued to take place. Such displays were nevertheless only made possible by the communicative power of the international telegraph system. The first line between India and Europe had been opened in January 1856. . . . Before leaving Buckingham Palace for her Diamond Jubilee procession, Victoria sent a special telegraph message rippling across the empire reading "From my heart I thank my beloved people. God bless them!" Contemporary writers and critics were well aware of the imperial role of the telegraph network. . . . The telegraph network made the Queen-Empress's demise one of the first truly global media events. The latest bulletins upon her health were carried to every corner of the British Empire. Crowds gathered at telegraph stations as far apart as Melbourne, Bombay, and Montreal. (240–241)

Later, the BBC would continue this influence through international conflicts involving the British Empire and in many more subtle ways such as continuing focus on British concerns in the post-Empire environments of many newly independent states.

COLONIZATION AND CULTURAL (RE)INVENTIONS

This role of media in yesterday's Empire, today's globalization (however construed) and culture (however imagined) has been both pivotal and under-represented in modern thought. This is true of the modern context of mediated globalization of cultures and, perhaps more importantly, it is also true of the historical context of the evolution of modern society in which mediated messages both fashioned and supported images of reality (e.g., wartime news reels, travelogues, and international news wires). Ongoing systems of mediated representations of reality that influence cultures include international news flows and the cultural products of dominant nations that are distributed worldwide. While there has been some scholarly attention to these issues in fields such as mass communication and cultural studies, the scope of analysis has generally tended to be somewhat narrow—examining current and recent social issues and generally ignoring tremendously long-standing and lingering cross-cultural influences—some of which lead to paradoxes in our analysis of media and cultural issues.

COLONIALISM AND INDIAN MEDIA

The conservatism of Indian media in the context of India's rich and ancient history of sexual expression provides one such seeming paradox. The second largest producer of feature films in the world, Indian cinema is notable for its international reach, its lavish productions, and also for its aversion to direct representations of sexual activity including the portrayal of kissing (Rampal 2001). Valentine's Day is also an annual source of contention with some conservative groups holding protests and even (more recently) turning to threats of violence against couples observing the event (Doniger 2009).

In the ancient times of the Vedas, the Indian deity Lord Krishna was sought after by many women and famously enjoyed the delights of sexual encounters. In *India before Europe*, Asher and Talbot (2006, 111) cited two ancient Hindu writers who "focused on Krishna as an adolescent, when he had frequent amorous adventures with the cowherding women (gopis) of Vrindavan village, near Mathura. Night after night, the gopis are said to have left their sleeping families behind and hurried to secret liaisons with Krishna." In the same vein, the authors also cited an eleventh-century erotic Indian poem with illustrations called the "Chaurapanchashika, Fifty Stanzas of a Love Thief" telling of the seduction of a young princess by her tutor. They noted that "the illustrations are bold in their portrayal of seductive acts, as the teacher lifts his pupil's skirt to educate her in ways far beyond her parents' expectations" (111).

Many centuries ago, religious-minded Indians produced highly erotic temple carvings on a cluster of some twenty-five temples at Khajuraho in Madhya Pradesh state. Mitter (2001, 69) described the carvings as containing "various poses and scenes ranging from lovemaking couples to group sex and bestiality." Writing of the Nayaka kingdoms of the seventeenth century in India, Asher and Talbot (2006, 178) noted that

> the [Nayaka] kings are depicted in literature not so much as warrior-heroes or even as moral exemplars but rather as semi-divine and highly erotic individuals. . . . There is no shortage of (erotic) images rendered on calicos, in ivory, and on stucco adorning local temples. A Nayaka courtier, for instance, is shown in an ivory statue embracing a voluptuous woman.

Comparisons with a relative prudishness of modern Indian media expressions reveal apparent contradictions in attitudes to sexuality that have at times been explained with some reference to the colonial influences of British Victorian sexual attitudes (Arondekar 2000; Singh 1996) and in terms of what Tambe (2000, 586) has characterized as a "consonance between Victorian sexual Puritanism" and "Indian religious revivalism." Bhatia (2003) argued, for example, that even the attire of Indian women was the result of colonial influences mixed with local traditions. Like other cultural issues, this is a contentious one with tremendously detailed and nuanced arguments subsumed within larger questions about forms of colonial domination, but it is not unreasonable to suggest that there was some relationship between Victorian social mores and inherited Indian norms of public sexual expression.

Doniger (2009, paras. 11–13) captured something of the complexity of the relationship between local culture and colonial influence writing that

> Some of the British, especially in the early colonial period, admired and celebrated the sensuality of Hinduism. Others, particularly but not only the later Protestant missionaries, despised what they regarded as Hindu excesses. Unfortunately, many educated Hindus took their cues from the second sort of Brit and became ashamed of the sensuous aspects of their own religion, aping the Victorians (who were, after all, very Victorian), becoming more Protestant than thou. It is not fair to blame the British for the Puritanical strain in Hinduism; it began much earlier. But they certainly made it a lot worse.

Whether or not one agrees that British Victorian sexuality influenced modern Indian sexual expression (and despite debate about the extent of any such influence) it is clear that British colonialism left a cultural legacy in India. British rule, for example, imparted the Indian subcontinent with English as a lingua franca. This remnant of British colonialism benefits Indian culture and society today externally (particularly in India's ability to leverage itself in international business). It is sometimes less obvious that the introduction of

English also provided a tool of national integration for India's diverse linguistic groups with their hundreds of dialects and variations. This is particularly true since Hindi had never evolved to the status of a national tongue.

This is not to contest the basic notion that in all cases of conquest, the conquered culture suffers upheaval, erosion, and loss of much that it once treasured. India continues to suffer the throes of cultural upheaval stemming from and trailing after centuries of British colonial rule. Yet, Indian culture in its many forms is known to be vibrant and deeply entrenched. No one would argue that Indian culture was destroyed by the British occupation—though it was certainly changed.

Under colonial rule cultural dislocation is always a possibility, cultural synthesis is commonplace, and cultural change is inevitable. At the same time, it was a learned ascetic with a decidedly traditional approach who would lead the drive toward Indian independence. We will revisit this interplay of colonial influences and traditional cultures in later chapters.

As is true here in the case of the British Empire we do often tend to forget that forms of mass-mediated communication did actually exist long before our modern satellites and Internet. Hoodfar (2005, 411–412) pointed to the role of books, for example, in promoting and maintaining the concept of colonial superiority:

> In a century and a half, 1800 to 1950, an estimated sixty thousand books were published in the West on the Arab orient alone. The primary mission of these writings was to depict the colonized Arabs/Muslims as inferior/backward and urgently in need of progress offered to them by the colonial superiors.

While the British Empire and other European powers depended on the printed word, the telegraph, and then on radio, other empires in the past depended on parchment and even architecture to spread the messages of colonization and cultural influence (Innis [1950] 2007; Scarre and Fagan 2003). The consequences and legacies of such cultural influences continue till today in the form of legal precedents, linguistic turns, religious ideas, and more. Bonsu (2009), for example, provided evidence from consumer interpretations of advertising images to argue that old colonial ideas and imagery surrounding (and subjugating) Africa linger in the presentations and readings of global advertising. It is also important for us to note that modern colonial enterprise has frequently been deeply intertwined with early notions of global capital that tended to conflate ideas of religion, race, and conquest (Campbell 1999).

Chapter Four

Neo-imperialism, Media, and Culture

The field of communication studies has evolved into several different areas of specialization including international and intercultural communications. These specializations as well as the field's concern with mass media and "new media" are central to the processes associated with globalization, as are emerging issues of the blurring of mass and interpersonal communications.

Despite being guilty of a lack of leadership, communications scholarship has not been ignorant of globalization nor has it been negligent in addressing the issue. Even before globalization had become a "hot" topic, communications scholars were concerned with the effects of unbalanced information flows among nations. One of the key concepts to emerge from communication scholarship of the past few decades was one that associated the traditions of colonialism with the information relationships among modern nations. These relationships were characterized as "neo-imperialism" and suggested that the new forms of imperialism were primarily cultural.

These notions of neo-imperialism or cultural imperialism were popularized by scholars such as Herbert Schiller (1976) and Thomas McPhail (1981) who used terms such as "cultural domination" and "electronic colonialism" to describe a process in which international powers now exercise cultural influence over "the other" without the tiresome need for invasion, occupation, administration, and governance. Croteau and Hoynes (2003, 260) outlined the basic tenets of the cultural imperialism thesis as follows:

> Western media products introduced into other countries, especially "developing" countries, contributed to a decline in local traditional values and promoted, instead, values associated with capitalism. In addition, ownership and control over media were maintained in US hands, and other nations became more dependent on the United States for cultural production.

Similar, but often much more esoteric analysis could be found from the pen of Noam Chomsky. Not that these were the only scholars expounding such ideas, mind you, just that they were the ones who got the most press—being from the same powerful countries and economies that they were criticizing and all. Many so-called third world scholars including the likes of Hamid Mowlana, Walter Rodney, and George Beckford were also analyzing the persistent and debilitating social, cultural, and economic legacies of colonialism and its methods of regeneration (but—somewhat ironically—they received far less attention).

One particular manifestation of the skewed relationships of production and control of information was what Drahos and Braithwaite (2002) termed "information feudalism." They gave an example of how the communication policies of dominant nations could be used as trade weapons even in a globalized trading environment. During the early 1980s the Caribbean islands saw a booming trade in satellite dishes and receivers since it became apparent that US broadcasters were beaming signals with footprints that spread well beyond the borders of the United States. The US broadcasters and the US administration never particularly accepted the view of many in the region that the signals, far from being US property at the point of reception, were actually violating sovereign territory by presenting themselves in foreign nations uninvited. Far from it, US producers made the argument that the owners of the signals were to be paid for the unauthorized reception of their signals. What seems a given in today's producer-dominated intellectual property environment was not so cut and dry back then. So a little muscle was needed to enforce the producers' point of view and it came in the form of trade policy. The nations of the Caribbean are not only in the satellite footprint of the United States but also in the backyard of the world's most powerful economy. They depend on this market for their survival in terms of goods and services, and in many of the islands, this trade is focused on tourism.

Action on the issue of satellite signal reception (or interception) came from the top and it came hard. The opportunity came in 1983 when the signing of a major trade and assistance deal between the Caribbean region and the United States was being finalized. It was known as the Caribbean Basin Economic Recovery Act, or more popularly, the Caribbean Basin Initiative and included duty concessions and several other trade incentives. If we are to believe the stories of that time in the Caribbean region, intellectual property provisions were written into the agreement at the last minute at the behest of the US entertainment industry with which the then-President Reagan had strong ties.

According to Drahos and Braithwaite (2002, 83),

the president was obliged to refuse a country this benefit if a government owned entity in it was broadcasting copyrighted material without the consent of the US copyright owners. Other provisions required the President not to designate a country for benefits if it had taken steps in relation to intellectual property that amounted to the nationalization or expropriation of that property. The Act gave the president some flexibility to overlook a state's record on intellectual property on the grounds of national economic and security interests. But it was also made clear in the background reports relating to the Act that the president was not to do deals with Caribbean states that would lessen the protection of US copyright owners.

In addition to the imposition of the copyright rules on these states, the US government also forced them to find copyright law experts to draft such laws. The experts also came from the United States:

> Several Caribbean states like the Dominican Republic found themselves having to acquire copyright law in a hurry in order to get entry into the US market on favorable terms. Finding the necessary local expertise to do the job was something of a problem since intellectual property protection had not been a high domestic priority. US copyright experts soon found themselves on flights bound for the Caribbean, where they drafted the necessary legislation. Inevitably they produced laws based on US models. The process of imprinting US intellectual property standards on the world had begun. (Drahos and Braithwaite 2002, 83)

Despite such evidence of the abuses of information and communication policies, ideas such as cultural imperialism and intellectual feudalism have been roundly criticized by a large number of scholars. Croteau and Hoynes (2003, 206), for example, echoed the frequently expressed notion that cultural imperialism was (and is) a conspiracy theory of sorts, suggesting that cultural imperialism analysis somehow argued that "US-owned media hardware and programs were part of a plan to culturally subjugate the world." Not surprisingly, many of the critics of cultural imperialism are also from the powerful developed countries. Also not surprisingly, the corporate media has often given more attention to the criticisms of cultural imperialism than to the actual charges made by the likes of Schiller and Chomsky.

The phenomena associated with cultural imperialism have not gone away. They have, in fact, become worse. Schiller and McPhail had little more to worry about than taped foreign television programs, pop music, and the occasional satellite feed. Their cross-border flows did not include the Internet. Their global marketing did not include podcasts. They were not getting troubleshooting advice for their PC from "Alfred" (not his real name) in Bangalore.

The regeneration of cultural (and other forms of) imperialism has come with a different name—globalization. Martin-Barbero (2000, 36) compared the evolution of globalization to traditional imperialism:

> Contrary to the process that until the 1970s was called imperialism, the globalization of the economy redefines center/periphery relations: what "globalization" means is no longer invasions but transformations produced from and within the national and even the local sphere. It is from within each country that not only economies but cultures are being globalized.

If we take a step back, it becomes apparent that both imperialism and modern globalization have somewhat more ancient roots than are usually evident. Part of the reason for the ongoing process of globalization has to do with its deep roots. In their book *Communication and Empire: Media, Markets, and Globalization, 1860–1930*, Winseck and Pike (2007, 1) chose 1860 as their starting date with the following rationale:

> Our starting point of 1860 reflects a number of factors, including the extra-European focus of capital flows that emerged in the last few decades of the nineteenth century, the parallel rise of multinational corporate and financial institutions, the emergence of new technologies and business models that became the basis of what we call the global media system, and the advent of modernity.

Trouillot (2003, 29) asserted that "the world became global in the sixteenth century," adding that

> the rise of the west, , the conquest of the Americas, plantation slavery, the Industrial Revolution, and the population flows of the nineteenth century can be summarized as "a first movement of globality," an Atlantic moment culminating in US hegemony after World War II.

Globalization, as an ongoing and gradual process, can also be seen as a continuation of the cultural imperialism of past decades and the actual imperialism of the past centuries. Further, the processes and principles of globalization are also destructive to the very nation-states that they try to incorporate. Martin-Barbero (2000, 36) pointed to the "social and political disintegration of the national sphere" where the rules are determined "not by the state but by the market transformed into an organizing principle of society."

Interestingly enough, even among wealthy countries, there is still concern over the impact of foreign media. Gathercole (1987, 80) noted, for example, that from watching US television, Canadian schoolchildren think the FBI is a Canadian institution and know more about the laws and legal systems of the United States than those of Canada.

This perceived impact of foreign media portrayals has been widely examined (Ang 1985; Tan, Tan, and Gibson 2003; Liebes and Katz 1993) with an enduring concern for the extent to which foreign media can be said to influence receiving audiences and their respective cultures. Elasmar and Hunter (2003) conducted a meta-analysis of thirty-six cross-border studies of US television broadcasting in the period 1960 to 1995 and found considerable evidence of effects on the attitudes, values, and beliefs of receiving audiences, though they noted that these were varied, often subtle, the results of active audiences and often inconsistent with the dominant cultural imperialism paradigm of the period. The impact of foreign media (however theorized) has also been empirically demonstrated. Madanat, Brown, and Hawks (2007, 1039), for example, in a study of Jordanian women, argued that "Western advertising and media were associated with restrained and emotional eating, desired weight loss, and disordered eating attitudes and behaviors."

There are numerous studies that point to active audiences who translate and adapt the meanings of foreign contents to suit their needs. Liebes and Katz (1993), for example, examined the worldwide popularity of the US television soap opera *Dallas*. They identified "primordiality" (connections with fundamental or universal mythologies regarding ideas about kinship, good, and evil) and "seriality" (continuing interest in the story as it unfolds) as two of the factors that prompted viewers abroad to consume this American product. In their analysis, Liebes and Katz questioned the process of cultural imperialism. They warned against the notion of a passive viewer in this cross-cultural context, suggesting that foreign viewers of US television can be quite critical in their readings of content.

Another perspective on this issue may be found in the literature on so-called textual transparency or narrative transparency commonly associated with the work of Scott R. Olson. In this context, transparency may be defined as a "textual apparatus that allows audiences to project their indigenous values, beliefs, and rituals into imported media" (Olson 1999, 5). In keeping with the notion of an active audience, this transparency perspective suggests that audiences are capable of ascribing their own meanings to media content regardless of what the producers intended. Chitnis et al. (2006, 133) explained that textual transparency or "narrative transparency theory" argues that "a cross-cultural understanding of the text may take place because the audience interprets a foreign text using their own cultural beliefs and values." An example of this comes from a study of American popular music in China in which Rupke and Blank (2009, 143) concluded that

> local audiences pick and choose those American cultural elements that reso-
> nate most closely with their life, their needs, and their personal goals. Some
> elements of American culture don't fit well and they are discarded. Powerful

local institutions play a role by supporting some elements but not others. This sort of pushing and pulling reshapes American popular culture to fit the local context. There is American influence, of course, but it is mitigated, altered, and molded by the local culture.

Given these realities, when the names of multinational media giants are mentioned today, the one-way nature of information flows as imagined by the cultural imperialism thesis becomes somewhat more complicated by the complexities of the modern globalized media market. Jenkins (2004, 119), for example, noted that

> major media companies, such as Bertelsmann, Sony, and Universal Vivendi, contract talent worldwide, catering to the tastes of local markets rather than pursuing nationalistic interests; their economic structure engages them not only to serve as intermediaries between different Asian markets but also to bring Asian content into Western countries. Many American children are more familiar with the characters of Pokeman than they are with those from the Brothers Grimm or Hans Christian Andersen, and a growing portion of American youth are dancing to Asian beats.

Further, American films and television content are not unique in the possession of narrative transparency. Bainbridge and Norris (2008) argued, for example, that Japanese animated comic books including anime and manga forms demonstrate the same or similar qualities. They argued that these Japanese exports function in ways that are similar to those asserted by Olson about American movies and television programs. The deeper question to be addressed in this context is not whether various texts are transparent, but rather, how relevant is the question of transparency in a globalized production environment? The 2009 success of *Slumdog Millionaire*, for example, involved a British production team creating a movie in India that went on to win a United States' best picture academy award. More and more, the globalized scope of film and television production is matched by globalized reception conventions. This produces an international form of media literacy, conventionalized over time and through repeated experience. Where more and more film and television production is undertaken with the global scope of media markets in mind, a broad subscription to and recognition of the elements of narrative transparency that serves only to widen potential market appeal is not bad for business.

Whether produced with transparency in mind or not, examples of broad appeal of (non-American) foreign content can be found in the recent popularity of Turkish soap operas in the Arabian Gulf and wider Middle East and the popularity of Indian movies in Nigeria (Larkin 2008). This spread of nonindigenous (and non–United States) programming begs the question of whether the notion of narrative transparency has legitimate roots in American media production or whether Olson has simply identified the broad parameters of intertextual recognition that can be applied to any media. The focus on US media may be more of a historical fact related to the domination of the production industries in past decades than to some special narrative or textual transparency of American content as Olson seems to suggest.

Still, questions remain about the fundamental assumptions of a perspective such as narrative transparency. Whereas it contains an implicit understanding of the interconnectedness of various texts, it appears to presume that such texts are inherently separate to begin with. While this is entirely consistent with the insular perspectives of traditional cultural analysis, it may find less relevance in a global (and globalized) media environment. Here, while the contexts maybe local, the themes and, indeed, the mythologies are increasingly likely to be universal.

The literature on transparency is rooted in Olsen's attempt to explain what he perceived as Hollywood's competitive advantage in film and television. It argues that audiences are able to reinterpret Hollywood content because it excels in areas such as verisimilitude (the sense of realism), inclusion (a sense of participation in the unfolding of the plot relating to their own lives), and ellipticality (allowing the spectator to speculate on what may be going on, and thus "completing" the picture in their own minds). Some scholars question this presumed superiority of US content on these and several other dimensions. Feng (2008, 1), for example, concluded that transparency is simply "a vehicle of reinforcing the American cultural hegemony with the disguise of multiculturalism."

Outside of continuing concerns about hegemony and neo-imperialism, other analyses have emphasized voluntary reception and discretionary internalization of commingled global influences. Kraidy (2005) has used "hybridity" to label the idea that new hybrid identities develop out of multiple and competing identity-building forces in modern societies. This concept has gained currency in discussions of modern cultures including Bollywood weddings (Kapur, 2009), reality television in Saudi Arabia (Kraidy, 2009), and Chinese martial arts films (Wang, 2008).

Despite its popularity, the concept of hybridity also presents several difficulties. Straubhaar (2008) pointed out that people rarely identify themselves as cultural hybrids, describing instead a set of cultural layers and spaces that they define and express. Another perspective on hybridity argues that despite outward shows of hybrid influences, audiences' core values and identities may remain unaffected. Scrase (2002), for example, argued that members of the Bengali middle class maintained their core traditional cultural identities despite adopting (or appearing to espouse) more contemporary identities from exposure to foreign television. Puri (2004) went a step further in interrogation of hybridity, arguing that the term "hybridity" is itself value laden with particular racial and paternalistic ideas that create biases in analyses falling under its scope.

NEW MEDIA, GLOBALIZATION, AND CULTURES IN CONFLICT

So-called new information and communication technologies have not ushered in a new utopia. While communication is important in avoiding or mitigating conflict, it is a necessary but not sufficient condition. Rubin (2002) argued that the globalized systems arising from these communication networks actually support conflicts such as those in Afghanistan, the Congo, and Angola. Webster (2001, 3) suggested that this same globalization has led to a decline in national sovereignty, writing of the decline of the nation-state in the following terms:

> No longer capable of effectively controlling affairs inside its territorial boundaries, for example because financial relationships transcend frontiers and take place instantaneously or because decisions taken by super states such as the European Union or United Nations may take precedence over national desires, the days of the sovereign nation-state seem to have passed.

The challenges of sovereignty and politics are exacerbated by an increasingly global scale of reference in which broad international coverage of events spawns more widespread public perception and stimulates opinion on a global scale. Hatchen (1999, 114) emphasized the role of media in the perceptions of international politics and thus on emerging global public opinion, noting that

> a significant portion of international political rivalries and frictions are refracted through the prism of international broadcasting—the nationalistic and ethnic animosities in the post–Cold War world, the Arab-versus-Israeli tensions as well as those between moderate and radical Arab regimes, the North-South disputes between rich and poor nations, plus dozens of smaller regional controversies and disagreements between neighboring nations.

However, increased global flows of information both at the mass and interpersonal levels do little to directly affect international conflict, particularly as traditional biases and selective focus continue to dominate. Additionally, issues of representation continue to be pertinent since a few nations dominate the international media and the news and information disseminated by these media reflect the cultural and political biases of those nations. Lundsten and

Stocchetti (2004), for example, argued that transnational broadcasters such as CNN and BBC can establish specific interpretations of global events to global audiences through the frames of their own national and cultural biases.

CULTURE, CORPORATIONS, AND THE GLOBAL

Traditional separation, or even opposition, between the domains of politics and corporate business becomes less evident and less meaningful in the globalized corporate environment. Menninger (1985, 208) examined the implications of viewing the corporation from political scientists' point of view and suggested that

> the corporation is economic activity through the establishment of systematic, organized rule of the many by the few. Employees are ruled by supervisors and managers, stockholders' assets are ruled by corporate directors, customers and suppliers are ruled by an industrial sector's entrenched giants. This occurs with no formal rationale or social contract that explicitly legitimizes such rule, and individuals seem to have little choice about accepting or rejecting the situation in a meaningful fashion. Countervailing forces such as government regulation of industry, subject to changes in administration and policy perspective, are insignificant checks to corporate power.

The corporation therefore employs a (not too attractive) system of politics within its specific environments. What happens when that system becomes the dominant paradigm of both society and leadership?

German thinker Max Weber (1964–1920) identified three typologies of authority, namely charismatic domination, traditional domination, and legal domination. Weber saw the loci of power as moving from charismatic individuals and traditions to formal states and legal systems. Weber was also famous for identifying what he termed the Protestant work ethic with the development of capitalism—a fact which bolsters the case for the power of religion as a (former) dominant social institution. The effects of dominant social institutions on culture are well known. In the past, several types of institutions have dominated various cultures to the point of bending culture to their whims. In each case, the institutions have had a basis for domination and they have created a class of dominant personalities who have also introduced their own whims to the process of domination.

In our own age, many argue that the predominant cultural force is the corporate multinational production or extraction institution. Corporate media is not simply a servant of the larger corporate ideology but also its chief foot-soldier—advancing a crusade-like set of basic beliefs about markets, economies, and consumption to ever-increasing crowds of faithful believers. The multinational corporation is also a kind of shape-shifter, which, for many decades, has been able to represent itself as different things to different people when necessary. Winseck and Pike (2007, 5) noted that even in the late nineteenth century:

> The most interesting multinationals saw national identity as something that could be changed pretty much on an as needed basis. The US-based Commercial Cable Company was the master at this, owning a stake in the German Atlantic Telegraph Company claiming to be British as it sought subsidies for two "British" companies that it owned—the Halifax and Bermudas Company (1890) and the Direct West India Company (1898)—and "all-American" when standing before the US Congress to promote why it should be chosen to lay a US-owned cable across the Pacific (1904) and as it fronted—for another firm—the US and Haiti Telegraph Company (1896) that was registered in New York but in reality owned by French interests. The company also formed alliances with European companies to offer services in the Euro-American market. Given that such relationships were the norm rather than the exception, it seems questionable to assume that the nationality of corporate actors was easy to establish or highly relevant.

Religion

Humankind is all too familiar with the social and political domination of religious institutions. The influence of the Holy Roman Empire on Europe for many centuries is only one example. It is also important to note that the intertwining of corporate, religious, and political powers is nothing new. According to Innis ([1950] 2007, 133),

> In 313 the so-called edict of Milan secured the privileges of a licensed cult for Christianity, recognized the church as a corporation by authorizing it to hold property, and dethroned paganism as a state religion. The Lord's Day Act of 321 suggested that the divorce between religion and politics could not be maintained.

Even today, there are entire countries ruled by theocratic institutions and regions dominated by religious thinking. Within these contexts religious leaders and thinkers who are a part of the ruling structure sometimes exercise a virtual stranglehold on thought and expression, as well as the material elements of human existence. Often with such religious domination, it is difficult to separate religion from culture—and indeed one often becomes the other. Where religious rules dominate they also intertwine with politics. Tessler (2002) suggests, for example, that politics in the Middle East can never be completely separated from Islam despite many efforts at reform in the region.

Consideration of religious domination of culture is important since it presents two important questions. The first has to do with the extent to which religion may be considered culture, and the other is the question of religious reform.

The connection between religions and culture is a difficult one. For many Western observers, it is easy to refer, for example, to Islamic culture when many in the Muslim world would not understand what that means. For example, to equate the cultures of Egypt with those of Indonesia (both largely Islamic countries) would be absurd.

It is not possible in many cases to demarcate where lines between religion and culture may be drawn. Take, for example, the ongoing debate on religion in the ostensibly secular United States focused on whether the United States is a "Christian nation" (Giroux [2004] presents a detailed treatment of this debate and its evolution under George W. Bush's presidency).

Lambert (2003, 3) argued that the "Christian nation" movement erroneously (and, perhaps deliberately) blurs the religious ideas of the Puritan fathers (who aspired to the one true faith based on their interpretation of the Bible) with those of the Founding Fathers since:

> The Founding Fathers had a radically different conception of religious freedom. Influenced by the Enlightenment, they had great confidence in the individual's ability to understand the world and its most fundamental laws through the exercise of his or her reason. To them, true religion was not something handed down by a church or contained in the Bible but rather was to be found through free rational inquiry. . . . The framers sought to secure their idea of religious freedom by barring any alliance between church and state.

There is rampant speculation and some evidence from contemporaries that several of the key figures in the early development of American government including George Washington were in fact not traditional Christians in the sense that the Puritans would recognize, but Deists, influenced heavily by seventeenth- and eighteenth-century philosophers (Dershowitz 2007).

Returning to the present day, and despite the views of the Christian nation crowd, it might be convenient (and largely accurate) to point out that the church does not in fact rule the United States. However, the influence of religious groups on US politics and cultural life should not be underestimated. Many attribute the ascension of George Bush to the support he received from religious leaders in the southern states—including political speeches from the pulpits of some churches. Jerry Falwell's "Moral Majority" was a major force in the election of Ronald Reagan who rewarded that group with the Meese Commission on Pornography. The institution of the Hollywood Motion Picture Production Code was not only instigated by the Catholic Church but also later enforced by strict Catholic moralist Joe Breen. At the turn of the twentieth-century religious zealot Anthony J. Comstock caused new laws to be introduced to curtail what he perceived as smut in the United States. He also fought (literally to the death—as he died of influenza during the trials) to prevent family planning pioneer Margaret Sanger from publishing educational pamphlets on women's reproductive health. From evidence such as this we may confidently argue that vital social and cultural questions of political leadership, creative expression (and even sexual and reproductive rights) have been determined in part by religious forces in the United States.

The power of religious institutions in most modern Western nations, however, is checked by a history of reformation in which cultural changes have also affected religion. From the economic and political implications of the Protestant reformation to the social implications of women as priests in many denominations, the West has benefited from numerous social influences on religion over the years. Awareness of this has also prompted many to call for reformations in other geographical regions, though such changes in modern theocracies have been less than spectacular to date. Places such as Iran, Somalia and Afghanistan have seen drastic (and disastrous) returns to fundamental religious rule in the face of cultural challenges.

Religion has been responsible for tremendous cultural change over the centuries of human existence. However, religion is also, often, a part of culture. Religious forces and ideas have been responsible for the destruction of particular cultures (consider the eradication of so-called pagan rituals in Europe by the Catholic Church and the replacement of traditional Egyptian religion by Islam). At the same time, religion as part of culture has been a major force in the development of culture. Consider, for example, the role of religion in the development of legal systems in most countries. Religious ideas may guide the most basic elements of culture, including such minute details as personal conduct and belief.

Traditional definitions and conceptualizations of culture have often failed to adequately account for the politics of leadership, administration, jurisprudence and governance as part of culture. This is partly due to a modern tendency toward secularity in government. However, the relationships between culture (including—of particular interest to us here—religion) and governance are often quite obvious. For example, laws in most "Western" nations specifically outlaw bigamy and polygamy based on Judeo-Christian traditions (as interpreted today) whereas laws in many countries of the Middle East not only allow for polygamy (based on certain Qur'anic interpretations) but also provide regulations for the practice. Conversely, many Middle East governments ban alcohol from their societies based on religious tradition, while the same substance is quite legal in Western nations with rules for consumption including age restrictions and sanctions for improper use. In both instances, cultural tradition is a major factor in legal matters and consequently local politics. But traditional religions may not be all that we need to worry about in the globalized economy.

Jay McDaniel (1997) has argued that modern corporate culture and practice possesses all of the essential defining properties of a religion including a priestly class of economists shrouded in both mystique and trust, missionaries (the advertising industry), and churches (stores and shopping malls). To this we may add functions such as prophecy in the form of economic forecasting, faith expressed as confidence in the eternal strength of the market, and salvation expressed as liberation from (through satisfaction of) material needs. Harvey Cox (1999, 18) further suggested that the language of business publications such as the *Wall Street Journal* and the business sections of popular magazines, upon examination "turned out to bear a striking resemblance to Genesis, the Epistle to the Romans, and Saint Augustine's City of God," comparing what he found in their pages to religious "myths of origin, legends of the fall, and doctrines of sin and redemption." Cox also pointed out (somewhat tongue-in-cheek) that he observed one contradiction between what he calls the religion of The Market and the "traditional religions"— namely, that "the traditional religions teach that human beings are finite creatures and that there are limits to any earthly enterprise" (23). Schultze (1991) similarly argues that business has learned from both the techniques and substance of evangelism, using advertising to promise salvation from everyday burdens. Robert H. Nelson (2003) described the social dominance of this particular kind of thinking as the product of an economic priesthood of sorts, saying that

> economists are still the modern priests of economic progress. Many of them still believe . . . that the elimination of economic deprivation will lead to a great improvement in the human condition, morally as well as materially. That is a main reason for entering the field of economics. The role of economists as the pre-eminent profession among the social sciences is justified by economists' possession of the key scientific knowledge required to bring about a modern heaven on earth.

The domination of corporate interests in metropolitan countries and all around the world can be seen in the creation and fostering of marketing opportunities in the guise of cultural events. Here we need to envisage the global cultural event—marketed by the corporations to create predictable consumption patterns and selling opportunities. Many in the United States recognize the corporate exploitation that characterizes so much of Christmas celebrations. The credit card bills associated with the pressures of corporate advertising are no longer limited to toys for the kids. Strangelove (2005) pointed out, in fact, that some 40 percent of all diamond jewelry sales in the United States are made during the Christmas shopping season. Jones (2006) contended that many "appurtenances of modern Christmases were adoptions or inventions often devised by the commercial world" (55).

Like the religious forces of the past, corporate interests today engage in fortune-telling. This is often described as forecasting or market analysis but most frequently attempts to produce predictions of future market or consumer behavior. Corporations as well as investment firms produce outlooks based on a combination of scientific measurements and pseudo-scientific speculation. Traditional tools such as statistics are used along with more avant-garde analyses like chaos theory. All of this is put together with a touch of corporate spin to describe the outlook for a company, a sector, a market, or an economy. The problem is that much of the forecasting is biased, intended to create the very conditions it predicts and heavily influenced by factors such as corporate lobbying and vested financial interests.

Corporate ventures continue to get away with this kind of fortune telling because of the amount of money involved in and affected by their pronouncements. On the screens of CNBC and MSNBC and other news outlets, investment bank representatives (they were there with Enron, they were there with the dot.com boom) explain that they were told to toe the line to investors because so much money was at risk. Related to this is the corporate definition or redefinition of morality. While tax evasion and fraud are serious moral and legal issues for individuals, corporations seem to be quite immune. In early 2007, in the midst of ongoing debates in the United States about funding for George Bush's Iraq adventure, the Halliburton Corporation (a major player in the war effort) announced that it was moving its headquarters to tax-free Dubai in the United Arab Emirates (BBCNews.com 2007).

A somewhat less obvious facet of the infiltration of corporations into the role of religion may be found in the increasingly corporate nature of churches in the United States and elsewhere. Run as corporations, these religious entities focus on extracting value out of their followers and other consumers while enjoying the traditional privileges of religious bodies. Among the benefits of such corporate structures are increased resources to produce evangelical materials that aid their proselytizing. The transnational nature of evangelical churches today also bears the mark of corporate interests. Hefner (1998, 97) argued that

> the tie of Christianity to Western modernity rarely slackens entirely. The necktie, Coca-Cola, and calico dresses appear again and again. . . . The forces at work in these instances are stronger than missions and evangelicals alone. They are evidence of the cultural hegemony of the United States and Western Europe in global capitalism, consumption, and communications.

Knowledge

Harold Innis ([1950] 2007) outlined the role of knowledge and knowledge monopolies in the creation and maintenance of empires. He suggested, for example, that the ability to measure time and predict floods accurately became the basis of power in Egypt. Additionally, knowledge as the basis of ruling has been intertwined with religion. Part of the power of religion to provide the basis for rule has been in the notion of privileged knowledge belonging to religious institutions and persons. This could range from knowledge of herbs and medicines to knowledge of God (or gods) and the nature of the universe. A major element of European enlightenment and reformation lay in the liberation of knowledge from the religious and privileged classes in part due to advances in printing technology associated with Johannes Gutenberg. This is perhaps our earliest evidence that mass media can work against established cultural norms. Merriman (2004, 127) reflected on the role of both mass media and commerce in the reformation, noting,

> The Protestant Reformation began as a religious reaction against established abuses within the Church. But it also reflected profound changes in European society. The Reformation followed not only the discovery of the printing press but also the expansion of commerce, the arteries of which became the conduit of reform. . . . The printing of Luther's works facilitated their rapid diffusion, with perhaps a million copies circulating through the German states by the mid-1520s.

Giroux (2000, 50) characterized knowledge as capital in today's corporate culture which is "privileged as a form of investment in the economy but appears to have little value when linked to the power of self-definition, social responsibility, or the capacities of individuals to expand the scope of freedom, justice, and the operations of democracy." The importance of knowledge in today's society and its importance as a basis for the dominance of corporate enterprise can be seen in proprietary knowledge, the importance of so-called information technology (read "knowledge" technology) and the strategic importance of so-called intelligence both in corporate and governmental terms. Cameron and Gross-Stein (2000, S18) argued that in the globalized economy, knowledge has gained primacy:

> Knowledge has replaced other factors of production as the most important commodity. Unlike commodities that were important at earlier phases in the history of the international economy, knowledge is an infinitely renewable resource, only loosely related to geographic space.

The notion of the information or knowledge society is often traced back to the work of economist Fritz Machlup in the United States who suggested that the essential structure of production in the modern economy has shifted from being primarily about the production of goods to the development of, trade in, and consumption of information. Machlup and his confederates measured the relative contribution to the US economy of particular industries they identified as knowledge or information based. Machlup's figures indeed demonstrated an increase in the relative value of information or knowledge industries in the data which originally ran up to the 1960s. However, it is not difficult to argue that some of the findings are the result of a very broad definition of information or knowledge-based industries. Detractors of the original information society thesis pointed to the inclusion of teaching, retail service and other debatable fields as information-producing industries.

Whether or not Machlup's figures were flawed seems of little consequence today, when few would argue that the production, distribution, protection, and consumption of information have become primary elements of the modern economy. While being aware of the potential for debate regarding the differences between information and knowledge, it is still possible to see how the information rich are more likely to be found in the ruling classes of today's societies. Indeed, the very notion of the information rich and information power has engaged scholars researching the so-called digital divide both within and among various countries.

Successive official "digital divide" surveys by the US government have contended that the divide has been bridged with widespread diffusion of the new digital technologies. However, there remains some doubt as to whether even in the United States, the gaps in access and use of the technologies have really been bridged.

Clinard (1990) has noted that the budgets of multinational petroleum companies sometimes exceed the national budgets of the countries they do business with. Yet there is more than this fiscal imbalance that is tilted heavily in the favor of the corporations. There is as well, a knowledge differential that determines the stakes of the game.

In 1993, while working on a television special, I was granted an interview with the minister of energy on a small Caribbean island to discuss his country's energy sector. He showed me maps and charts of various prospective energy projects and talked about negotiations with the foreign multinational petroleum companies. Something from that interview has stayed with me ever since. It was the fact that this (very senior) government official did not in fact know for sure where the oil and natural gas resources were buried. That information belonged to the multinational energy corporations who, through satellite and other survey methods, had already determined the best places to drill. Using this proprietary knowledge, the foreign multinationals could enter into treaties that served their own best interest. Such is the effect of the knowledge differential and the role of knowledge in the current world corporate culture.

Ancestry/Tradition

The power of ancestry has also served as the basis for the creation of ruling classes and institutions. European monarchies were generally predicated on the so-called divine rights of kings and nobility was (and still is) passed on from generation to generation. Most modern states have moved beyond the rule of the ancestors. Part of this shift necessarily emerged from the Industrial Revolution in Europe during which the emergent wealthy merchants and factory owners were able to eclipse the social power of the "blue bloods." When common people were able to amass wealth and power there was no reason to continue to vest the ancestral nobility with power. In Europe today, most traditional monarchies are mere symbolic vestiges of the ancestral-centered past.

Ancestry would fall within Weber's early determinants of authority, the charismatic and the traditional. Weber's analysis could not escape the influence of European history and the rapid advancements of the Industrial Revolution which featured the fall of the old order with its emphases on social status and nobility in favor of wealth and innovation associated with the new order. The role of ancestry and tradition in the dominance of modern multinational corporations can be traced back to the roots of the capital accumulations in their various home economies, particularly with regard to imperialism, colonialism, and (in many cases) slavery.

Wealth

Trouillot (2003, 57) expressed concern about the increasingly polarized concentration of resources and wealth in a few hands globally. He noted that

> in 1998, 74 of the 200 top international corporations were based in the United States, 41 in Japan, 23 in Germany, 19 in France, and 13 in the United Kingdom [Clairmont 2000]. The turnover for only half of them then exceeded France's national product and dwarfed Mexico by a ratio of six to one.

Clinard (1990, 37) similarly noted that

> the American oil industry is the largest as well as the richest in the world; it does $200 billion in business each year. In 1988, three of the top 10 US industrial corporations were oil companies. . . . Exxon, with sales of over $79 billion, was the third largest industrial concern in the United States and also the world.

Wealth in its many forms has also been a criterion and a means for the development of social influence and the consolidation of ruling classes. Whatever the definition of wealth in a society (e.g., money, land, cattle, or shells), those in possession or control of such wealth or the means by which to amass it have often formed, either implicitly or explicitly, a ruling class or similar institution. When the church held sway as the principal organizing institution of European society, wealthy families were buying their sons into important positions in the priesthood.

Adam Smith in his work "The Wealth of Nations" extended this notion of the power of wealth within single societies to the power and influence of wealth in the geopolitical schemes of European colonialism. He suggested, for example, that the quest for what he called "bullion" in the form of gold and resources was the primary motivating factor for European nations to seek to exploit other lands or even to compete among themselves.

It is perhaps from this basis that the corporation most clearly arises as the principal organizing institution of modern society. Part of the mythos of corporate wealth is the notion that when corporations are wealthy, their societies and communities are also wealthy. Thus corporate wealth is widely accepted as a fundamentally good thing. Governments like wealthy corporations because they can offer (or at least appear to offer) employment. Even economists and planners like wealthy corporations because they can show how devices such as the Keynesian multiplier effect can be good for sagging economies.

The power of corporate interests (whether domestic or foreign) to provide jobs and economic multipliers is often enough to sway government policies. In the late 1980s and early 1990s, based on these very concerns, the government of Jamaica agreed to allow foreign corporations to operate manufacturing plants in special zones in Kingston (somewhat ironically called "free-zones") in the hopes that these plants would provide much needed employment and stimulate the domestic economy (Green 1998, 34). These "free-zones" were guaranteed to be free of organized labor and free of restrictions on the foreign companies. The cruelest irony perhaps came in the eventual mistreatment of the Jamaican workers who described the free-zone as having slavery-like conditions, an accusation corroborated by Green, who described the operators as "notorious for their exploitative, even brutal labor practices and anti-union antics."

THE CORPORATION AS THE DOMINANT PARADIGM

It is easy to appreciate the amount of political influence that large corporations can exert in their home societies. However, the intervention of foreign corporations in the politics of nations around the world has even greater cultural implications. The process known as globalization (often a euphemism for the simple and rapid spread of global corporate power) involves the spread of corporate power to such an extent that the very concept of the nation state is now brought into question. One approach to globalization called the hyper-globalization thesis suggests that "traditional nation states have become unnatural, even impossible business units in a global economy" (Ohmae 1995, 5). Lacher (2006, 1), similarly argued that

> the movements of money, goods, services, ideas, and communications across state borders are just too fluid for states to be able to control them. States thus become increasingly incompetent in the face of global transactions; their ability to fulfill basic state functions is thrown into question. Effective authority leaks away from the state, and political power is consequently absorbed by other organizations.

Large multinational (and even powerful domestic) corporations are among those "other organizations" that Lacher and others see absorbing and usurping traditional state political power. In doing so, corporate power is seen to dominate both politics and thinking, which raises concerns about the establishment of the hegemony of corporate capital.

HEGEMONY

Amin and Luckin (1996, 218) described the dominance of the thinking associated with international corporate capital and its implications, saying that

> the dominant social thought is economistic in the sense which sets off from the idea that there are economic laws which are "incontrovertible," that these laws dictate the functioning, change and "progress" of systems of production, which among other things imposes increasing interdependence of national sub-systems on the global level. This strand of thought, however, goes much further; through the interpretation, right or wrong, of these economic realities as forces which impose themselves on history whether we want them to or not, it calls on us to submit to them. It is said that states' polices must—or should—be adjusted to the strategies of private firms and submit to their interests, which transgress national borders.

The processes by which this dominant social thought (or dominant ideology) of the corporations is expounded and accepted are by no means simple. They involve a complex interplay of such factors as mediated messages, trade flows, emergent markets, historical and cultural realities, and various types of politics. There are several explanatory frameworks that seek to characterize these processes including the cultural imperialism thesis and the related notion of hegemony.

The term "hegemony" evolved from the work of Marxist writer Antonio Gramsci but has since moved into the common vernacular of academics in areas such a critical communication studies and international relations. The incompetence of states and the lack of authority cited by Lacher above can be explained in terms of hegemony. Gramsci (1971) argued that ruling groups or classes can exert power through force, consent, or a combination of the two. Implicit in this is the use of power to spread the dominant ideology of powerful groups. However, the notion of hegemony goes beyond simply spreading that dominant ideology into making the ideas contained within that ideology into given or assumed knowledge. When hegemony is achieved, the dominant ideology is no longer an ideology but rather the stuff of intuition and common sense. The power to question the dominant ideology is removed since the vast majority of people no longer see the ideology but rather operate within its confines. Like with Foucault's panopticon, there is little need to impose the rules of this ideology as the adherents have accepted its tenets so completely as to impose it upon themselves.

This sense of hegemony is important in the analysis of the spread of corporate power around the world. While many media analysts have spent a lot of time and attention on how the powerful media arms of corporations affect foreign markets and individuals, the paradox of so many of these analyses is that fact that the supposedly innocent victims of this corporate propaganda all seem perfectly willing to participate in their own exploitation. The notion of hegemony provides us with a possible explanation of the paradox.

When the first Burger King outlet was opened in Kuwait, there were lines outside stretching for hundreds of meters. Was Burger King's marketing so irresistible that wealthy Kuwaitis could not control themselves? What accounts for so many people being so eager to engage the corporations so willingly? What accounts for the same reaction in so many other places (the TGIF franchise was sold out for weeks when it opened in Trinidad and Tobago). The academics ask—do they not see that this is just one more example of globalization and that they are allowing their cultures to be overrun? Yet the lines continue to stretch outside Burger King in Kuwait. During Ramadan, traffic jams are frequent around the outlets as Kuwaitis flock for the breaking of their daily fast (*footoor*) with a Whopper.

The audiences/consumers for corporate product respond to the marketing and to the goods and services of the corporations particularly because the corporations have established a certain hegemony in their target markets. The person lining up for that Burger King or McDonald's burger has already been exposed many times to the product even if he or she has never tasted one. The presence of the item as a part of the consumer lifestyle has been entrenched in every Western television program and movie the person has seen and with which they have come to identify; the desirability of the item is not in question, the quality of the item is not in question, the price of the item is assumed to be fair and worthwhile. All of these assumptions are the result of corporate hegemony—wrought by multinational advertising, media texts, and physical presence. The success of the strategy is not that the consumer fails to question this process, but rather that it never occurs to him or her to do so.

DIMENSIONS OF CORPORATE CULTURE

The term "corporate culture" is used broadly to refer to any number of phenomena and issues surrounding the social dimensions of intra-corporation, inter-corporation, and extra-corporation relationships. Giroux (2000, 41) contended that "as corporations have gained more and more power in the United States, democratic culture becomes corporate culture, the rightful ideological heir to the victory over socialism." He described corporate culture as "an ensemble of ideological and institutional forces that functions politically and pedagogically to both govern organizational life through senior managerial control and to produce compliant workers, depoliticized consumers, and passive citizens" arguing that in this process, "the substance of critical democracy is emptied out and replaced by a democracy of goods, consumer lifestyles, shopping malls, and the increasing expansion of the cultural and political power of corporations throughout the world."

Davis (1984, 1) defined corporate culture as "the pattern of shared beliefs and values that gives the members of an institution meaning, and provides them with the rules for behavior in their organization." Though several closely related terms are often used interchangeably, the term "corporate culture" is often used to refer to (1) the "culture" of a particular corporation, business, or organization (often termed "organizational culture") and (2) the norms, beliefs, and practices of corporations in general. It is this second sense of the term that concerns us most directly in the present analysis.

Deeks (1993, 23) argued that elements of corporate culture such as the modern concept of the market have crossed over from "moral pariah to moral principle." Deeks noted the cultural dimension of modern corporations; he pointed out that major elements of modern life ranging from media products to technology and travel not only reflect but also constitute culture and these same elements are in fact the results of corporate business decisions. He argued that

> so integral is business activity to our way of life that we can play with, and explore, the idea that our culture is a "business culture." In such a culture business practices and values dominate the material, intellectual and spiritual life of the whole community. (1)

Deeks, like many media critics, has argued that businesses create and affect language, noting that the language of advertising creates what he termed a "bizarre bazaar" (67). He argued that in fields such as fashion, literature, communication, sport, and tourism the will of corporations has had enormous impact on modern culture.

Another strange, ironic, and troubling dimension of the notion of corporate culture is hidden from view and requires something of an insider's perspective to expose it. Gordon (1995, 3) hinted at the beginnings of the problem:

> Culture was "discovered" in the late 1970s and 1980s by the academic human sciences and the business corporation. These two sites have little communication with each other and have developed distinct understandings of what culture means and how it works.

They have not, however, remained separate. When corporate culture stands in for the study of cultures itself in fields such as anthropology and intercultural communication, the corporate perspective on culture can influence the very meanings of culture itself. Such a situation is not simply hypothetical. It exists today quite clearly in the study of cultures and intercultural communication. In textbooks and in seminars, and in business communication courses taught in MBA programs across the world. Students are fed on a diet of intercultural communication that has more to do with corporate culture than it does with human culture in the traditional sense.

The rise to prominence of the field known as intercultural communication has been due in part to the increased popularization of this concept in the realm of global businesses or businesses with global aspirations. Whereas numerous poor naïve academics and anthropologists have studied the interactions of cultural groups over the years, their work has not been given quite as much attention as the work of one corporate-funded researcher when it comes to the idea of intercultural communication.

Imagine my surprise when students in a class in intercultural communication had never heard of the work of Edward T. Hall who just happened to be a founding father of the field. No, these students were weaned on the work of another scholar, one funded by the IBM Corporation to further its operations among different countries and cultures. It did not help that their teacher for the course was a former corporate trainer in intercultural communications. He had never heard of Edward T. Hall either.

An increasing majority of intercultural communication courses are now exclusively focused on the corporate-inspired analyses of Geert Hofstede. None of this is to deny that the IBM-funded research of the great Geert Hofstede has been useful to the field. However, the very notion of this research was corporate inspired and its objectives and analyses were primarily focused on creating more profitable working environments for the corporation in question. The unfortunate result of this has been a force-fitting of variables from the corporation to variables in broader society. The assumption that one equates the other is rarely questioned in the textbooks or coursework. In this case even what passes for academia is clearly and openly funded by and focused on the welfare of the corporation.

Hofstede's analysis has always carried a certain weight for another reason. Unlike the work of Hall and many anthropologists, Hofstede's analysis claimed numerical support. While the notion of empiricism involves more than just numbers, the corporate logic is one that values numerical proof.

Chapter Five

New Mythology, New Media, and the Globalization of Culture

THE MYTHOLOGY OF CORPORATE GLOBALIZATION

Myth is not the same as falsehood. Myth is the basis of thought, text, and expression in culture. Authors such as Joseph Campbell have made this broader notion of mythology popular in recent decades. In this sense of myth, the dominant culture is not perceived to be mythical. It is perceived as fact. Myth is usually only recognizable after a culture has passed. In its time myth is reality. Thus, our view of Hindu mythology or Greek mythology is retrospective but clearly focused on mythology in the traditional sense of an untrue story. We seek the messages in the stories but they remain just stories. We perceive our own everyday lives as being far more concrete, relevant, and grounded in fact.

However, there is a danger here in not recognizing that mythologies are lived. On the one hand, past mythologies are taken as true and their messages (or their substance) are followed. For example, there are many faithful people today who hold to absolutely literal readings of ancient texts despite the mounting and overwhelming contradiction of the historic or scientific accuracy of those texts. On the other hand, mythologies of the day are often treated as fact. The science of today, for example, may seem more like the alchemy of yesterday when viewed by future generations. It is only our lack of knowledge that prevents us from seeing the weaknesses of our assumptions about the world around us.

Even our objective science of the day will eventually yield to greater ideas. Thomas Kuhn (1962) clearly demonstrated the passing and evolution of scientific paradigms. We would be both egotistical and mistaken to assume that the science of today is the lasting scientific paradigm of human-kind. Future generations may scoff, for example, at our most advanced work with atoms after some more fundamental organizing principle of matter is unearthed. Thus our science may even pass into mythology.

There is also another dimension of everyday mythology that lies between our confidence in modern science and our regard for ancient stories. It is a body of mythology that lurks in the fields of corporate endeavor and analysis and passes itself off variously as fact, science, or common sense. Like any dominant culture, the corporate culture has its own mythology. Like other dominant cultures, the corporate culture has great influence over which myths are accepted as true and which are scoffed at as false.

NEW MYTHS FOR A NEW CULTURE

In this globalized network, the mythologies of the past are rendered quaint, if not completely irrelevant. Whereas the European Church dangled salvation before its masses, today's dominant social institution, the globalized corporate culture, needs new myths to mobilize its adherents.

The Sovereign Consumer

Strangelove (2005, 30) argued that one of the primary myths of the modern market economy is the notion of the sovereign consumer—one who makes rational and informed choices in the market. He suggested, citing Galbraith's critique of the role of media persuasion in consumer behavior, that "consumer sovereignty over action and belief is limited by a massive persuasion system that continually exposes individuals to marketplace images, messages, and values." This is a contentious point since few consumers would like to feel that they are manipulated into purchases.

Most consumers consider themselves above the influence of advertising and would like to think that they only allow commercial persuasion to affect them at their own discretion. However, the very breadth of marketing and advertising in modern society makes it difficult to clarify our own wants and needs from those mediated to us. Herbert Marcuse (2002, 11) called this latter category "created needs" and suggested that they are necessary to en-sure that the surpluses of modern society are duly consumed. He suggested, further, that the distinction between "true and false needs" cannot be made by individuals as long as they are manipulated and indoctrinated, with the mass media being one of the tools of manipulation and indoctrination. He asked, for example, "Can one really distinguish between the mass media as instru-ments of information and entertainment, and as agents of manipulation and indoctrination?"

Strangelove (2005, 31) contended that economists are reluctant to admit this central role of corporate media in the determination of customer wants but suggested that communication theorists have been more insightful:

> In 1948, early communication theorists Paul Lazarsfeld and Robert K. Merton suggested that "organized business" used a new type of social control to manage opinions and beliefs—propaganda. . . . As early adopters of propaganda (soon to be renamed "public relations"), business aggressively manipulated the mass audience.

Smart (2003, 77) went further to make the case that this manipulation creates something more akin to a form of modern serfdom, arguing that

> the consumer is not "sovereign," but more like a "postmodern serf"—not bound to the land, but bound to consume. With the growth of branded consumption it is not the products that are being marketed and sold but increasingly, lifestyles, experiences and identities.

Yet, these characterizations miss an essential reality of the modern media environment in its local and global manifestations, and that is the presentation of consumers back to themselves in an ever-emerging set of image identities. Therefore, as the market influences the consumer, the consumer also influences the market and so the images portrayed must also reflect the changes wrought. The transnational self-presentation is a difficult one indeed and overt differences in dress, language, and environment are still realities that are difficult to overcome. I make this point to indicate that the consumer or audience member cannot be excluded from the equation. While we may debate the sovereignty of the consumer (of products or information) it would be unrealistic to suggest that the consumer is at the same time powerless. Whether the commodity is soap or television viewership, the consumer still has choices. The international corporate-driven media must constantly battle to win the allegiance of the consumer and thus is also in a race to represent the consumer back to himself or herself.

One of the implicit assumptions of critical analyses of the role of the corporate media (as we have demonstrated above) is that they are always successful in marketing to viewers and consumers. The truth is that they are not. Consider the fact that even McDonald's, the oft-cited harbinger of all things globalized, has not succeeded in every market it has entered (the franchise failed in Trinidad and Tobago after about four years of operation), nor did it always succeed in convincing the local markets of its desirability (it faced opposition from Hindus in India during its introduction).

Free Markets / Competition

Global corporate culture operates on the assumption and mythology of the existence of and desirability of free markets. It is the holy grail of international businesses to have free markets. However, the same corporations are frequently the beneficiaries (either directly or indirectly) of market controls in their favor at home or abroad as well as corporate welfare in the form of tax incentives abroad, tax breaks, and various other forms of corporate subsidies at home. On the much-vaunted advances from Silicon Valley, Deeks (1993, 45) noted that much of this had to do with nonmarket forces:

> Notwithstanding the euphoria about private enterprise, many of these high-tech ventures were dependent upon military and government funding. They developed guidance systems for missiles and communications systems for military intelligence.

Martinez (2009) pointed out that despite the almost unanimous support of free market economics among economists and policymakers, the reality of most modern market economics is deeply connected to politics and politically influenced government regulation. Some opponents to the Iraq war have even argued that it is a case of the invisible hand of the free market being imposed through the iron fist of military intervention. Absent this extreme, a much more subtle form of this kind of influence comes in the relationship between trade and information policy; previously considered examples of the CBI provisions in the Caribbean and the general spread of intellectual property provisions in US trade agreements are instructive here.

The very notion of the market is itself fundamentally flawed despite numerous economic treatises on its almost divine power to bring buyers and sellers together. It is beyond the scope of the present discussion to enter into a complete critique of the market as a fundamental social structure, but let us examine just a few of the many concerns about the ascension of the so-called free market as the primary arbiter of value and exchange.

Seabrook (1996, 9) argued that the term "market" itself agglomerates traditional familiar notions about marketplaces with the idea of the entire economy, creating a abstraction that is at once comforting and "beyond contestation." He further suggested that the market economy has become "the object of a quasi religious cult" (11) replacing older religious influences and that markets are imbued with both human and superhuman characteristics (e.g., caprice, strength, weakness, and hesitation).

Among the more popular critiques of the market is the notion that markets and market ideas based on extraction and exploitation are potentially damaging to the environment. While we might think that today's generation came up with these ideas, Perelman (2003, 68) noted that the environmental implications of market forces have been realized (and even documented) for centuries, noting that

> one of the first hints that market forces are inimical to environmental sustainability came from a British surveyor named John Richards in 1730. Richards estimated the annual yield from allowing a 50-year-old oak tree to survive an additional 50 years to maturity. Comparing the timber yield from the 50-year-old and 100-year-old tree, Richards calculated an increase equivalent to a little more than 3 percent per year. Since the prevailing interest rate at the time was almost double that, economic logic suggested that harvesting the tree at 50 years was preferable to allowing it to survive to maturity.

One of the strongest ideological claims of the market is its implicit claim to nonideology. We are lead to believe that the market is at once sacrosanct and secular. Willetts (1994, 52) interrogated this tendency, writing that

> many market theorists have written of the market as if it floats free of any cultural or institutional constraints. It is just a world of rational economic agents entering into contracts with each other. But perhaps the most interesting aspect of thinking about the market nowadays is the willingness of at least some economic liberals to recognize that the market is constrained both from above and from below. The market operates within a series of external constraints—cultural, moral and legal—which define its area of activity. Similarly, there comes a point at which micro institutions—firms, families etc.—cease to apply market principles to their own internal organizations.

Even in the preceding excerpt, where the author critiques the unfaltering acceptance of market principles, one can still find the notion that families, for example, should (presumably at some point before they "cease") apply market principles to their own internal organizations. Such an assertion is steeped in the assumptions of the naturalness of the market and its acceptability in all facets of life. Though the market is supposed to be value free and unbiased, failure to adhere to its rules in modern society can not only prevent you from doing business, but also, mark you as a threat to the social order. Even internationally, the accepted stance of modern nations is in favor of free markets. While many nations practice some kind of protectionism in their own national interests, they have great difficulty justifying such practices in the present climate of neoliberal market dominance.

The deeply rooted ideological components of markets and market philosophy are well camouflaged in a charade that presents the market as somehow natural and also as the only way to conduct business and (often, by extension) society. Notions of democracy and modernity are often tied to ideas about the market and are reproduced every day by corporate-owned media in general and by specific media dedicated to covering corporate business. According to Croteau and Hoynes (2003, 171),

> news coverage of economic issues is remarkable in the way it reproduces a profoundly ideological view of the world. Most news coverage of the economy is by and about the business community. . . . Economic news focuses overwhelmingly on the activities and interests of investors. One of the most striking examples of this phenomenon is the fact that virtually every newspaper has a Business section, while almost none has a Consumer or Labor section.

The spectacular meltdown of US and world financial markets in 2008 drove home the relationship between market ideology and government policies only too well. In the face of widespread failures of much-touted free market policies, the selfsame proponents of free markets including several Western governments and multiple corporate multinationals vociferously backed plans to hand over taxpayer dollars in the form of various corporate bailouts. This corporate welfare was readily handed over to firms whose management had demonstrated callous disregard for the fate of investors, unrestrained greed in exploitation of consumers and obscene indulgence in their executive wages and perks.

The sudden about-face in which pseudo-nationalization and government subsidies suddenly became acceptable in the "public interest" went largely unscrutinized by the corporate media and most mainstream media around the world. In all of this, there was also no question of the wisdom of leaving economies to be run primarily on free market principles despite widespread concession that the market alone could not be relied on to solve the crises.

Thomas Frank (2000) described this blind reliance and trust in market forces endorsed by corporate and business interests as market populism and characterized it as America's new secular religion. He suggested that powerful forces in business and the media actively promote capital and other markets as the natural and democratic mechanisms of progress and modern life. Bobbitt (2003) went somewhat further in describing the evolution of what he called the "market-state." This particular tack has some meaning in the United States in the context of another common example of the weakness of the market—its irrelevance (even danger) when applied to the provision of health care. The market for health provision is a dangerous idea. Demand is almost completely inelastic and supply is heavily controlled, hence any commercial health system is bound to be highly politicized in terms of control.

Few would argue with the notion that serious problems exist in the US health care system, where despite the availability of high levels of care, access to basic services can often be elusive. However, we have witnessed a continuing push for market determination of health care needs to the benefit of large pharmaceutical companies, vast insurance empires, and other industry players. While these industry players ply politicians in Washington's lobby system, they also characterize government involvement in health care with a very powerful term—"socialist." In this discourse, Canada, Britain, and other important industrialized nations are characterized as socialist. The health lobby also continually revisits the idea that participants in government-provided health care systems lack basic services and must wait months for routine procedures. While the merits of either system may well be debated, it is the ideological color of the discourse in the United States that is most troubling. The use of terms such as "socialism" appeals to the heavily ingrained fear of socialism cultivated over many years of Cold War rhetoric into many of those who are most desperately in need of affordable health care in the United States. Despite all of this, the US government is in the business of providing some level of health service or access through programs like Medicaid and Medicare, an implicit concession to the inability of the market to fully serve this sector.

Intellectual Property

Ronald Bettig (1996, 35) presented a Marxist analysis of the role of communication in capitalist society, writing that

> Marx and Engels took it for granted that within capitalism the ruling class owns and controls the means of communication and is therefore able to manage the production and distribution of information and culture. They recognized that with this control the dominant class is privileged in the struggles over the making of meaning in the cultural and ideological realms; they stressed in particular how this class is able to represent its specific interests as the general interests of society as a whole.

Without necessarily taking a fully Marxist view or adopting an economic determinism, Stuart Hall (1997) extended this idea of mediated influence by suggesting that the ways of making and fixing meaning extend beyond what is produced and presented in the media. He suggested at various points in his work that the absence of certain ideas and images also serves to fix meaning in favor of the powerful. Thus in what is presented and what is omitted, the corporate purveyors of meaning entrench their control.

These relationships of power and communication become even more important when they move beyond domestic boundaries into international relationships—sometimes in more complex ways than we might expect. Much has been written, of course, on the influence of US media on foreign cultures, but less notice is paid to the interlocking relationships of power and influence that serve to further the interests of US media corporations abroad. Drahos and Braithwaite (2002, 83) demonstrated the indirect influence of US media corporations in their description of how US trade incentives were tied to US media power in Reagan-era horse trading:

> Of itself the Caribbean Basin Initiative on intellectual property was not particularly economically significant. Ronald Reagan, perhaps remembering his thespian roots, had helped out the movie industry by approving legislation that allowed the United States to pull a lever against Caribbean states if their hotels continued to intercept satellite signals of US movies without paying a license fee. This market was not vast. In any case the hotels presumably would pass on the cost of the license fees to their customers, many of whom would have been visiting US tourists.
>
> The deeper significance of the events in the Caribbean Basin lay in the realization by key individuals in the US that the rules of trade and intellectual property could be re-written in order to form a global partnership between the trading and intellectual property regimes. This partnership could bring with it access to new markets and vastly increased or royalty incomes.

THE MARKET, ADVERTISING, AND CULTURE

Advertising and marketing are often cast as economic, socially neutral enterprises. However, these enterprises are in fact intimately connected to processes of social and cultural change in favor of the advertisers who pay vast sums of money to influence the public not only to buy their products but also to accept the ideological notions of consumerism and the market economy as well. According to Croteau and Hoynes (2003, 187),

> mass advertising emerged in the 1920s when leaders of the business community began to see the need for a coordinated ideological effort to complement their control of the workplace. Advertising would become the centerpiece of a program to sell not only products but also a new American way of life in which consumption erased differences, integrated immigrants into the mainstream of American life, and made buying the equivalent of voting.

Similarly, Potter (1954, 188) argued that advertising changes views and attitudes, saying that

> the most important effects of this powerful institution are not upon the economics of our distributive system; they are upon the values of our society. If the economic effect is to make the purchaser like what he buys, the social effect is, in a parallel but broader sense, to make the individual like what he gets, to enforce already existing attitudes, to diminish the range and variety of choices, and in terms of abundance, to exalt the materialistic virtues of consumption.

This cultural influence extended also into the perceptions of "the other." Cultural distortion and stereotypes have been part of the repertoire of marketing and advertising. O'Barr (1994) noted, for example, that US advertisers frequently associate images of foreign lands or cultures to sell products designed, made, and intended for use in the American market. Such portrayals can have lasting effects on the persons or cultures portrayed and, at the very least, serve to perpetuate stereotypes both in the United States and internationally.

In modern globalized society whether we are in Saudi Arabia or St. Vincent or Miami, we understand advertising as an integral component of both the economy and everyday life. It lays claim to an information function that is perceived as essential to consumer behavior. In a (somewhat overstated— one might concede) critique of advertising, Seabrook (1996, 21) argued that despite its claims to being informative, advertising instead cultivates a deliberate kind of ignorance that is itself essential to the consumer economy:

> Its insistence upon the value and desirability of the commodity or service spirits away all concern with its origin, content, the suffering involved in its production and the consequences of its sale. The purpose of advertising is to sanctify all purchases, any purchases. It sacralizes all transactions of buying and selling, blesses the act of acquisition with the noise and show and excitement it generates around each fresh marketed item. A cloud of unknowing envelopes the mysterious communion between vendor and buyer, conjuring away all the awkward questions, such as whose mouths have been denied food to furnish succulent milk-fed chickens or corn-fed beef to supermarket shoppers; or who might have been dispossessed of the land where women once grew food for subsistence, ousted for the sake of out-of-season fruits and vegetables exported to the West; or who might have been driven by landlessness to leave the home village, walk two hundred miles for the privilege of work in a sweat-shop to produce some fashionable export garment destined to be tomorrow's rags.

THE CHURCH, THE CORPORATION, AND CULTURAL CHANGE

The awesome power of the corporate institutions and their media arms to influence both popular and traditional culture can be fear-inspiring. We have previously established the broad scope of modern corporate power and the sprawling influence of modern media (not that it is that hard to do). From these ideas, the conclusion that there will be cultural erosion is rather an obvious one. But the obvious, as we have seen, is not always true. Everyone assumes, for example, that television violence somehow causes real violence. It is somewhat more difficult to establish cause and effect, however, and the research on this connection as well as the research on video games and violence continues to be inconclusive despite the best efforts of a few crusaders who champion the obvious as though it must be true. In the same way that the flat earth is obvious to our eyes, the obvious can often be wrong.

The power of the modern global corporate system is vast indeed, but the much touted power of this system is not completely without precedent. Consider the power of the church in Europe and throughout the known world at different times. The Christian church, and more properly the Holy Roman Empire wielded throughout Europe vast and insurmountable power for centuries. Harold Innis ([1950] 2007, 134) wrote that

> in [the] election of a new capital at Constantinople, dedicated on 11 May 330, Constantine was concerned with its possibilities of a military defense and with the prospect of support from the large Christian population of Asia minor and from proximity to the most important centers of Hellenistic culture. He emphasized a strong centralized authority and joined a powerful ecclesiastical interest to a military bureaucracy. Caesaropapism implied authority of the emperor over the church. Christianity became the religion of conquerors and Constantine rather than Christ was to Christianize Europe.

Even when the power of this institution had waned, it still influenced conquest and colonization throughout the world. As I will argue in due course, we are still feeling the effects of this power today. It is also important to note that the Christian church's rise to dominance took place gradually starting during Roman rule. According to Nagel (2006, 409),

> in the Roman Empire, Christians were, at least initially, at the lower (though not the lowest) end of the social spectrum and suffered centuries of on-again off-again persecution before they finally found themselves in a position of power. By then the traditions of the relationship between the Christian Church and the Roman imperial administration, and between Christian and pagan cultures had been well established.

In the Christian revolution, Jenkins (2008, 382) described the reach, power, and cultural influence of the Christian church as a dominant social institution in the following terms:

> Medieval people readily spoke of "Christendom," the *Res Publica Christiana*, as a true overarching unity and the focus of loyalty transcending mere kingdoms or empires. Kingdoms like Burgundy, Wessex, or Saxony might last for only a century or two before they were replaced by new states and dynasties, but any rational person knew that Christendom simply endured. This perception had political consequences. While the laws of individual nations lasted only as long as the nations themselves, Christendom offered a higher set of standards and mores, which alone could claim to be universal. Although it rarely possessed any potential for common political action, Christendom was a primary form of cultural reference.

Nagel (2006, 410) argued that this rise to dominance came after centuries of cultural exchange during which the religion absorbed guiding principles of empire and the empire absorbed religious tenets of Christendom:

> Christian doctrine was subsequently shaped by centuries of Christian thinkers applying Greek philosophic and linguistic conventions to the religion of Jesus. Educated pagan converts attempted to translate the message of Christianity into a language and a form compatible with their traditional cultural conventions. Roman law and political and organizational principles were, in turn, absorbed by the nascent Church and became part of its administrative structure.

Such was the power of the early church that it had the power to appoint kings, controlled vast resources, and influenced public policy both directly and indirectly. Mayr-Harting (2002, 110) argued that the Christian church revolutionized the political scene in Europe:

> During the eighth and ninth centuries the Christian church effected nothing short of a revolution in the forms of Western politics. Put briefly, there developed an idea of the pervasive religious and moral responsibility of the ruler. Christianity enormously expanded the perspectives in which rulers could think of themselves, and these perspectives in turn became an engine of expanded royal government.

The experience of the Crusades—a global movement of sorts in its early form, concerned with cultural (in religious guise) preservation was one of the many factors that brought the Church to its overwhelming position of dominance. The *Magna Carta* of the early thirteenth century (issued with changes at dates such as 1216 and 1225) attempted to create a separation between church and state partly because the power, influence, and resources of the church were seen as being in direct competition with that of the Crown (King John at the time).

We are told by Moore (1990) that, earlier, the Holy Roman Empire under the Emperor Constantine consolidated its power by specifically excluding non-Catholics from any benefits and condemning them to penalties, including servitude. Such attitudes and the use of the empire to spread (relatively new) religious and cultural ideas are testimony to the power of the early European church.

With this power came corruption. The excesses of the church often warped the very same moral and cultural values that the institution sought to champion. Well known in the popular folklore of Europe were practices such as the purchase of priestly positions by the sons of European nobles, and the practice of appointing the illicit sons of priests to such positions as well.

Several Popes including John XII (955–963) and Alexander VI (1492–1503) were even known to have illegitimate children while holding the position of pontiff.

During the crusades, the church actively worked to convince commoners and nobles alike that by undertaking support and participation for the crusade effort they would be guaranteed paradise. Munro (1895, 8) noted that Pope Urban II at the Council of Clermont said, "Undertake this journey for the remission of your sins, with the assurance of the imperishable glory of the Kingdom of Heaven." Gibbon ([1776] 2003, 1054) noted that "in the council of Clermont, [Pope Urban the second] proclaimed a *plenary indulgence* to those who should enlist under the banner of the cross; the absolution of *all* their sins, and a full receipt for *all* that might be due of canonical penance." However, none of the practices or cultural distortions of the Church were so prominent and would come to be so pivotal as the use (and abuse) of the indulgence. According to Gibbon,

> a year of penance was appreciated at twenty-six solidi of silver, about four pounds sterling, for the rich; at three solidi, or nine shillings, for the indigent: and these alms were soon appropriated to the use of the church, which derived from the redemption of sins an inexhaustible source of opulence and dominion. (1053)

Church power in its different forms was cross-culture and empirewide, expanding in later eras as part of European colonial enterprise from countries such as Spain to the newly invaded lands of Latin America for example. That power included the infliction of torture and death upon the non-Christian masses encountered during colonial conquest as well as ongoing psychological influence on the conquered populations, setting up the invaders and their gods as superior, and the adoption of their religion as a means to survival.

By comparison, even today's most dire evaluations of the cultural influence of the global media and multinational corporations are quite benign. The truth is that the dominant social institution will always dominate and distort the culture. Our mistake is in thinking that this is somehow anathema to culture. This is culture. The cultural distortions of the past are in fact the culture of today. Doty (2004, 135) contended that even basic mythologies and foundational tales of a culture are subject to change over time:

> Every retelling is a transmission that adds or subtracts something from an earlier version. It is shaped for the particular hearers or readers, so much so that it is almost impossible to speak of exact repetition: even if the words of a second telling are precisely the same, the performance (another form of ritualization) will vary as the teller takes into account the interests and situations of the listeners.

Much of the writing on culture, couched in scientific terms may simply reflect religious and ethnic biases in dealing with non-dominant cultures. Our entire conception of differences may have more to do with religious dogma than we normally acknowledge. Indeed, history is replete with religious influences on culture and even science with some of the worst outcomes in mankind's histories. Hobson (2004, 167), for example, pointed out that "Europeans came to believe that African slavery was natural because it was divinely sanctioned" and traced this orientation into the development of what he terms Europe's "scientific racism" in which doubtful science was later invoked to justify the religiously sanctioned social practice of slavery. Various Islamic sources indicate that the practice of slavery was widespread during early Islam and continued as part of its practice over the centuries. Apologists note that several Islamic laws provide for the protection of slaves and stress the virtues of granting freedom to slaves, but these arguments only serve to further elucidate the acceptance of slavery in Islamic religion and culture—an acceptance that has yet to be reformed or repudiated in any meaningful way by Islamic jurists and scholars. Troubling too, is the fact that Muslim states such as Saudi Arabia have lagged behind the rest of the world in outlawing slavery and continue to be scrutinized for human trafficking and other human rights offenses pertaining to foreign labor.

In places and times where religious institutions have dominated society and culture, everyday realities and practices were, quite subtly, a function of religion. To the extent that corporate will today dominates society and culture, the many subtle influences of corporate ideas, spread by global media, may similarly dominate our everyday realities and practices.

NOT SO GLOBAL AFTER ALL?

Yet it is easy to go too far with ideas about corporate dominance and to overemphasize the role of corporate power as a determinant of modern culture. One must also consider the possibility that many of the ideas about globalization may simply be part of the emerging corporate mythology.

Frances Cairncross (1997) wrote one of the seminal works on the global impact of the new digital information technologies, entitled *The Death of Distance*. In that book she contended that anyone with a telephone and a credit card can become part of the communications revolution and part of the globalized economic system. While that may hold true in many cases, several examples will quickly disabuse us of that notion.

The first is what I call the case of the Cuban cigar. A cigar is a relatively harmless item in global economic terms (though not so much in terms of personal health). Why, then, should a Cuban cigar prove to be a thorny impediment to the notion of a global economy where anyone with a phone and a credit card can participate? Well, if you are sitting in the United States, no telephone and no credit card (even one with membership privileges) can help you get a Cuban cigar. You may be able to buy it online from an international dealer somewhere, but now try getting it physically to you. US customs laws prohibit entry of Cuban cigars into the United States for sale or trade. The fines run as high as $50,000 per violation. For reasons having to do completely with ideology and politics, the global market falls flat when it comes to Cuban cigars.

A few hundred miles to the west of Cuba lies the island of Jamaica. The Jamaican national dish is "ackee and saltfish," which comprises a fruit called "ackee" (scientific name *Blighia sapida*) and "saltfish" (dried salted cod). Even ackees exemplify the continuing distortions of the global market. While you can buy canned ackees, in the United States, it costs about ten times what it does in Jamaica. The two countries are relatively close together and the shipping does not explain the price differential. What does explain the price difference is that fact that the US Food and Drug Administration (2007) places controls on the importation of this item because of the naturally occurring toxins hypoglycin A and hypoglycin B.

This seems reasonable enough since the potential for illness and even death is well known in Jamaica as well. The US Food and Drug Administration limits the imports of this item to cans originating from particular plants in Jamaica that have demonstrated that they have the proper equipment for processing the ackee in a manner that renders it (relatively) harmless. This all seems quite well-reasoned and even highly warranted until you consider that the climate and vegetation of South Florida are very similar to the climate and vegetation of Jamaica and that ackee trees (while relatively rare) are increasingly being used as decorative foliage in South Florida landscaping (Crane and Balerdi 2008).

These simple examples do not even consider the numerous other tariffs, customs duties, trade bans and other formal barriers to trade that are part of the international economy. These are well-established limitations on globalization of trade and markets that meet with less and less support in the globalized environment but persist despite acknowledged limitations on their effectiveness. The US Department of Agriculture noted in "A Review of US Trade Restrictions and Grain Exports" (2003) that

> economic sanctions can be powerful foreign policy tools targeted to further US foreign policy and national security objectives. Trade restrictions imposed by the US Government, however well-justified, do impact US commodity exporters and consequently the entire agricultural sector. Furthermore, the effects of these restrictions are not limited to just the markets that US exporters are prohibited from trading with: other exporters change their marketing strategies to the detriment of the US.

So whether it is a can of ackees, a Cuban cigar, or shipments of wheat, there are many aspects of the globalized economy that do not allow anyone with a phone and a credit card to jump on the global bandwagon. The message here may be that what seems obvious may not be so clear.

NOT MUCH OF A REVOLUTION?

Obviousness is again questioned when we look at the evaluation of this modern corporatized information revolution by Peter F. Drucker. In a 1999 article in the *Atlantic Monthly*, Drucker argued that the current changes in technology and society were not as drastic as many would believe and that such changes have happened many times before. He referred to the current changes as primarily a routinization of traditional activities rather than real transformation of society. He argued,

> Like the Industrial Revolution two centuries ago, the Information Revolution so far—that is, since the first computers, in the mid-1940s—has only transformed processes that were here all along. In fact, the real impact of the Information Revolution has not been in the form of "information" at all. Almost none of the effects of information envisaged forty years ago have actually happened. For instance, there has been practically no change in the way major decisions are made in business or government. But the Information Revolution has routinized traditional processes in an untold number of areas. (4)

While Drucker warned of too much hype over any one technology—citing the eventual failure of steamship technology—considered all the vogue in its inception, he did not discount the importance of the new information technologies. He suggested, for example, that while the railroad changed the mental geography of its time, today's globalized e-commerce may have eliminated geography altogether. Drucker and others point also to the fact that the globalized approach to business has led to cultural changes not only within commercial production and distribution but also in the markets and communities that are inevitably drawn into the globalized network of trade and communication.

NEW MEDIA, SUBVERSION, AND THE GLOBALIZATION OF CULTURE

The term "new media" is an ill-defined one in both popular and academic usage. However, definitional problems do not generally prevent commentators and scholars from casting blame on the World Wide Web, Instant Messaging, and other forms of "new media" for being the latest form of the general assault on culture wrought by media and globalization as a whole. Kellner (1995, 16), for example, argued that

> the new media technologies also provide powerful forms of social control through more efficient, subtly concealed techniques of indoctrination and manipulation. Indeed, their very existence might sap political energies and keep people safely ensconced within the confines of their home entertainment centers, far from the madding crowds and sites of mass political action.

These new media, with their increasingly global reach, underline the scope of influence of modern media and suggest both a far-reaching and deeply rooted set of challenges to cultural continuity and survival. In past decades, media scholars such as Schiller and Tunstall conceived of global media as relatively monolithic institutions with few producers and clear messages. These media were fairly easy to observe in the form of trans-border television transmissions or foreign films.

The "new" media are somewhat more insidious. Without the need for mass transmissions, the new media more subtly influence users at the individual level. Private web surfing, online chats, and media consumption in the form of online videos and games open a new realm of media effects previously unexplored by those concerned with global media and cultural decline.

The experience of new media for many small and/or developing countries has included several threats to national values, culture, and even laws and security. In several countries where censorship is practiced, press laws are easily subverted by the use of the World Wide Web and the Internet. In numerous cases, attempts to control citizens' access to and use of particular types of content are rendered laughable by the new media technologies.

Kuwait, a small oil-rich emirate in the Arabian Gulf, attempts to control its citizens' access to material deemed offensive to its core religious and cultural values. To do this, several censorship systems are run by the government, among them a system of censorship of foreign movies before they are allowed to be shown in Kuwaiti cinemas. This system frequently results in films that are too seriously butchered to be coherent by the time they are shown, and even the complete banning of many titles. As with all examples of censorship, this particular case demonstrates several quirks that point to the flaws in the system quite directly. For example, in the release *Pirates of the Caribbean*, each kiss was edited out by the censors, but the lead character's alcohol consumption and persistent drunkenness managed to get left intact. Censorship, based on the strict moral and religious norms of Kuwait, seems strangely fixated on matters of sex (which is not forbidden) but allows alcohol (strictly prohibited by their culture) right on through.

As for those films completely banned, the list includes a few seemingly unlikely candidates such as Michael Moore's *Fahrenheit 911*. In this case, the film was banned on what appear to be purely political grounds. It is no secret that the leadership of Kuwait had been indebted to successive Bush administrations for protection against their neighbor Saddam Hussein.

The quirks of censorship aside, the futility of the Kuwaiti government's efforts become evident in the context of new digital media forms. While the government is busy employing mullahs to cut out pecks from the movies, their citizens can buy the same titles fully intact from bootleg vendors on the streets who thrive on the digital replicability of the new media. Those titles that are not available from the DVD bootleg vendors are, of course, available on file-sharing systems online.

The Kuwaiti government, aware of its citizens' tech-savvy ways, attempts to ban persons in Kuwait from accessing these and other sites that the government deems objectionable. Since most file-sharing sites in recent years use a system of "torrents" to index and track shared files, the government has placed most of the popular torrent search portals on their blacklist. Any attempt to access such a site results in a message saying that access has been blocked by the ISP at the request of the ministry of communications.

Not to be outdone, Kuwaiti browsers, then return to the new media technologies and employ the use of proxy sites to find their torrents and then download the files using their torrent clients. The government has not yet figured out a way to block the actual downloads.

While one can hardly sympathize with the Kuwait government and its mullahs, the potential and actual subversion of their efforts in the name of their culture are quite clear. A broader examination of new media in general reveals that a common thread of subversion is evident.

We might begin with notable subversives like Johannes Gutenberg, whose contributions to printing technology led to the subversion of church power in Europe, or the subversive medium of film that so threatened early-twentieth-century social values, the Payne Fund Studies were launched to investigate their effects on the young. But wait, those are not what we usually mean by "new media." Hmm, back to that definitional problem again.

So what is (or are) new media? New as a chronological notion is not sufficient to delineate what we mean by new media as all media were at one time new and all new media will eventually cease to be new. It is possible, and perhaps desirable, to define the term "new media" more in terms of effects than chronology. Here we return to the notion of subversion from above as an examination of all "new" media reveals that the definition of their "new"-ness often coincides with their ability to change or subvert some existing social, moral, or economic order.

An examination of subversion and new media could start almost anywhere in history as we have seen with the case of Gutenberg. However, to bring things a little closer to our time, let us start with a fellow named Anthony Comstock who was most decidedly not a subversive. Born 1844 in Connecticut into a strict religious family, Anthony Comstock was a famous crusader for morality and Victorian-styled social order. He was the key player in the passage of the 1873 Act for the Suppression of Trade in, and Circulation of, Obscene Literature and Articles of Immoral Use.

In Comstock's view, society and the moral order of the day were under threat from smut and the peddlers of pornography. While his definition of these items tended to be quite broad, he was particularly troubled by certain minor developments in communications and media technology that threatened his vision of the Victorian social order. Bear in mind that under that social order, images of the erotic were perceived as being moral threats to particular groups of persons but allowed for consumption by privileged classes. In Victorian England, for example, erotic artifacts on display at the British Museum were restricted to viewing by males of the noble classes only. The idea being that women and the common folk were morally weak. In the United States, Comstock and others were troubled at the easy availability of visual pornography in the new medium of the erotic postcard (or French postcard). Sources indicate that these were available in metropolitan centers for the price of a penny at the turn of the twentieth century and, at this price, were consumed by the working people of the day. Here, the prevailing social and moral order, embodied by Comstock, was being subverted by this new medium.

On a smaller scale, and even earlier, Standage (1998, 128) described how in 1848, a young couple used new media to subvert not only prevailing conventions but also specific geographic (and parental) limitations:

> The daughter of a wealthy Boston merchant had fallen in love with Mr. B., a clerk in her father's countinghouse. Although her father had promised her hand to someone else, she decided to disregard his intentions and marry Mr. B. instead. When her father found out, he put the young man on a ship and sent him away on business to England. The ship made a stopover in New York, where the young woman sent her intended a message, asking him to present himself at the telegraph office with a magistrate at an agreed-upon time. At the appointed hour she was at the other end of the wire in Boston telegraph office, and with the telegraph operators relaying their words to and fro in Morse code, the two were duly wed by the magistrate.

The marriage was successful and held as legally binding despite the girl's father's objections.

In more recent times, Deborah Wheeler (2001, 2006) has chronicled how Middle Eastern female students use today's new media to subvert their local social and cultural conventions, particularly those having to do with their interactions with the opposite sex. Despite parental and social restrictions on young men and women socializing, young people use instant messaging, social networking sites, and even text messaging to conduct active social lives. Eickelman (2003) further chronicled how fax campaigns in Saudi Arabia were successful in bypassing government restrictions on certain printed materials and even a simple and widespread technology like photocopying was used for the same purpose in Saudi Arabia and Egypt. Similar observations have been made concerning the use of cassette tapes in the 1990s and prior in the Middle East to distribute speeches and other materials deemed unacceptable by various governments.

Chapter Six

Corporate Domination of Cultural Product

COMMODITIZATION OF CULTURES

Critical theorists such as Theodor Adorno and Max Horkheimer have addressed what they call the "culture industry." Thompson (1990, 98) explains the term as referring to "the commodification of cultural forms brought about by the rise of the entertainment industries in Europe and the United States in the late nineteenth and early twentieth centuries." Herbert Schiller, Thomas McPhail, and others have extended this notion, critiquing the international aspects of this culture industry. In this latter view, the globalized multinational information giants spread their particular brand of culture in order to sell their own cultural products. A direct result of this, Schiller and others would contend, is the acculturation of foreign people into foreign markets.

The impact of the culture industry is to change culture from that which is lived into that which is purchased. The very notion of pop culture suggests commercial involvement and the usurpation of the cultural sphere by corporate interests. In one sense this is inevitable, with the increasing significance of corporate interests necessarily comes an increase in the corporate involvement with culture. Corporations have become part of the culture, therefore they are to be expected to feature in the culture.

However, to the extent that the corporations are involved in the creation of cultural ideas (not only about buying and selling but also about morality and aspirations), the relationship is less than a natural one. When corporate will warps and bends culture to its whims and in the interest of increased

sales, the impact on culture is detrimental. When the culture doing the bending is a foreign-owned multinational giant (or wholly owned subsidiary)
corporation, the impact is downright frightening.

Within the domestic context of most countries as well, cultural practices
are increasingly the result of market forces and the commercial potential of
cultural events. Rook (1985, 255), for example, pointed to this trend, noting
that "while some ritual occasions have declined in popularity, new rituals
have emerged to take their place, if not replace them." His example of a new
ritual, however, is telling when he described "Super Bowl Sunday" as "one
of the largest ritualized celebrations on the planet." His comparison of the
modern cultural practice to a commodity is also clear in his assertion that
"like most marketplace products, rituals are also subject to life cycle forces"
(255).

Hannerz (1992, 106–7) argued that commoditized meaning makes a fiction of the very principles of market freedom that it often claims to embody:

> Over time, being at the receiving end of the commoditized flow of meaning
> also means having one's perspective shaped by it, being culturally constructed
> by it; no longer just taking possession of that culture, that is, but perhaps
> becoming possessed by it. And when this happens, the freedom of the market
> becomes a fiction; the consumers are hooked, incapable of warding off what-
> ever is the ideological import of cultural commodities. As a state may mold its
> citizens, the market may thus to some degree mold its customers.

However, if we are tempted to think of commoditization (commodification)
as an invention of modern marketing and globalization, we are reminded by
Jackson (1999, 99) that

> in Victorian Britain, the extension of overseas trade was justified by a cul-
> ture . . . that associated whiteness with cleanliness and purity at home, in
> contrast to the associations of blackness with dirt and pollution abroad. The
> resulting entanglements between ideologies of domesticity and imperialism
> underline the artificiality involved in making any clear distinction between
> 'culture' and the commodity form.

CORPORATE CULTURE AND LANGUAGE

Every dominant cultural institution is reflected in the everyday language of
its sphere of influence. Language of corporate origin is increasingly easing
its way into the general lexicon. Together with the spread of English as the
lingua franca of international business, changes in English as a result of
corporate influence are also widespread.

Cultural investigators from anthropologists to linguists have had an enduring interest in the interplay of language and culture. This interest is reflected in the so-called Sapir-Whorf hypothesis that is widely interpreted and debated. The hypothesis sought to relate differences in language to differences in culture and even differences in the thought process of the speakers. This hypothesis is the source of the popular idea that "Eskimos" have many words for snow while "Arabs" have many words for sand. In reality, the hypothesis and the debates are somewhat more complicated, particularly because of the implications of the suggested relationship between thought and language. Moore (2004, 89) summed up the implications thusly:

> The Sapir-Whorf hypothesis implies that different languages mark different systems of perception and that the differences between societies' cultural behavior are communicated by and codified in the structure of linguistic meaning. The study of another culture's language is more than an investigation into how they speak; it is an inquiry into how cultural existence is created.

The hypothesis and associated debates have led to a division of views on the role of language in culture. On the one hand there is the view sometimes labeled "linguistic determinism." In this view of the Sapir-Whorf hypothesis, language is a determinant of culture. The words that do exist within a language enable members of that linguistic group to discuss and to think about the concepts associated with them. The lack of such words effectively eliminates not only debate but also thoughts about concepts not linguistically defined. An example of this is the existence of extended definitions of family members in modern Indian languages. Therefore a maternal aunt and a paternal aunt have two different designations in many Indian languages while in English we would simply tag each as an aunt. The lack of linguistic tools to make the distinction means that it is difficult for most speakers of only English to conceive of the distinction and to discuss it. The linguistic determinism argument holds that the existence or lack of words for particular concepts is not just a reflection of the cultural realities of the language group but rather a determinant of what the group includes in their discourse and, by extension, their cultural existence.

Critiques of this deterministic view of Sapir-Whorf focus on the implication that thought about a subject is impossible without the necessary vocabulary. At its simplest level, it is obvious that a person can perceive the color orange and even have discussions about it even if their language only has words for black and white. Further, the dynamic nature of language and its morphology suggests that linguistic referents evolve wherever there is a need for them. So an increased interest in violent incidents on the roads prompts the popularization of the term "road rage." While this process of linguistic innovation is quite rapid today due to the mass media, it is quite evident throughout the history of languages. Thus, for many analysts, the linguistic determinism form of the Sapir-Whorf hypothesis goes too far in the importance assigned to language and fails to account for the dynamism and reciprocity of the language-culture relationship.

A second and much more widely held view is found in what is sometimes called the "linguistic relativism" view of the Sapir-Whorf hypothesis. In this view there are dynamic reciprocal relationships between language and culture. Words evolve to reflect the cultural realities of a linguistic group and those words in turn help to reinforce the same cultural realities. In Western societies increased female participation in the workplace after the end of World War II marked an important cultural change. With that cultural change came the need for linguistic change and the evolution of terms such as "glass ceiling" and "sexual harassment" followed in later years. The emergence of these and other terms in turn enabled social discourse and even legal debate on issues related to female workforce participation within Western culture and in most modern societies.

Whether deterministic or relative, it is difficult to escape the influences of corporate language on modern culture. Two separate categories of corporate language are evident. The first (and more frequently studied) category is what we may term formal corporate language. This is the material that is attributable to corporations in their advertising and marketing efforts. Under formal corporate language file McDonald's "I'm loving it" and Nike's "Just do it." This category of corporate language is evident and clearly tagged as a form of corporate expression.

The second category is what we might call informal corporate language. Informal corporate language comprises all those terms and expressions entering the popular vernacular that derive from corporate sources. This is a much larger category with arguably more influence than simple advertising. Someone selling their house to buy a smaller one now speaks of "downsizing"; when we meet new people, we are "networking"; we encourage "lateral thinking" or "thinking outside the box." All of these terms and more derive either directly or indirectly from the jargon of corporations. Many started out as formal corporate language and made their way into the vernacular. For example, the well-known corporate euphemisms around job cuts used in news releases have evolved over the years from layoffs to downsizing and rightsizing.

Seabrook (1996, 12) examined the spread of what he called "the language of the market," writing that it "colonizes ever new areas of experience" including romantic relationships in that "relationships become transactions; we shop around, or are in the market for a new affair or perhaps a long-term relationship, or even a one-night stand."

Trouillot (2003, 35) gave examples of terms considered standard in modern language and thought that are derived from the North Atlantic historical and social experience and described how those terms are loaded. He labeled terms such as "development," "progress," "democracy," and "nation state" as "North Atlantic Universals" and contended that they

> are not merely descriptive or referential. They do not describe the world; they offer visions of the world. The appear to refer to things as they exist, but rooted as they are in a particular history they are evocative of multiple layers of sensibilities, persuasions, cultural and ideological choices tied to that localized history. They come to us loaded with aesthetic and stylistic sensibilities, religious and philosophical persuasions, cultural assumptions ranging from what it means to be a human being to the proper relationship between humans and the natural world, ideological choices ranging from the nature of the political to its possibilities of transformation.

The relevance of the Sapir-Whorf hypothesis here is its concern with the relationship between language and thought. Trouillot (2003) argued that North Atlantic history conditions our thinking about basic ideas through its influence on language. It follows then, that the influx of corporate language into the vernacular reflects not only the influence of the corporate culture on society but also its influence on individual and social thought. Therefore, when we use language of the corporate culture, we are in some regards acceding to that culture and becoming part of it. Further, when we use the words of that culture we are more likely to think along the lines that are defined by that vocabulary. Therefore, as one example, when we adopt the term "rightsizing" in whatever context, we adopt with it the positive spin loaded into the concept. With the use of the term "right" it becomes more difficult for us to conceive of this term as meaning firing and job losses and ruin for families. At the end of the day, when we adopt these terms not only has corporate power changed language, it has also changed thinking.

ENTERTAINMENT AS CORPORATE CULTURE

The international proliferation of entertainment products including television, movies, web content, and video games marks the hyper-development of a legitimate industry. There is no reason to question the fact that people are willing to pay for entertainment. However, there are several facets of the entertainment industry that mark it as more than simply producers of mass entertainment.

Chapter 6

At the most obvious level, scholars have identified a "transmission" function. The entertainment industry is widely understood to be a tool of cultural transmission. In fact, Katz, Curran, and Gurevitch (1972) identified cultural transmission as one of the uses and expected gratifications of mass media. The guiding principles and underlying assumptions of the vast majority of screen content, particularly from metropolitan countries help to replicate the tacit assumptions about the market and market economies in which their production and distribution are steeped. Some of these ideas are as obvious as the acceptability of the notion of pop celebrity. They may also be as subtle as the underlying assumption that actors and actresses (who are highly compensated by the production companies) are more expert on the films they star in than the producers, writers, and directors. Even more subtly transmitted is the idea that it is morally acceptable to expend vast resources on the production of mere fantasies with those resources then being recovered from audiences (some in poor countries) and reinvested in the production of more fantasies.

Another function of the entertainment industry is what we may term the distraction function. The entertainment industry also serves to distract its audiences from major issues of the day. Entertainment media fantasies and fictions engage audiences who might otherwise be contemplating or (importantly) discussing the failings of governments and corporations. News media present selective coverage of issues that may or may not be the most important but rather the ones that sell the most advertising. The saying is echoed in many newsrooms across the world—if it bleeds it leads.

CORPORATE LANGUAGE AND CORPORATE SPIN: CELEBRITY AS CORPORATE SPEECH

The nature of modern celebrity is often puzzling. Marshall (1997, 4) suggested that the use of the term in earlier times included "an affinity with piety and religion" but has evolved into "some modern sense of false value" and that while once associated with the church, "celebrity" has now come to be associated with modern capitalism. He further suggested that there is indeed an "ideological function" (246) to the celebrity system. Today, some people rise to fame on merit that is true. However, we have repeatedly seen the ascent of dubious celebs to say the least, giving the distinct impression that celebrity is often a deliberate creation of the media industries rather than a function of either personal achievement or social importance. Rothenbuhler (2005, 95) examined inter alia the view of celebrity creation as a kind of "ideological displacement" that presents celebrities as "heroes" who may be portrayed as "glamorously different from us ordinary folks; just like us in most ways, but different nevertheless; as selected by luck; or as fated, magically endowed, or inexplicably special."

The shift from the celebration of actual achievement to celebrity for its own sake can be explained in part by what Gamson (1994, 64) called "celebrity-making," which he described as "an established commercial enterprise" in which "as carriers of the central commodity (attention-getting capacity), celebrity performers are themselves products."

Celebrity is, in today's popular culture, largely a function of how much money corporate interests think they can make from a personality. This can range from the ability to sell CDs and movies based on the celebrity's actual performances (however much augmented by technology and publicity) or the ability to sell newspapers over "controversies" generated by the personalities. The quaint case of a talk show host being sued for slandering a common food product probably had less to do with the merits of the case and more to do with the economic potential of news coverage of the case.

In *Illusions of Immortality*, Giles (2000, 25) argued that the prevalence of celebrity is both a unique and unifying aspect of modern Western culture, writing that

> there is little doubt that the phenomenon of fame, transformed through media technology into celebrity, has created a common Western culture today which is, historically, highly unusual. The sheer number of famous names and faces is without precedent. As media outlets (newspapers, magazines, TV channels) increase in number there is a concurrent increase in the number of "special people" who provide so much of their material. And even the people who work within these media become famous, often deliberately so.

But it is not only the media practitioners who are propelled to celebrity status. The associations between capital and celebrity are evident in the celebrity standing of people whose only claim to fame is their wealth and social status. Dubious celebrities such as Paris Hilton have no particular record of talents that should endear them to the public, nor indeed do they have particularly notable records of achievements in humanitarianism, science, the arts, or politics. The primary basis for her celebrity begins with her association with vast capital resources. The endowment of the British Royals with celebrity status, especially in the case of the late Diana—Princess of Wales has in large part been because of the idea of their capital worth since there is little political power left in that monarchy.

The imagined social achievements of any of these celebrities and their wide international followings have less to do with their actual achievements and more to do with the money that media giants can make from pictures of them with their latest lovers. When such celebrities are touted as ambassadors for various causes, it is often only because of their attention-getting potential which has itself been created by media hype. Their charity and benevolence, spinoffs of their celebrity, then become all tied up with their images that are further projected to willing masses internationally.

THE GLOBAL VILLAGE?

In 1967, Marshall McLuhan (63) wrote, "We now live in a global village." In 1967, the ARPAnet—precursor to the modern Internet—had not yet been developed.

McLuhan envisaged a world in which electronic communications, as extensions of humankind, would eliminate distance and bring communities together. When he wrote these words, McLuhan was thinking primarily about traditional mass media such as radio and television coupled with the power of the communications satellite. McLuhan saw these media as extensions of the human being that were fundamentally different from print. He saw in print the tendency to "detribalize" human beings into separateness because each individual experiences print separately. Electronic mass media, however, would "re-tribalize" humanity through shared experience.

Today, the notion of the global village is an attractive one in an age where instantaneous global communications is possible at an individual level, especially where individual users of communications media can have access to global audiences once connected. Though not explicitly stated, this utopic concept as articulated in popular culture also seems to presuppose that the integration enabled by communications technology would reduce or eliminate barriers to cooperation, trade, and coexistence.

However, not everyone believes in this global village. In fact, many scholars argue that the opposite is happening. Instead of a global village emerging with equal access and use of information and communication technologies (ICT), some scholars argue that continuing and worsening disparities in access to and use of ICT are leading to worsening disparities of wealth and development (Scott 2001). Further, they warn of the increasing influence of large multinational information and communication companies and their power to shape public opinion and market behavior.

Access to technology has long been an issue in areas such as international communication and studies of cross-border information flows. Colonial powers such as England and France in the early half of the twentieth century used shortwave radio service such as the BBC and RFI to spread the point of view of their respective empires. In the latter half of the twentieth century, newly independent ex-colonies found that their limited access to communications technology limited their ability to be heard on the international stage. To make matters worse, reporting done by media in large and powerful countries about many smaller and poorer countries tended to promote a biased view in which famines and natural disasters were the only events to come out of developing notions.

Carlsson (2003) described the debate during the 1970s as unprecedented in their passion and played out primarily at the United Nations with UNESCO being the main forum. Here, highly industrialized nations argued for a free flow of information (widely interpreted as information policy open to foreign imports of information) while mostly newly independent developing nations argued for information sovereignty (seen by the developed nations as a front for censorship and information control). Added to all of this was the fact that most developing nations recognized some role for media as a tool of national development at that time—rendering liberal approaches to foreign content a dangerous threat to such ideas as national identity.

In more recent times a related debate has sprung up around the development of, deployment of, and access to modern information and communication technologies—with particular regard to the Internet and associated technologies. Sadowsky (1996) suggested that new technologies such as the Internet held tremendous promise for developing nations despite problems with implementation and diffusion.

Sadowsky (1996) outlined some of the problems developing countries face with regard to implementation of Internet and related technologies including such factors as physical and human resources infrastructure, national income, development and rate of growth, availability and the amount of international assistance directed toward technology transfer. These factors account, in part, for the observed differences in technological development between developed and developing nations.

Third World theorists and thinkers have identified this discrepancy in technological development as an international "digital divide"—in which the disparities between rich and poor countries' access to information technologies tended to increase with time (Chandrasekaran 2001). The United Nations has explicitly recognized the information technology gap and initiated work in some larger developing countries including Tanzania, South Africa, Romania, and Bolivia to address the gap between richer and poorer nations. The programs were intended to help those countries increase Internet access and other communications capabilities.

Despite the acknowledged gaps in technology, the new communications technologies have yet implanted themselves in many lesser-developed nations. In a rural Cambodian village, for example, the technologies are responsible for changes in the villagers' lifestyles and "residents know the changes are the result of a few never-before-seen contraptions at the village schoolhouse—a couple of desktop computers, a set of solar panels, and a satellite dish—that have connected the village to something called the Internet" (Chandrasekaran 2001). In Borongan, a small town in the Philippines, residents use a church-provided Internet cafe to surf the web and send e-mail, and "the church plans to set up Internet centers in 79 dioceses across this nation of 7,000 islands" (McFarland 2001).

For developing nations, there is still some question of how worldwide the web actually is. Halavais (2000, 7), for example, concluded that

> the organization of the world wide web conforms to some degree to traditional national borders. Web sites are, in most cases more likely to link to another site hosted in the same country than to cross national borders. When they do cross national borders, they are more likely to lead to pages hosted in the United States than to pages anywhere else in the world.

In practical terms, many scholars map the oppressive power of global media corporations on small and poor countries. Edward Herman and Robert W. McChesney (1998), for example, characterized media influences on Barbados, Jamaica, and the Caribbean islands as "decolonization aborted" saying that the islands have evolved from British colonial dependency only to exchange this for a new kind of dependence on the United States fostered through heavy information and trade flows including heavy dependence on tourism. Additionally, they also point to the fact that the islands have also handed their telecommunications infrastructure back over to the traditional colonial powers, particularly in the handover of national telephone systems in many islands to the British telecom giant Cable and Wireless. They note, as do several other studies, that Caribbean schoolchildren frequently demonstrate better knowledge of US geography and politics than the geography and politics of their own small nations and argue that the continuing media influences are part of the push for migration from these islands to the United States and Canada. They also echoed several Caribbean theorists in the notion that even local media tend to closely mimic US form and content, reducing the possibilities of identity preservation that are sometimes imagined as possible outcomes of such productions.

Relevant to these and similarly small and highly vulnerable nations as well, are developing notions of space as a mythic rather than corporeal function in global culture. Whereas small nations have often been overlooked on the world stage, their relegation to the roadside of history is further guaranteed by the effects of globalized mediated culture. In the mythic space of this culture, hosts on internationally broadcast cooking shows regularly speak of "island" cooking and music programs promote "island" music as though all islands have common traits. This mythic space is evident in Piller's (2001, 164) explanation of the relationship between international marketing and mythic place:

Some products do not have an explicit connection to the US but have traditionally been associated with an American lifestyle, such as blue jeans or cigarettes. "Come to Marlboro Country" thus does not invite the reader into an international realm but into the American West. The mythic American West with its wild horses, pristine nature, tough guys, frontier spirit, and freedom can be conjured up in the most unlikely places.

Chapter Seven

Cultural Erosion and Globalization

One of the places where the forces of culture, capital, and globalization most clearly intersect is international tourism. The creation of cultural spectacles for the benefit of foreign viewers and with commercial motivation leads to cultural distortions and social dislocation.

TOURISM, CULTURAL EXPOSURE, AND CULTURAL EROSION

Tourism in its many forms carries dual and opposing potentials for cultural education and cultural erosion. On the one hand the tourist experience can be a valuable tool of education and provide insights into other ways of being. On the other hand, this same experience can come at heavy costs to the host culture or environment.

Visitors to the historical rock city of Petra in Jordan, for example, cannot help but notice local Bedouin boys and girls at the site. While these children harangue the tourist into taking a ride on a "Bedouin taxi" (donkey), the visitor is quickly impressed at the propensity of these children to speak multiple languages and to bargain with tourists from all over the world. It is easy to forget, however, that these children are all of school age. Few tourist guides will explore this issue though it represents not just what we might think of as cultural erosion—but also a human cost in education and potential when these children are enticed to sacrifice their education for plying menial jobs on the tourist circuit.

At a much broader level, the very concept of international tourism raises several issues for the discussion of the globalization of culture. The Briton Thomas Cook (a familiar name to those who have ever purchased travelers checks) is often credited with the development of modern tourism. This is because he became famous for offering package tours in the middle of the nineteenth century. However, Erve Chambers (2000), in *Native Tours*, noted that the idea of the tour to a distant place had already been well developed in Europe by that time particularly with the experience of religious pilgrimages and even secular group tours of distant places. Chambers attributes Cook's success and the development of modern tourism to rapid industrial development and to the related development of rapid forms of transit such as the steamship and the railway.

Chambers later introduced us to a fellow by the name of Fred Harvey whom he credited (alongside the early railroad companies) with the development of tourism in the southwest United States. Harvey was born in London in 1835 and moved to the United States when he was fifteen years old. He started off working in restaurants but switched to the railway industry later in life. While traveling on the trains he noticed the need for proper food services to the traveling public and convinced railroad officials to allow him to open restaurants in the railroad stations. From this start, he developed not only more restaurants and hotels but also a system of tourism that involved the "commodification" of local cultures. Chambers (2000, 94) defined commodification as "a process whereby goods and services that were once considered to be outside the realm of direct economic value and exchange are transformed into commodities that can be bought and sold." A similar term used to refer to this process elsewhere in the literature is "commoditization."

Harvey provides us with a valuable set of insights into how tourism can become a stage for packaged culture. According to Weigle (1989), Harvey created what he called "Indian Detours" where he staged re-creations of Native American life for tourists who paid a fee for the privilege of witnessing the "authentic" display. In and around his hotels such as the Alvarado Hotel in Albuquerque similar agglomerations of native people and artisans were encouraged for the benefit of the tourists. This early experience mirrors much of what happens today in the modern tourist trade.

Chambers (2000) identified culture and heritage as being among the most rapidly growing commodities of modern tourism along with indigenous crafts and traditional spaces. His somewhat deadpan delivery of this concept belies a much more dramatic set of forces at work in this process of commodification—which is arguably not just about selling culture but also reducing culture to the saleable. In making this distinction one can argue that selling a tour to a place where an ancient festival is about to be observed is commodification of the culture, but a decision to stage that festival for the tourist trade is reducing culture to the saleable. The real issue here, then, in terms of globalization and culture is that in many instances, the economic power of tourism tends to warp the local culture in ways that better fit the needs of the tourist trade. This results in a cultural product that meets the needs and expectations of the visitor rather than fulfilling the cultural needs or reflecting the cultural realities of the local population.

An example of this may be found in the work of Wilk (1999, 251) who argued that what constitutes the national cultural definition of Belizean food is actually a function of tourism and other global (and globalizing) influences:

> Belizean restaurants in the United States, cookbooks, public festivities where food is served, and the expensive dining rooms of foreign-owned luxury hotels were all crucial stages where ideas about Belizean food were tried out. By 1990, many dishes that were once markers of rural poverty had been converted into national cuisine. Others had quietly disappeared. Foreigners, expatriates, tourists, and emigrants were crucial agents in formulating and valuing the local.

This particular example is fraught with even deeper irony given the fact that the Belizean cultural matrix includes not only the cultural influence of African slaves and colonial domination but also the ongoing influence of several surviving native (or first peoples) communities of the region.

A November 2008 release from the US Virgin Islands tourism authorities ("St. Croix to Welcome First Ship of the Season" 2008) read in part:

> Welcome festivities planned by the Department of Tourism begin at 9:00 a.m. and continue until the ship's departure at 6:00 p.m. Entertainment includes performances by the Rising Stars Steel Pan Orchestra, The Guardians of Culture *Mocko Jumbies*, the St. Croix Educational Complex Quelbe Band and the St. Croix Heritage Dancers. As the 684 cruise passengers disembark, they will be greeted by mocko jumbies dancing to the sounds of steel pan music as well as greeters from the Department of Tourism offering recommendations on the day's activities, souvenirs and Cruzan rum samples.

While the Mocko Jumbies (traditional stilt walkers) are instructive as an example of cultural ebb and flow—having been brought to the region by African slaves during the Triangular Trade, it is also interesting to see cruise ship visitors in Caribbean islands like Jamaica or St. Croix greeted by steel drum ("steel pan") players when the steel drum or steel pan is not native to these places. It is borrowed from a neighbor to the south—Trinidad. A few moments of logical exploration would reveal, for example, that steel drums are so called because they were originally (and often still are) made from steel containers used to store petroleum. Since most of these islands are not petroleum producers, it would seem odd that the steel drum would be used in their tourist industry. Since the steel drum is not, by and large, a part of Jamaican culture, why is it used to greet visitors to Jamaica and featured prominently in the tourist offerings of so many Caribbean islands?

In part, this is due to the ebb and flow of cultural influences which so clearly undermine notions of authenticity and uniqueness in the globalized environment. However, we must also return to the notion of commodification through globalized media as the steel drum band (steel band) is a spectacle that can be sold to the tourist imagination. What is presented to the visitor has more to do with what the visitor has come to imagine and expect than the reality of the cultural landscape they have just entered. Thus the sound of the steel pan is associated in marketing, in Hollywood, and on television with the tropics and the visitor's imagination is satisfied when this sound is presented on arrival. The instrument's association with the location is a cultural misplacement deliberately employed to enhance the sense of "tropical"-ness in the visitor. To make the charade more complete, many natives in brightly colored dresses and Bermuda-style shorts must also run around excitedly to greet the ship. With maracas in hand and straw hats on their heads, hand-picked to be of a certain physical type, these people are a complete figment of the tourist imagination—bearing no relationship to the everyday life and culture of the locals. This cultural misrepresentation continues in numerous forms throughout the visitor's stay, and results in a hybrid tourist offering that keeps the most profitable practices over the most authentic.

The interplay of tourist expectations and cultural expressions create curious situations. Local entrepreneurship can often lead to the creation of cultural events with imagined histories designed to capture tourist dollars. This can range from tours to spectacles of dubious historical or cultural significance. Adams (1997, 391) noted a concern in the academic literature about the notion that certain forms of tourism can engender "staged authenticity." In her particular study in Indonesia she noted that "large-scale Torajan funerals are increasingly sculpted to address the needs and expectations of visiting tourist dignitaries."

At the same time that local culture may be warped to fit foreign expectations, the influence of the tourist presence itself is seen as a deculturizing or culturally erosive force. Writing about tourism in a particular area of Nepal, Pandey et al. (1995, 34) suggested that

> imitation of tourists' fashions and hairstyles is pervasive among the younger generation of Ghandruk. The traditional dress—kamlo, kamchad bhoto and pants—has been replaced by more modern garb imported from the West. Even the Nepali cap, the most important element of the national dress, has been abandoned. The youngsters have distanced themselves from their traditional cultural identity and even display disrespect towards their elders.

A NONTRADITIONAL TAKE ON TRADITION AND AUTHENTICITY

The question of authenticity is one that we often ask when we encounter such items as "dream catcher" souvenirs for sale at Kmart and made in China. While the retailer cannot be accused of trying to offer "authentic" Native American artifacts, the purchaser cannot escape the irony. Cultural authenticity is a tiresome and often indefensible concept in the light of what we have called interculturality. If, for the sake of argument only, we may define "cultural authenticity" as the extent to which an idea or practice actually originates from within a cultural group. We must note that, over time, every culture experiences a cumulative formation including completely "inauthentic" cultural innovations (built in a process of what we might call "cultural accumulation"). Over time and with adjustments, this accumulation leads to cultural entrenchment (innovation) that then assumes the status of tradition.

Simply put, it may be that we overrate tradition and authenticity. Let us return to the steel pan for a minute. Further examination reveals an interesting history that is important to our discussion of globalization and culture. While we may grumble about the authenticity of the steel pan at cruise ship arrivals in other islands, it is also important to note that the authentic origins of the steel pan are equally bound up in international trade and global practices. For the steel pan it begins with another kind of ship—an oil tanker. The steel pan itself would not exist in its present form if not for the multinational petroleum industry that introduced the steel containers to the islands of Trinidad and Tobago. From the 1850s early attempts at drilling for oil were being made in Trinidad. By the turn of the century petroleum production was well under way and large multinational corporations would later become the major players in the industry. The multinational petroleum corporations active on the island used 55-gallon barrels to store and ship crude petroleum and they were a relatively common part of the everyday cultural landscape—refashioned quite frequently as containers for collecting rainwater for domestic use (with a coating of tar to prevent rusting). Gay (2000) also suggested that the geopolitical realities including the presence of US forces in Trinidad during World War II were also associated with the prevalence of the containers on the island. Around 1947 the empty steel containers were first modified to be used as musical instruments by persons including Winston "Spree" Simon (Seeger 1958).

Thus we must be aware of placing too much emphasis on some pure cultural product emerging out of a single cultural experience. The steel pan which is very much a symbol of Trinidad and Tobago's nationhood and culture, symbolic of both African roots and colonial resistance, is equally a product of global petro-capitalism and global geopolitics. Richard Handler (1986, 2) warned of the danger of over-emphasizing some sort of imagined authenticity:

> I take "authenticity" to be a cultural construct of the modern Western world. . . . Our search for authentic cultural experience—for the unspoiled, pristine, genuine, untouched and traditional—says more about us than about others.

Even in the domestic context, the question of authenticity is a contested one. Lindholm (2008, 80), for example, argued that

> despite Italians' own beliefs, the identification of true Italianness with pasta is not ancient. On the contrary, it is largely a result of the huge outpouring of poor Italian immigrants in the nineteenth century. In lieu of other obvious national markers, these workers were identified as, and began to identify themselves as, pasta eaters. The connection between being Italian and eating pasta was then carried back to the home country by returnees.

Without doubt, international exchanges have impacted both the practices and concepts of culture and authenticity. Morley and Robins (1995, 108) argued that the forces of trade, migration, conquest, and imperialism have resulted in the globalization of capitalism with profound cultural consequences. They suggested that

> global capitalism has in reality been about Westernization—the export of Western commodities, values, priorities, ways of life. In a process of unequal cultural encounter, "foreign" populations have been compelled to be the subjects and subalterns of Western empire, while, no less significantly, the West has come to face with the "alien" and exotic culture of its "Other." Globalization, as it dissolves the barriers of distance, makes the encounter of colonial center and colonized periphery immediate and intense.

Tomlinson (1999) argued for an understanding of globalization as a set of multivalent connections that have increased in various social and technical realms. However, more than its measurable qualities, he was more concerned with its myriad effects which, he argued, include cultural change. From these and similar discourses, globalization raises two primary issues related to culture, namely identity and homogenization. These two are, of course, interrelated. To the extent that identity is eroded, homogenization is expected to occur. Yet, we cannot miss the simplistic nature of this assumption in today's mediated and globalized cultural environment. An example of how complicated the relationships can be arose in early 2009 between two Caribbean neighbors.

On February 10, 2009, the *Jamaica Gleaner* reported that the country's Broadcasting Commission had decided to uphold a ban on Dancehall Reggae songs containing certain kinds of sexual lyrics (Luton 2009). This led to national debate and some people called the move an attack on dancehall by the authorities. It was not the first time that various elements of Jamaican society had clashed on what was appropriate for broadcast and what was not. What was particularly interesting about the case was another facet of the debate that arose out of several decades of cultural exchange between Jamaicans and their southern neighbors Trinidad. Starting with the importation of Trinidad carnival into Jamaica by wealthy Jamaicans in the early 1980s and the subsequent spread of Trinidadian soca music onto the Jamaican airwaves, an uneasy relationship developed between the two music industries.

Thus, when the chairman of the Jamaica Broadcasting Commission, Hopeton Dunn, indicated that the February 2009 ban on lewd dancehall songs would stand, there was an almost immediate backlash against the imported soca music. The very next day, the front page of the *Trinidad Express* announced "Call for Soca Ban" and the lead story carried reports of Jamaicans calling for the banning of soca music on the Jamaican airwaves as the contents were called worse than anything Dancehall Reggae could inflict on the Jamaican listeners (Bowman 2009). This cross-border shootout took place via local newspapers who reported in print and in their Internet editions, issues of mediated content with cultural implications for each country and for the relationships between them. What might have otherwise been an internal cultural issue cannot now be separated from the global reality of the interconnectedness of media systems and cultural exchange. Nor is this an isolated incident since even powerful countries such as France maintain cultural protection policies including quotas on importation of foreign media including music, television programs, and movies as well as subsidies to local producers of such media (Lieber and Weisberg 2002). Canada has maintained cultural quotas in media since 1956 and actively promotes Canadian film production by economic incentives. Somewhat ironically, European Union policy has been to promote television exchange among members while allowing quotas on media from outside—indicating a sort of political and economic definition of European identity that can be supported by cross-border information flows to the exclusion of non-European content. The history of Europe belies any specific pan-European identity, however, and makes the whole thing look rather contrived even if we ignore the language differences that hamper such cross-border flows.

Chapter Eight

Counterculture and Cultural Imaginations

HISTORICAL CONTEXT OF COUNTERCULTURE

Culture has never been a still pond. The shape and form of every culture has been wrought from conflicting influences. Whether these influences are Mithraism and Christianity on the Romans or the influence of Christianity and Judaism on sixth-century Arabia, our snapshots of ancient cultures often fail to properly account for the myriad influences within each culture. Part of this is because dominant cultures often craft the histories of a people or place by controlling not only official policies but also official recordings of events.

Yet, it is clear that the small but vociferous group of Christians that challenged the Roman Empire in the first three centuries AD were an influential counterculture (as it turned out). There were others. When Muhammad began his preaching in Arabia in the seventh century, he and his small group of followers were viewed as an upstart gang of counterculture rebels. We may define countercultures, therefore, as subcultures that hold views and aspirations that fundamentally differ from those of the dominant social paradigm.

Obvious examples of counterculture movements exist in our times. Interestingly enough, many of these counterculture movements either implicitly or explicitly address some form of corporate domination of the culture—often defining corporate culture as the de facto culture of modern society. An episode of the PBS *Frontline* series captured the angst of the "counterculture" music group Insane Killer Clown Posse and their throngs of face-painted, mostly young, mostly white, mostly male followers. The posse stood against corporate control of music and the appropriation of youth culture by large corporations. Though by the end of the documentary we learned that in yet another sweep of the youth market—the corporations had managed to buy up the IKCP and had signed them to a major corporate label.

Yet, it is conceivable, indeed plausible, that even this is a normal process of cultural evolution and development. John Clarke (1991, 99) described processes such as this in terms of cultural revitalization and suggests that the "appropriation of the vernacular" by the dominant social forces, rather than supplanting or eroding indigenous or authentic culture, is part of the process of creation of national popular culture. Thus counterculture, even in its co-option by corporate media and business forces, is a part of the *process* that we usually refer to as culture. Clarke suggested that the process of appropriation in this form results in self-contradictory ensembles of elements reflecting both the vernacular culture and the dominant forces that have adopted it. He also suggested that, often, the vernacular or local elements can find themselves both nationalized and internationalized. From our perspective here, we may add that this happens through the mechanisms of the corporate global media.

Counterculture can express itself in relatively informal ways. Urban legends about corporations are one example of an informal response to their perceived (and sometimes feared) cultural domination. Fine (1985, 64) called these "mercantile legends" and suggested that they "typically posit a connection between a corporation and some harmful situation or event." His examples of these legends include the Kentucky fried rat, worms in McDonald's hamburgers, and Jockey shorts that cause sterility. These legends go further than just suspicions about the products themselves to include concerns about the conduct of the corporations and their key figures. In this regard Fine noted urban legends about a former president of McDonald's being a member of the Church of Satan, suggesting that Uncle Ben's (rice) gives money to the Palestine Liberation Organization or that Procter & Gamble is owned by a satanic cult. He concluded that

> the popularity of mercantile legends suggests that the public is sensitive to the nuances of corporate capitalism. . . . These stories not only inform us about the dynamics of memory but also about the perception of the economic order. Most of these narratives are identical thematically: there is danger from corporations and danger in mass-produced and mass distributed products. . . . The stories revolve around the enormous size, power, control, and wealth of the corporation. (79)

ETHNOGENESIS: SPONTANEOUS IDENTITIES AND IMAGINED COMMUNITIES

Sollors (1987) wrote of a phenomenon called "ethnogenesis." It is not a very complimentary term when applied to cultural groups—with the suggestion being that many notions of cultural resurgence among modern groups tend to involve imagined identities associated with fictional histories. Thus Sollors might cast a negative shadow on observations such as the West Indian (as in the West Indies in the Caribbean—not Western India) Labor Day carnival in Brooklyn, New York, and the Notting Hill carnival in England that have been mentioned previously. In these festivities, an imagined Caribbean identity is portrayed by migrants who left those islands behind and who would, in their traditional settings, have no contact with one another (Cohen 1993; Harrison 1999, 12). Harrison outlined the process of identity creation by the Notting Hill carnival participants and organizers in these terms:

> Their appropriation (but to them, repossession) of the carnival as a symbol of identity eventually came to be legitimized by a revision of its history. From the start, a white community worker had been acknowledged by everyone as the carnival's originator and as its leader for its first few years. But in the mid-1980s, some of the West Indian leaders "discovered" that the carnival had actually been founded by a West Indian woman in the late 1950s.

Without getting into the value or validity of specific observances, it is interesting to note the extent to which such ethnic and cultural imaginings have been rampant in recent years. This is a process that I have termed "retroconstruction." Meyer and Geschiere (1999) contended that the very awareness of being involved in global cultural flows leads to a desire to "fix" oneself and one's identity against the flux. Retroconstruction is a common strategy in pursuit of such objectives. It is the strategy of refashioning relatively recent cultural inventions with a sense of tradition (since we prefer our traditions to be more . . . well, traditional). It is achieved in many ways involving manipulation of symbols, selective transmission of details or (as we have seen in the example above) even good old-fashioned bending of facts. This process is somewhat akin to the (admittedly curious) modern habit of buying new items and modifying them through cosmetic procedures to appear "antique."

We've noted above that Mother's Day was not created by Hallmark, nor any other card company for that matter. It bears noting, however, that the formal institution of the observance was of fairly recent vintage (1914 to be exact). To see retroconstruction in action, you could visit the website MothersDayCentral.com, which not only implies an ancient and traditional context to Mother's Day but even goes so far as to link its origins to ancient Egypt, saying that

> the highly traditional practice of honoring of Motherhood is rooted in antiqui-
> ty, and past rites typically had strong symbolic and spiritual overtones; soci-
> eties tended to celebrate Goddesses and symbols rather than actual Moth-
> ers. . . . One of the earliest historical records of a society celebrating a Mother
> deity can be found among the ancient Egyptians, who held an annual festival
> to honor the goddess Isis, who was commonly regarded as the Mother of the
> pharaohs.

In fairness to the site, they actually do a good job of providing an overview
of many similar observances worldwide; they even recount Anna Jarvis's
campaigns against commercialization of Mother's Day. Our interest here,
however, is in how they seek to legitimize and even exaggerate the historical
and traditional context, reconstructing it in histories that most certainly did
not directly relate to the modern observance. Nor are they unique in this
regard, as many of our traditions have similarly "antiqued" finishes rather
than being genuine antiques.

"FUNDAMENTAL" RESPONSES

Movements such as the antiglobalization movement are highly visible re-
sponses to the largely unchallenged domination of global corporations—
endorsed by both complicit governments and multinational regulatory agencies. However, other counterculture movements are less obvious. It is possible, for example, to see the rise of conservatism both in the East and the
West as a response to the spread of global corporate culture. In short, they are
reinventions and retroconstructions that fit a modern mold while appealing to
an imagined past.

In the United States and other Western countries so-called moral and
religious voices have aligned themselves with particular political movements
to create a neoconservative ideology that has included among its subscribers
Jerry Falwell's Moral Majority in the 1980s and the so-called Religious
Right in the United States that powered the self-professed born-again Christian George W. Bush twice into the White House. In the East, fundamentalist
religious movements have arisen in recent years.

These movements, partly in response to the influence of globalization and
external cultures on their societies, have sought to impose religious strictures
on their societies—not all of which are really traditional in nature. Much has
been written, for example, of the rise of the so-called Wahabi movement in
various Muslim nations. Lane (2006, 89) argued that "Islamic fundamentalism is reinforced by the globalization drive and its manifestations." To call
this fundamentalism, however, is somewhat of a misnomer, in the same way
that calling the religious right in the US fundamentalist is a misnomer. None

of this is a return to fundamental principles of anyone's traditional religious or cultural beliefs. The vast majority of the theologies being preached by so-called fundamentalists are heavily selective re-interpretations, and sometimes novel interpretations of religion based on an imagined time of greater adherence or purity. The problem extends even to the generally accepted mainstream sources of Islamic history which Berkey (2003, 40) suggested were "put together and used by Muslims to settle later controversies and to justify retrospectively an Islamic *Heilsgeschichte* [salvation history], and so reflect more what later Muslims wanted to remember than what was necessarily historically accurate."

But along with the tendency to reinterpret original records, comes the tendency to further reinterpret them later on with a view to filling some new need or responding to some new imperative. In colonial era Arabia, resistance provided such an imperative to a return and refashioning once more of an already tampered-with notion of religious heritage and history. Indeed, Saikal (2003, 34) suggested that in the Muslim lands colonized by the West, their fundamentalist movements emerged in part "to challenge colonial powers or their local allies and pro-Western modernity." He added that

> some of the Islamic elements were decidedly puritanical, calling for a return to the basic teachings and values of Islam as enshrined, in their view in the Qur'an and Hadith; some even advocated extremism as the medium for change. . . . One of the prominent early examples of this cluster was Mohammed ibn Abd al-Wahab (1703–87) of the Arabian peninsula, the founder of the Wahabi movement, which through an alliance with the ruling Ibn Saud dynasty continues to be a central player in the politics and society of the modern Saudi state. . . .
>
> Another example of this clustering were Madhists or followers of those Islamic leaders who claimed to be Madhis (the "divinely guided" or "awaited" ones sent by God) and who mounted revolts against European colonialism in different parts of the Muslim domain. They too essentially wanted a return to what they regarded as the true and uncorrupted Islam as opposed to European political cultural hegemony.

Roy (2008, 366) concurred with this assessment, noting that "re-Islamisation is part of a process of deculturation (that is, of the crisis of pristine cultures giving way to westernization and reconstructed identities)."

In this sense fundamentalism is a cultural and political idea. It does not in fact involve a return to fundamental values but rather to reimagined traditional (often false) identities. The anxiety with which fundamentalism of any kind approaches modern media and the social discourse engendered by the globalization belies a direct conflict. In 2005, for example, Hollywood movie studios began to express concern about a service that provided edited versions of major movies for religious conservatives who objected to the sex and violence in the movies (well, let's be fair—mostly just the sex).

Yet the imagined identities do not stop with religious beliefs. Corporate culture and the gurus of marketing within its halls have created even more powerful imagined identities for consumers.

IMAGINED CULTURE, CREATED TRADITIONS

Media and technology have long been associated with cultural and social change. For one of the first and finest examples of this we may look to a jeweler named Johannes Gutenberg. He had a knack for getting in trouble, owed quite some debts, and even got in trouble over a marriage promise. His connection with printing came somewhat obliquely but was related to his skills with metals.

Printing was in fact already well known by Gutenberg's time. The principles of printing had existed for many years (the Chinese were known to use both ceramic and metal moveable type by the middle of the eleventh century) though it never really caught on in Europe until Gutenberg. One of the main reasons for this was the materials and process involved in woodblock printing of the time in Europe. Each page to be printed would have to be laboriously etched in relief out of wood (laterally inverted or "mirrored") and the resulting "plate" would only be good for a few impressions until it softened and became unusable—hardly a tool for mass production. By the time the famous Gutenberg bible was produced in 1455, Gutenberg had brought together press technology (often likened to the sort of devices used in pressing olives) and moveable type made of metal. With these two developments printing became a more feasible and practical alternative to handwriting of books and pamphlets.

Drucker (1999, 4) identified Gutenberg's improvements to the printing process as "the first of the technological revolutions that created the modern world." He went on to suggest that Gutenberg's development of reusable moveable type led to a social and cultural revolution in Europe thusly:

> The printing revolution swept Europe and completely changed its economy and its psychology. . . . In its first fifty years printing made available—and increasingly cheap—traditional information and communication products. But then, some sixty years after Gutenberg, came Luther's German Bible—thousands and thousands of copies sold almost immediately at an unbelievably low price. With Luther's Bible the new printing technology ushered in a new society. It ushered in Protestantism, which conquered half of Europe and, within another twenty years, forced the Catholic Church to reform itself in the

other half. Luther used the new medium of print deliberately to restore religion to the center of individual life and of society. And this unleashed a century and a half of religious reform, religious revolt, religious wars.

It is ironic that the notion of Gutenberg inventing printing is itself evidence of distortion as a part of culture, but more on that later. Printing press technology had many different impacts on European and world culture. From the spread of literacy due to the falling costs of books, to the political impact of learning being spread among the masses, this communication technology was, arguably, more revolutionary than our Internet or satellite. The development and spread of the technology also finds parallels with our more recent information technology.

In the infancy of the Internet's public spread, many scholars and policy makers picked up the habit of touting the democratizing power of the Internet through which information consumers would become information producers and "talk back" to the media. When video technology spread to the home market in the late 1980s a similar idea was circulated, suggesting that a new group of movie producers would develop through the availability of the technology. Some of this did happen, the Internet has in fact created some democratization especially in some limited areas like social networking sites in which the users produce the content. A few decades after the introduction of home video cameras, digital video technology (integrated with the personal computer) has evolved to the point where small-scale production can yield useful content without the need for hundreds of thousands of dollars of camera and editing equipment. Yet, there has never been a complete revolution and major corporate forces still dominate both the Internet and the video industries.

We can cite parallel developments in Europe of Gutenberg's time. The availability of reading materials at lower costs enabled a vastly improved spread of information, encouraged literacy, and literacy encouraged learning. According to Merriman (2004, 128), though religious literature was the predominant type of material in the early days of mass printing, there were several other offshoots that resulted in the spread of learning:

> Other favored themes of books and pamphlets included nature, the discoveries of the explorers, the acquisition of technical skills (such as medical skills from self-help medical handbooks), manuals of self-instruction (such as how to defend oneself in court, or how to make beer and wine), and everyday morality. Visual, often satirical images such as woodcut illustrations and broadsheets, directed at those who could not read, probably reached far more people than did printed tracts.

However, both information and learning were still largely controlled by the church. To make matters worse, the same technology that promised (and delivered) enlightenment was quickly co-opted by the church both for propaganda and for political abuses. Not only was the printing press used by the church to print up indulgences (according to some sources, with the encouragement of a profit-driven Gutenberg), but it was also used by the church to strengthen its grip on information control and standardization of texts. Merriman (2004, 128) described one method by which this was pursued during the period known as the reformation:

> Princes and ecclesiastical leaders intensified their efforts to secure religious conformity by controlling what people read. The "blue library" (so called because small books or pamphlets were wrapped in blue paper) helped diffuse orthodoxy through pamphlets deemed acceptable and sold by itinerant peddlers. Each Western European country had such a "literature of bits and pieces" Didactic stories were meant to instruct people about religious events, saints, and ideals approved by the Church, and to distance them from the "superstitions" of popular culture.

It would be something of an irony, however, that the church's monopoly on information would eventually be undermined by the same technology it was so eager to use for the printing of indulgences. Even more so, it was a particular turn of fate that saw printed versions of Luther's *Disputation of Martin Luther on the Power and Efficacy of Indulgences* (also called *The 95 Theses*) posted on church doors and according to Brecht (1985) quickly translated and spread among the intelligentsia of the time.

This connection between the communication technology of the fifteenth century and social change in Europe of that time (and the periods following) bears lessons for us today. Factors such as the rate of information distribution, the content and the propensity for intermediation (or lack thereof) that defined the spread of printing technology and its effects also affect us today. Our information flows are somewhat greater than in the time of Gutenberg, but the impact of information on our culture may be just as meaningful.

COLUMBUS STORIES AND FICTIONAL OSMOSIS

The impact of these vast flows of information in the modern globalized and hypermediated reality raises questions about what makes its way into popular discourse. Given the size of the universe of potential information, is it possible to always distinguish between reliable information and complete falsehoods? Here I propose to introduce and explain a process I have termed "fictional osmosis." This is the process by which fictions are merged into popular discourse and then into cultural beliefs. Often this happens because fictional stories become popular and so work their way not just into storytelling but also into the matrix of texts and cultural expressions. Once integrated, it is difficult to extricate fictions from truth and they meld into cultural expression.

One example of fictional osmosis is the prevailing set of beliefs about Christopher Columbus. Historians have attempted to demonstrate that many of the ideas about Columbus found in popular thought (and even some textbooks) are not true. Columbus did not set out to prove that the earth is round nor did he set sail with a crew of criminals. These are not matters of historical debate either, because these and other erroneous ideas quite clearly arise from a quasi-fictional work—*The Life and Voyages of Christopher Columbus*, by Washington Irving (1828). Irving was also the author of *Rip Van Winkle* and the *Legend of Sleepy Hollow* (1820, 1917).

Another treasured American cultural tale finds its origin in fiction as well. Mason Locke Weems ([1806] 2009, para. 24) described George Washington's cherry tree episode in his book *A History of the Life and Death, Virtues and Exploits of General George Washington*:

> The following anecdote is a case in point. It is too valuable to be lost, and too true to be doubted; for it was communicated to me by the same excellent lady to whom I am indebted for the last.
>
> "When George," said she, "was about six years old, he was made the wealthy master of a hatchet! of which, like most little boys, he was immoderately fond, and was constantly going about chopping everything that came in his way. One day, in the garden, where he often amused himself hacking his mother's pea-sticks, he unluckily tried the edge of his hatchet on the body of a beautiful young English cherry-tree, which he barked so terribly, that I don't believe the tree ever got the better of it. The next morning the old gentleman, finding out what had befallen his tree, which, by the by, was a great favourite, came into the house; and with much warmth asked for the mischievous author, declaring at the same time, that he would not have taken five guineas for his tree. Nobody could tell him anything about it. Presently George and his hatchet made their appearance. 'George,' said his father, 'do you know who killed that beautiful little cherry tree yonder in the garden?' This was a tough question; and George staggered under it for a moment; but quickly recovered himself: and looking at his father, with the sweet face of youth brightened with the inexpressible charm of all-conquering truth, he bravely cried out, 'I can't tell a lie, Pa; you know I can't tell a lie. I did cut it with my hatchet.'—'Run to my arms, you dearest boy,' cried his father in transports, 'run to my arms; glad am I, George, that you killed my tree; for you have paid me for it a thousand fold. Such an act of heroism in my son is more worth than a thousand trees, though blossomed with silver, and their fruits of purest gold.'"

According to some sources, while the book itself was first published in 1800, the story of the cherry tree was absent—not added until an edition printed in 1806. There is no other account of this episode other than in Weems's book and it had never been mentioned until well after Washington's death. Weems's fanciful depictions included descriptions of Washington's last words that were contradicted by the accounts of Washington's own personal secretary and an account of Washington praying at Valley Forge. The latter scene made its way into the popular culture, featured on stamps and other official expressions. There is some contention as to the actual form of Washington's personal faith but, setting that aside, there is no corroboration of Weems' account of the praying general.

Fictional osmosis is aided by a process of compounding, in which the fictions become retold and then take on the ring of truth when combined with fact or other fictions and when told in various versions over time. Nietzsche (2006, 15) noted that "as long as the soul of history is found in the great impulse that it gives to a powerful spirit, as long as the past is principally used as a model for imitation, it is always in danger of being a little altered and touched up and brought nearer to fiction." Such "touched up" history comes through the integration of erroneous stories, exaggerations, and other departures from fact into everyday culture and is evident by such measures as their appearance in government observances and in school textbooks, and eventually into everyday discourse and tales told. Marc Ferro's (2005) *The Use and Abuse of History or How the Past Is Taught to Children* explored the (somewhat subtle at times) propagation of semitruths, blind spots, and omissions of history through textbooks in different nations. Karim (2006, 269) referenced such national myth making and places the media squarely in the role of compounding such ideas, writing that

> national mass media systems emphasize the concept of the nation-state as the primary and natural form of polity. They play this role with the continual highlighting of national symbols ranging from the prominent portrayal of national leaders in regular news bulletins to the frequent retelling of tales gleaned from the national mythology in dramatic programs (to say nothing of the ubiquity of the national flag and references to national institutions).

As social beings we are resistant to the idea that culture, even our own culture can compromise outright fictions. The acceptance that fiction is a part of culture not only runs counter to notions of authenticity, but also makes us all very uncomfortable. This is particularly because of our emotional need to depend on our basic belief and value structures. Like a foreigner in a strange land, we are dislocated by the removal of the familiar and comforting—even if they are without basis. When the truth of these and similar stories is challenged, we are often inclined to keep the stories despite their untruth since their (often valuable) cultural functions have already been established.

The danger of the globalized media environment is that fictions flow more frequently and more directly into the popular culture and into formal culture and belief systems.

LEAD, LOAD, AND LAG

This high rate of information flow and the difficulties of processing information before it is replaced, lead us to consider some of the impacts of information flows on culture. Compared to the information flows of today, we might see the information flows of Gutenberg's time as insignificant. In absolute terms there is clearly more information flowing though our everyday lives than there would have been in Europe of the 1450s. Consider how many messages both personal and public that we receive (or are exposed to) on a daily basis. That number is easily hundreds of times greater than the information load of the average Johannes of Gutenberg's era and locale. Yet two mitigating factors must be considered here. The first is a dual faceted factor that I call the capacity/consumption factor. Here we should consider both the individual's capacity to receive and process information as well as the amount of that information processed.

In our modern globalized media environment we are bombarded with information—but we are also prepared to be bombarded by information. Our ability to process that information is as important as how much information we are exposed to. Widespread literacy, media choices, and audience discrimination all mean that the modern consumer of information is not necessarily inconvenienced by the unprecedented information volumes of our age. Comparatively speaking, the cultural impact of our vast information flows may be relatively small compared to information flows in the early days of the information revolution. The German villager who received a single message from abroad was probably more influenced by that message than we are today. In today's hypermediated environment, we also routinely transmit more than the amount of information a person can process in a single day. No one expects any of us to process all of it. Culturally, the impact of this globalized information flow is kept in check by the fact that the modern human being discriminates among the sources and messages available to him or her. We consume less information than is available to us for reasons of cost, time, and interest. Thus, I argue that on the basis of this capacity/consumption notion, estimates of the impact of the globalized information flows tend to be overstated.

Another factor in the comparison of the impact of information flows is that of uncertainty. This works in two ways as well. The German villager of the 1450s would have a limited number of sources of information and could only be certain of information to the extent that the sources were trusted. The modern Global Villager can check multiple sources to be as certain as possible (or as certain as needed). However, the load of each of these people would be extended in different ways. For the European villager of the 1450s there would be the challenge of determining the accuracy of information because of limited sources. Our Global Villager has a similar problem because of too many sources. In both cases the persons involved may reduce their information-seeking load by settling on particular sources that they identify as reliable. Consider your own preference for one news channel or another.

I suggest that the impact of our huge modern globalized information flows on their audiences can be understood in terms of three factors, namely lead, load, and lag.

Lead

This factor relates to the amount of time between an actual event and when news of that event reaches an individual either by mass media or interpersonal sources. Since we still do not experience most events in the world directly and immediately but through myriad mediated processes, the lead may be divided into two components—the time required to collect information about an event by information seekers (journalists or informers) in order to pass it on to the media channels or other individuals (typically kept to a minimum by news media) and the time between an event or issue being covered by the media and when the information consumer receives the information. As lead time decreases information becomes more difficult to process. Additionally, at the early stages of an event, preliminary information available on the media channels might be missing various crucial components and aspects of the event. It results in many questions being unanswered leading to confusion because of inadequate information. Today's increased emphasis on immediacy in media reporting results in shorter lead periods.

The problem is exacerbated when inadequate (sometimes incorrect) information is transmitted over different media channels and social media almost immediately all over the globe. The technological means and ease of disseminating information that is possible because of the Internet and satellite communication results in an instant transmission of visual and graphic details. The visual component of the event impacts the receivers and the inadequate information heightens a need for more details.

Load

This factor relates to the amount of information that is available about an event. It assumes crucial significance and is impacted as well as dependent on the first factor—lead. The concept of increased information load leading to decreased comprehension is well-known in communications literature (Carver 1973; King and Behnke 1989, 2000).

Load has three components: (1) volume of information, (2) consistency of information, and (3) valence of information (how much information on an event that an individual exposes himself or herself to). This is consistent with media research and measurements that attempt to quantify the level of media usage by audience members. It also, however, includes the information coming from interpersonal networks that are locally based or by interpersonal exchange of e-mails over larger distances. The concern associated with an event, or curiosity, as well as the economic or personal costs of obtaining the information.

Lag

The last factor pertains to the amount of time before information about a particular event is updated or changed or the amount of time until that event is eclipsed by another. The lag time impacts an individual's ability to check sources and to assimilate meaning about the event. There are two components to lag:

1. incremental lag, or how long it takes for every new piece of information to replace old pieces of information or to be added to the existing information about an event or issue; and
2. replacement lag, or how long it takes before the event or issue is replaced by another.

It is important to note that Klapp (1982) used the term "lag" to refer to the general outpacing of meaning creation by the speed of information production and reception. This returns us to the question of truth and misinformation as it influences culture. The information loads, lead and lag times of today tend to accelerate the processes of fictional osmosis more than ever before. This is easily seen in the spread of urban legends which tend to make their way into the popular culture. The popular "kidney in ice" urban legend, for example, prompted the New Orleans Police Department (1997) to issue the following bulletin in 1997:

January 30, 1997
Internet Subscribers:

Over the past six months the New Orleans Police Department has received
numerous inquiries from corporations and organizations around the United
States warning travelers about a well organized crime ring operating in New
Orleans. This information alleges that this ring steals kidneys from travelers,
after they have been provided alcohol to the point of unconsciousness.

After an investigation into these allegations, the New Orleans Police Department has found them to be COMPLETELY WITHOUT MERIT AND
WITHOUT FOUNDATION. The warnings that are being disseminated
through the Internet are FICTITIOUS and in violation of criminal statutes
concerning the issuance of erroneous and misleading information.

Reports such as this fit into a larger body of urban legends that suggest a
rampant trade in human organs worldwide. This is, of course, neither completely true nor completely false, but rather greatly exaggerated from uncer-
tain reports that spread via a combination of mass media and interpersonal
communications across the globe.

When a vast number of people believe these rumors they take on the
status of truth and become part of cultural assumptions about the world
around us, partly as we have seen, because of the speed and immediacy of
information. I use the terms speed and immediacy as distinct from each other
here. Whereas speed refers to how quickly the information spreads, immediacy suggests the extent to which the information can be made to appear as part
of the consciousness of the recipient. Thus, one may receive an e-mail message with attached pictures or video purports to show a young boy being
punished for stealing bread at a market. The message claims that the pictures
or video are taken in Iran, or Pakistan, or some other Islamic-sounding country and show a young boy having his arm run over by a car wheel. This
vicarious experience of the horrible event becomes real to the e-mail recipient due to the immediacy of the visual portrayal. Of course, a little investigation reveals that the images actually demonstrate little more than a street
performer's antics in a third-world market and that the last parts of the
sequence showing the boy emerging unscathed from the event is usually
omitted (snopes.com 2006).

In the context of such rapid and changing information flows it is tempting
to suggest that there are information classes defined by factors such as access
to information technologies and ability to decode information flows. However, while the political economists and some communications scholars have
pointed to such class distinctions in terms of resources and access, I would
tend to shy away from them in the present discussion. I do this because I
have witnessed some of the most educated and some of the wealthiest people
be taken in by false information distributed via the Internet and via word of
mouth. The ubiquity of technologies such as the mobile phone in modern
society makes it difficult to delineate classes based on access to information.
While the US government initially identified a so-called digital divide in the

United States, the divisions along economic, geographical, and even ethnic lines have consistently been reduced over the years since the 1990s when nationwide measurements of access were first made.

International distinctions among the information rich and information poor are still sometimes touted, but here again I would caution against making too much of a village not having Internet access. If we would label such a village as information poor, that would only be a sign of our own cultural bias. They are poor only in terms of the information we feel is enriching to them. Chances are that the same village has existed for centuries only because they are wealthy enough in the knowledge needed for their survival. The Internet may hold little benefit or interest for them.

Additionally, information richness itself becomes a problem in terms of the load factor on the individual. The burden of processing new and diverse information is a familiar one to most of us today. We often have to "check up" on information passed to us casually or electronically. Often, it becomes difficult to separate fact from fiction and many of us do not have the time to sort out each rumor.

IMMEDIACY AND FICTIONAL OSMOSIS IN THE MEDIA-GLOBALIZED ENVIRONMENT

The quest for speed in information is not a new one. Rosenberg and Feldman (2008, 35) argued that technological developments and speed of information have usually gone hand in hand:

> Speed was as much a driving impulse in the past as now. There must have been something about the way humans were hard wired even then that drove them to seek news at a faster and faster pace. The filmed weekly newsreel was just three years old in 1914 when Pathé sought to speed things up by offering a daily one. What made this possible was the use of what came to be called "safety film" which, unlike film made from nitrate, was nonflammable. That meant daily newsreels could be dispatched through the mail while the news itself was hot.

While much faster than the flows of Gutenberg's time, this is, of course, still a far cry from the almost immediate reporting and coverage of events in today's globalized media environment. Traditional media organizations such as BBC and CNN routinely provide live coverage from breaking news events around the world. A recent advertisement on BBC world reminded viewers, for example, that they have correspondents in more than fifty countries worldwide, so that when a story breaks—they are already there. Add to this, the variety of nontraditional news sources that also provide information to the mediasphere, including bloggers and, more recently, Facebook and tweets.

Among the many impacts of immediacy is the increasingly ability of false or doubtful information to enter the public discourse and make its way into cultural lore as true. This presents a contemporary, dynamic, and ongoing dimension of fictional osmosis. The cultural confusion arising out of Dan Brown's (2003) *Da Vinci Code* is an example of how fictional portrayals can affect culture. The novel spawned numerous other books and several websites dedicated to separating the truth from the fiction in the novel. Despite this, several questions about long-held assumptions entered the popular culture, including what may prove to be an enduring debate (see the present volume) on the role (and suppression) of females in religion. What is also interesting in the *Da Vinci Code* example is that the important contribution of religious skepticism which may have come from the novel may have been eclipsed by the wild and conspiratorial elements that many readers have also come to adopt. Thus it is Da Vinci's membership in a secret society and hidden messages in his mural of the Last Supper that capture the imagination and enter the cultural mix, rather than real and important questions about the role of women in the early church and the possibility of a plausible social context for the life of Jesus of Nazareth.

Yet, cultural impact by fictional osmosis is not limited to ostensible works of fiction. In October, 1990, after the invasion of Kuwait by Iraq, a news story emerged that was pivotal in turning US public opinion from indifference to concern for the Kuwaiti situation. The story featured a fifteen-year old Kuwaiti girl giving an account of Iraqi soldiers storming a hospital in Kuwait and dumping babies out of incubators.

According to Kitty (2005), US president George Bush, the United Nations, and Amnesty International were all taken in by this report. There was just one problem, the story was a plant originating with the public relations firm Hill and Knowlton. This is not to say that there was no evidence of brutality at the hands of Saddam's troops in Kuwait, but the specific instance that was carried here as news was actually a clever bit of public relations, released as a video news item and picked up by various media in the United States. The young woman on the screen was a member of the Kuwaiti royal family who had probably been flown out of the country very early in the progress of the invasion like so many other wealthy Kuwaitis at the time. Her performance was, in part, intended to win support for resistance to the invasion, but also in part to restore her family's hold on power. By the time the story had spread and garnered support from international agencies and the US public, debate about its truth of falsehood was a purely academic exercise. It was already in the culture.

Speed and coverage are also relevant to another incident, this time in 1998, when news coverage of a purportedly global phenomenon spread almost instantaneously across the world. The incident involved both rapid word-of-mouth transmission (direct and via electronic means) and mediated coverage (Singhal, Rogers, and Mahajan 1999) and created a worldwide stir when stone statues of Hindu deities were thought to be consuming milk offered by worshippers. The marvelous element of this particular news event was the video that often accompanied the stories, appearing to show the purported phenomenon. Several explanations have been offered for the phenomenon. According to one explanation, the natural absorbency of some of the materials used in carving the statues can account for some of the absorption of the liquids observed (which would also explain why the absorption of the milk eventually came to an end in many instances). Another quite obvious explanation is that the ardent worshippers were sometimes being exposed to little more than a cheap parlor trick. In either case, the hysteria generated in the community over the sudden and extensive mediated coverage of the event (including transatlantic telephone conversations on the issue) served to embed the (quite possibly pseudo-) event as a major religious occurrence. Subsequent debunking of the story serves little or no purpose to the true believer (or the media victim).

We might be tempted to venture the argument that in both cases above, the truth finally comes out and therefore the effects of immediacy are subject to revision—that is, we should not worry about it as it will correct itself in the long run. First, this is generally not the case for the reasons outlined above—including the information load on the individual and the replacement of the issue by others. Secondly, this would be to ignore the many other cases where the truth does not come out in the end and the misrepresentation simply continues on, to be weaved into the cultural framework.

The cultural distortions of the past are the culture of today—there is little to be gained by seeking either coherence or authenticity. We rationalize our present understanding with the notion that it has always been thus—another dimension of what I have called retroconstruction in earlier chapters. For example, we often think of Hinduism as both the religion and dominant cultural character of India. Yet Hefner (1998) argued that Hinduism as a unified religion or culture may be a relatively recent invention since it has traditionally been a set of diverse ideas spread in various ways across a large region through travel, trade, and political influence. King (1999, 146) suggested that "the notion of 'Hinduism' as a single world religion is a nineteenth century construction, largely dependent upon the Christian presuppositions of the early Western Orientalists." Additionally, Hefner pointed out that many Hindu religious sites were built with some influence from preexisting indigenous practices, likening the situation to that found in Latin

American Catholicism where some indigenous (and sometimes even African) figures still tend to show up in depictions and worship. Even the term "Hindu" is itself the product of external influences. According to King,

> the term "Hindu" is the Persian variant of the Sanskrit *sindhu*, referring to the Indus river, and was used by the Persians to denote the people of that region. The Arabic "Al-Hind," therefore, is a term denoting a particular geographical area. Although indigenous use of the term by Hindus themselves can be found as early as the fifteenth and sixteenth centuries, its usage was derivative of Persian Muslim influences and did not represent anything more than a distinction between "indigenous" or "native" and foreign. (162)

King (1999) also argued that the emphasis of particular texts as the core of Hindu tradition, for example, evolved out of colonial emphasis on the role of sacred texts as may be found in the Judeo-Christian tradition while the rich oral and musical/theatrical traditions of the region were denigrated as devolved aspects of the text or as superstition. Even Lorenzen (1999, 631) who disagreed with this idea of British colonial invention of Hinduism, managed to place it in the context of an earlier colonialism, suggesting that: "a Hindu religion theologically and devotionally grounded in texts such as the Bhagavad-gita, the Puranas, and philosophical commentaries on the six darsanas gradually acquired a much sharper self-conscious identity through the rivalry between Muslims and Hindus in the period between 1200 and 1500." At any rate, his arguments still support the idea that instead of a pure and indigenous (or authentic) system, Hinduism is (perhaps equally) the product of external influences. So that even considering the objections of some scholars, we can still safely assert that over the years of Mughal dominance and then British colonial rule, the concept of "Hindu" emerged out of the colonial dynamic and reflected perceptions of otherness from and to the Indian masses.

The real construction of Hindu identity then becomes masked by history and mass understanding into popular versions that have little to do with an objective or historical reality. Indeed, the constructions that evolve in the popular understanding are eventually highly romanticized, often developing long and illustrious (though usually imagined) traditions. Lorenzen (1999, 655) is guilty of retroconstruction even where he assigned the evolution of Hinduism to the contrasts and conflicts of Muslim rule in India, defining Hindus as a group at a time when neither the world nor the concept existed:

> What did happen during the centuries of rule by dynasties of Muslim sultans and emperors was that Hindus developed a consciousness of a shared religious identity based on the loose family resemblance among the variegated beliefs and practices of Hindus, whatever their sect, caste, chosen deity, or theological school.

Through such processes of retroconstruction—or the normalization and rationalizing of innovations into tradition we accept ideas such as Hinduism's natural association as part of Indian identity (though British colonials often spoke of Hindoo Muslims and Hindoo Christians). It is perhaps here that I should disclose that part of my own family is Hindu and I grew up listening to discourses about the pure evolution of a prehistorical Hinduism with its foundation in Sanskrit and its continuous practice for more than five thousand years. Either the British invention or the Mughal evolution hypotheses above are enough to question these popular assumptions.

Yet, retroconstruction gives us more than subtle identity associations. It also hands us many of the bizarre practices associated with religion today as though they have always been part of religion and, indeed, culture. Perhaps the most bizarre of these is rampant discrimination against women and repression of both sex and sexuality that continues in many religious traditions.

SEX AS SIN

Sex as sin is one of the outdated and barbaric ideas that continue to plague modern society in the guise of either culture or religion. As backward as these ideas are, their danger comes from their association not with some sort of divine aversion to sex but rather from the fact that there are deep misogynistic implications to these traditions. Scholars have traced the association of sex with sin to the work of early leaders of the Christian church including St. Augustine (Tannahill 1980) as well as to specific dictates from the church such as the ruling of Pope Siricius in 385 that upheld celibacy as a rule for clergy.

Sullivan (2006) argued that the problem begins with literal interpretations of the Judeo-Christian creation myth in which Adam and Eve are perceived as real people. Working within this fairly limited worldview, Augustine of Hippo (AD 354–430) developed and popularized ideas about original sin being transmitted via sex (specifically through semen) in his work *City of God*, or *De Civitate Dei* (Augustine [426] 1972). Bullough (1977, 185) argued that the medieval church adopted a stance on sex that reflected what he described as an intellectual hostility from previous social (though not dominant) thought systems; he placed the "sexually obsessed" Augustine as the "basic formulator of western Christian attitudes" and described him as a convert from Manicheanism who "was undergoing a crisis about his own inability to control his sexual desires," and who "became particularly offended by the act of coitus."

The roots of Augustine's asceticism may perhaps be found in the influence of the Persian figure of Mani to whom his early religious leanings were pointed. Augustine's adherence to Manicheanism and his inculcation of its tenets were not some youthful dalliance or passing phase. Glyn-Jones (1996, 172) wrote that Augustine, in fact, was a Manichean for fifteen years, noting that Mani "preached a doctrine of rival realms of darkness and of light" in which "pursuit of the realm of light required a rigorous asceticism."

Chidester (2000, 126) outlined something more of the history of Mani, who arose out of a community of followers of the Mesopotamian prophet Elchesai who, in a vision, was told that Jesus Christ would be re-born periodically on earth. The eclectic nature of Mani's experience and his particular religious teachings (sometimes characterized as Christian in nature, but probably only arguably so) are also evident in Chidester's account that tells us,

> After traveling for three years in India, Mani settled in Persia, where he proclaimed his "gospel of light," which wove together elements of Christianity, Buddhism, and the ancient Persian religion of Zarathustra.

Augustine's beliefs moved from the doctrines of Mani to the more mainstream Christian church after he moved to Milan and also following his disillusionment over his encounters and disagreements with the Manichean Bishop Faustus whom he had met during his time at Carthage. Chidester (2000) also indicated that during Augustine's movement from Manicheanism to mainstream Catholic orthodoxy, he was particularly taken with stories like that of Anthony the Great of Egypt, who was a renowned ascetic and generally known as a the father of Christian monasticism.

Thus Augustine, who went from Manichean convert to leader in church thought, brought inherited asceticism from Manichean thought and fascination with the monastic ascetics of mainstream Christianity to his own teachings. Even the inherited and admired asceticism were not sufficient for Augustine, who later took issue with Manichean attitudes toward sex. Clark (2000, 396), for example, suggested that it was "against Manichean theory," that "Augustine developed a pro-reproductive and anti-contraceptive marital ethic that became the hallmark of Catholic sexual teaching until our own century."

It was not only in matters of sex that Augustine's thinking was somewhat (let's say) idiosyncratic. By the time Augustine wrote influential works like the *City of God*, he also believed that peacock flesh did not decay, that goat's blood could destroy diamonds, and that mares could be impregnated by the wind (Augustine [426] 1972; cited extensively in Sullivan 2006). Augustine also seemed somewhat perturbed over the idea that men can control their limbs but have other elements of their body that they cannot control with the same certainty. Perhaps this goes some way in explaining why, according to Bullough (1977), Augustine hesitantly approved of brothels (despite finding them abhorrent) in order avoid the commission of even greater sins.

Sullivan (2006, 17) argued that numerous Christian scholars and statements of doctrine echo Augustine in the attitude toward sex as a vehicle of original sin and argues that this explains why such theologians "place a premium on Jesus' virgin birth" (more properly, his virginal conception) and says that "not having a human father combined with Mary's immaculate conception protected Jesus from the stain of original sin." He added that this kind of thinking has "steeped human sexuality in a marinade of sin and shame" (18). Beyond the problems of guilt, the male-dominated church (in line with the historic interpretation of Genesis) also associated women with the source of sexual temptation. This line of thought invariably led church writers and authorities over the years to associate women with moral weakness and temptation. According to Farley (1976, 168), Augustine established the inferiority of women not only in body but also in soul, though she notes the far more complex origins of such ideas:

> It comes as a surprise to many contemporary women that the present theological justifications for their inferior status in church and society derive in part from a history of strange and contorted doctrines and theories of evil and sin. Ancient myths identifying woman with chaos, darkness, mystery, matter, and sin echo clearly in Christian interpretations of concupiscence, of the body as defiled, of sexuality as contaminating, and thence of woman as temptress, as a symbol of sin.

While this explanation fits comfortably into our present notions of the interconnectedness of ancient and cultural influences, such a view accounts for and (perhaps) excuses the theological justifications of the negative view of women. Denike (2003, 16–17), however, was somewhat less charitable and laid the blame for religious misogyny squarely with the Christian church itself, writing that

> cast invariably as the "adversary of God" and the essence of man's sinful affliction, and deployed through tropes of women's weakness and impurity, the predominant conception of "evil" that was launched in the New Testament takes a form that radically departs from its Greco-Roman and Judaic predecessors. . . . This new "evil" is made manifest in Satan's conspiratorial and treasonous trickery, which is performed, first and foremost, through woman. . . . Strategically deployed through images of seduction, temptation, sacrifice, and conspiratorial pacts with the Devil himself, "evil" is inscribed with themes of sexual abjection, and it is cathected to, and incarnated as, the "weaker sex."

It was not only a set of beliefs or attitudes that emerged, as Denike (2003, 24), further, made the connection between attitudes and practice, arguing that

> as the source and perpetual threat to man's godly purity, the taint of woman's sex was enough for the Church Fathers, on the authority of Paul, to condemn her to silence and obedience, to forbid her to preach, or to administer the holy sacraments.

Here, we are less concerned with the merits of church doctrines and more concerned with the effects of these ideas (with all their ancient and confused baggage in tow) on cultures throughout much of the world, over the ages and till today. Phillipa Levine in *The British Empire: Sunrise to Sunset* (2007, 151) explored how this association between females, sex, and evil was spread through the British Empire, though the same could be claimed for other European Christian imperial outings. She notes that

> the imperial period was one of deep Christian orthodoxy, with its bifurcated understanding of sexuality as either sinful or procreative. There was already a long tradition in the Christian world of regarding women as dangerous temptresses, easily reinforced when British men encountered women unencumbered by the religious association between sin and sexuality.

The almost automatic association of sex with sin that pervades much of modern society owes more to the politics of the early church and the spread of these ideas by colonialism than to any natural association between religion and abstinence. Indeed Hindu philosophy still embraces (though often in veiled form) aspects of sexual worship including the celebration of the Shivalingam—a giant penis-form associated with the deity Shiva.

INVENTIONS AND CAMEL RACES

Cultural change (or what is increasingly termed "erosion") is an ongoing and inevitable process. Equally important is the notion of cultural invention. Cultural invention sounds self-contradictory because of our associations of "natural evolution" with cultural practice. Chambers (2000) argued, however, that such cultural inventions are common features of all societies and cultures. Cultural traditions may, indeed, often have been the result of relatively pragmatic inventions, fulfilling the needs of the communities rather than being simply symbolic or steeped in history.

Consider, for example, Khalaf's (2000, 249) analysis of what he called the "newly invented tradition" of camel racing and camel festivals in the United Arab Emirates and some other Arabian Gulf countries in which local "cultural traditions are changed, elaborated upon, and given new institutionalized forms." Complete with live televised coverage, entrants from several other countries and the presence of important political figures, such a festival, according to Khalaf, "provides links to the historical past of the Emirates' pastoral way of life that has been swept away by oil-triggered modernization" and also provides "the Emirates' political community with a ritually constructed theater to celebrate its own specific political ideology, cultural traditions, and values by invoking nationalist themes, symbols, metaphors, and language" (244).

The use and racing of camels have been features of local culture for many years in these areas. However, Khalaf (2000, 258) suggested that global influences and the UAE's participation in the international economy are the more important drivers of this modern (invented), mediated, and ritualized racing tradition; he writes,

> Within these cultural contexts and economic conditions, heritage preservation becomes significant for society, which turns to old cultural references and themes; in this case, revolving around the camel. Camel racing, a still-evolving invented tradition, represents a vehicle of cultural empowerment that helps the UAE construct its own image and sense of imagined community.

The presence of the political leaders of the region and many influential business persons (who own the camels) at these events demonstrates the pragmatism (and sometimes crass commercialism) involved in what we might term "cultural evolution." But it also causes the careful observer to question the very notion of authenticity—a difficult notion if we are to continue to hold dear not only the uniqueness of our own cultural ideals and practices, but also the imagined sanctity of these same things. Globalization has also played into the conduct of camel racing in the Arabian Gulf in even less savory ways. The use of child jockeys (from foreign countries) has been a major issue for several years (Child Workers in Asia Foundation 1997) with several cases of boys from Southeast Asian countries being injured while participating in the races. This abuse of the migrant labor environment and lax laws has resulted in the introduction of "robot jockeys" in some places (little more than a radio-controlled camel-beating device).

Each culture sees its own proclivities, attitudes, and practices as somehow "natural." The conflict arising from contemplating the proposition that our own cultures may be a mishmash of inventions from within and impositions from outside may lead us to question our own identities and to reject the notion of the "naturalness" of our own culture. Not a comforting thought—but a necessary one, particularly in a globalized world of constant (and accelerated) cultural borrowing and exchange.

Consider that even our notions of something as mundane as boredom may well be a cultural invention (and worse—tied to consumerism as well). This is precisely the point that Stearns (2001, 22) argued when he calls boredom "another eighteenth-century innovation." He suggested that the emerging consumerism of the day in Europe led people to new perceptions of being bored. While they may have been bored before (one can't imagine eighteenth-century Europe being frightfully exciting by any account), the changing commercial environment provided both a cure for boredom (i.e., either acquiring items, or just shopping for them) and a new perspective on it. Stearns noted, for example, that novelists of the time began, increasingly, to mention the concept of boredom in their works. Whether this constitutes a "profound" change in "human perception wrought by consumerism," as Stearns (23) suggested, is perhaps debatable, but it is clear that this change involved some cultural innovation, at least in terms of perception, of a mundane emotional state.

CUMULATIVE INNOVATION AS CULTURE

Bendix (1989) argued that, in tourism particularly, the notion of inventing tradition is not an exception but rather the rule. The importance of this observation, however, spills over outside of its context, as many of our cultural practices are also invented—whether by marketers or others. Watson (2008, 133), for example, describes how McDonald's was involved in promoting the idea of children's birthday parties in Hong Kong, where they were previously unknown:

> Until recently most people in Hong Kong did not even know, let alone celebrate, their birthdates in the Western calendrical sense; dates of birth according to the lunar calendar were recorded for divinatory purposes but were not noted in annual rites. By the late 1980s, however, birthday parties, complete with cakes and candles, were the rage in Hong Kong. Any child who was anyone had to have a party, and the most popular venue was a fast food restaurant with McDonald's ranked above all competitors. . . . McDonald's restaurants are packed every Saturday and Sunday with birthday parties, cycled through at the rate of one every hour. . . . For a small fee, celebrants receive printed invitation cards, photographs, a gift box containing toys and a discount coupon for future trips to McDonald's.

In what we can only take as a related strategy, Watson (2008, 133) also described how McDonald's uses local cultural cues to attract its audiences:

Television commercials portray Ronald McDonald leading birthday celebrants on exciting safaris and expeditions. The clown's Cantonese name, Mak Dong Lou Suk-Suk ("Uncle McDonald"), plays on the intimacy of kinship and has helped transform him into one of Hong Kong's most familiar cartoon figures.

THE INVENTION OF LOVE: THE COMMERCIALIZATION OF ROMANCE

Lest we be encouraged to think that only developing countries are subject to corporate and business influences on their cultures whether from outside or from within, we should also examine the role of corporate, business, and trading entities in US and European culture. David J. Cheal (1988, 150) argued, that in modern "mass societies" the relationships between and among members of society "must be deliberately constructed through invented traditions." Among these traditions he noted that "anniversaries, birthdays, Christmas, Easter, Father's Day, Mother's Day, and Valentine's Day are the principal occasions for the enactment of intimate traditions within small social worlds."

For example, the beloved Western traditions of the marriage proposal and its counterpart the diamond engagement ring may have more to do with the vagaries of business than the imperatives of romance. To be specific, they may have to do more with a glut on the diamond market in the early twentieth century than with eternal romance and everlasting love. Strangelove (2005) has recounted the story of how diamonds came to be entrenched in the modern cultural milieu. Partly traditional, the phenomenon is also partly advertising and business strategy. Strangelove placed this particular facet of modern courtship rituals with the 1947 US advertising campaign by the N.W. Ayers advertising agency that established the phrase "A diamond is forever" in the modern lexicon on behalf of its client De Beers in the context of a weak diamond market. The agency wrote that it wanted to strengthen the tradition so much as to make it a "psychological necessity." The advertising of the diamond tradition has also been taken worldwide. Kingston (2005, 53) argued that the De Beers diamond monopoly was "responsible for transforming a common, overmined gem into a symbol of eternal love." She added that

> the diamond engagement ring was sold as "a psychological necessity" without which a marriage proposal shouldn't be taken seriously. The message extended to Japan, where centuries of arranged marriages precluded the need for romantic symbols. In 1967, De Beers began using Western imagery to sell the diamond as visible sign of progressive, luxurious, Western values: by the 1990s, more than 70 percent of Japanese brides wore diamonds. (55)

Even the notion of spending two months' salary on the diamond engagement ring is a direct result of De Beers advertising campaigns in which it was suggested that the bride was "worth" two months' salary. Their advertising campaigns also promoted the surprise proposal because their research showed that when women were involved in selection of the rings they were more cautious purchasers than men. Kingston (2005) argued more broadly that media images of the wedding, the wedding proposal, and the engagement ring have all tended to support the notion that the bigger and more expensive the diamond, the stronger the proposer's love for the partner.

According to Strangelove (2005, 25), "sixty years later, global consumer attitudes to diamond rings remain highly engineered by the market's propaganda system." Indeed the United Kingdom's *Independent* newspaper quoted Nicky Oppenheimer, De Beers's chairman, as saying "diamonds are intrinsically worthless, except for the deep psychological need they fill" (Smith 1999).

To peer a little deeper into the realms of love and romance (whether with or without diamond rings), it is relevant to investigate the implicitness of these concepts in modern Western culture. As with most cultural phenomenon, we are never prone to questioning our implicit acceptance of the ideas of love and romance. Many of Hollywood's movies, for example, are based on the notion of romantic love. Bordwell, Staiger, and Thompson (1985) found that 95 percent of films made before 1960 had romance as their primary or secondary themes. This romantic love is often portrayed as being some sort of tangible force and is also often validated across cultural barriers as the natural yearning of the soul. Yet Bloch (1992, 8) described our Western conceptions of romantic love as "invented":

> If the expression "invention of Western romantic love" seems like a contradiction, it is because we so often assume love as we know it to be natural, to exist in some essential sense, that is, always to have existed. Nothing, however, could be further from the truth. . . . The terms that serve to define, or mediate, what we consider to this day to constitute romantic involvement were put into place definitively—at least for the time being—sometime between the beginning and the middle of the twelfth century, first in southern and then in northern France.

Not only are our particular conceptions of romantic love culturally rooted but they are also highly mediated. Wright-Wexman (1993, 8) argued that the "models of courtship and marriage put forward in Hollywood cinema make a significant contribution to the process of structuring the modern habitus regarding romantic love." Yet, from its beginnings (purportedly with the troubadors who sang popular songs about courtly love in the twelfth century) the association between romance and media has been strong. Increasingly today, forms of romantic love and expectations of romantic relationships are the product of both tradition and modern cultural (often mass-mediated) influences.

Marsden (2007) in a study of the romantic ideals of tribes native to the Chitral region of Pakistan, found that they were heavily influenced by their traditional form of love songs and poetry (called *ghazals*) as well as Sufi poetry. However, Bollywood songs (many popular Hindi movies contain some musical component) are also a major influence on their ideas. Marsden also noted that all of this exists in the context of an Islamized cultural environment which imposes several other constraints on beliefs and practices. Interestingly, Marsden's focus is also on elopement which frequently occurs when the prescriptions for marriage from family and community run counter to individual preferences and romantic attractions.

There is some controversy here as the contradictions of the Chitral tribes would suggest. Marsden (2007, 104) noted that despite evidence of ancient traditions of romantic love as seen here, "it is also widely held that romantic love is a novel aspiration among people experiencing the transformations of a newly globalized world." Certainly, the existence of stories of love in the Bible and other ancient texts also seems to provide us evidence of the universal and enduring character of romance. This leads some to argue that what we think of as romantic love has always existed. However, it would be something of a leap to equate Biblical romances with either our modern practices or our cultural expectations.

Of particular note here would be the notion of gay marriage so earnestly debated today in the United States, where the presumed logical outcome of love and romance is thought to be marriage (except, apparently, in some places, if you happen to be of the same gender as the person you are in love with). Historical and epic tales of love do suggest that something perceived as love or romance has existed over time, yet they do not suggest that they were identical to our particular modern Western conceptions of love. Part of the seeming paradox is that epics and legends tend to focus on the romances of nobility and divine figures while modern romance tends to suggest that such passion can fall to mere mortals. Further, Branden (2008, 1) added that our romantic figures of lore are also perhaps more properly seen as exceptions to the prevailing standards of romantic love rather than examples of them, writing that:

> The great love affairs of Lancelot and Guinevere, Heloise and Abelard, Romeo and Juliet live for us as symbols of physical passion and spiritual devotion. But such stories are tragedies—and tragedies of a very revealing kind. The lovers are impressive not because they typify their societies but because they rebel against them. . . . Their love challenges the moral and social codes of their

culture, and their stories are tragic because the lovers are defeated by those
codes. Implicit in the tragic nature of these love stories . . . is the fact that such
love was not regarded as a "normal" way of life or an accepted cultural ideal.

Thus, the love mythologies realized in today's real-life aspirations may not in
fact represent the general tenor of romantic practice even of the cultural icons
of love to which we subscribe. Romantic love as a cultural invention has also
been a cultural reinvention, and as we have argued, a commodity for sale.
The insistence of so many Western movies on the superiority of individual
choice in romantic and marriage unions (also a familiar theme wherever
persons of other cultures are mentioned), the assumed relationships between
love and marriage, and even the assumed heterosexuality of such phenomena
are heavily culture-bound. Some go as far as to equate the modern Western
ideal of romantic love with the demands of modern capitalism. This perspective considers the move to individual choice of mates as a prelude to the
formation of a buying partnership that supports the consumer economy. This
is in contrast to the collective economy of resources that would support a
socially determined union of reproductive partners that would best suit the
needs of the collective social group. Noting the correlations between the two
may well constitute an apt observation, but to say that the capital consumer
economy somehow determines the form of romance is too unromantic even
for a cynic like the present author.

CHRISTMAS, SHOPPING, AND CULTURE

Much has been written on the commercialization of Christmas and in the
popular culture today it is well understood that much of the secular practice
of Christmas is a largely commercial venture. Yet, even on the religious
tenets of Christmas there is considerable mixing of the secular and commercial in the popular imagination, as Kovacs (2008, 3) pointed out:

> To start, none of the following items are mentioned in the bible concerning the
> birth of Jesus: the word *Christmas*; a Christmas tree (or any tree, for that
> matter); hanging ornaments; December; the exact date, or even year Jesus was
> born; three wise men; a little drummer boy; winter; snow; yule; yule logs;
> wreaths; boughs of holly; mistletoe; colorful lights; eggnog; candy canes;
> parties; drinking; shopping; reindeer; St. Nick; Santa Claus; elves; toys; wrap-
> ping paper; caroling; cookies; plum pudding; chimneys; stockings; colors of
> red, green, and white; Bing Crosby; Jimmy Stewart; or children coveting a
> Red Ryder BB gun.

Recognition of the invented nature of much of modern Christmas tradition is not a particularly new phenomenon. The *Science News-letter* in 1954 called Christmas "a warm mixture of pre-Christian customs, religious rites and modern invention" ("Christmas Is Tradition" 1954, 378) adding that

> whether it was to pay homage to pagan gods or to drive away evil spirits, man practiced many of the customs that we now associate with this holiday more than 5,000 years before the birth of Christ. And to these he has added ritual and, much later, new innovations born of his contemporary world. From the dark woods of north Europe to the hot lands of India, early worshippers decorated evergreen trees, hung boughs of holly and mistletoe and burned logs to celebrate the first day of winter, which they called Yuletide. This was the time when the sun seemingly stood still, and the light of day was shortest.

To return to the question of commercialization of Christmas, Cheal (1988, 155) noted that this phenomenon has created two major problems, which he described in the following terms:

> Firstly, there is the fact that religious messages have been used to sell consumer goods, with the result that their contents have been trivialized. . . . The other objection that devout Christians often have to secular Christmas is that the expansion of gift giving and related interpersonal rituals, has resulted in an enormous collective expenditure that serves no religious purpose.

A traditional quasi-religious notion of the profanity of commerce lingers in this evaluation as profiteering from a religious occasion may be seen as inherently irreligious. Yet Schmidt (1997, 20) noted that since medieval times "the confluence of people for church festivals provided an ideal occasion for haggling and trade, and often wares were peddled in the churchyard or even at the church door." With this notion in mind, Schmidt traced the development of Easter observances in their modern form to the United States between 1860 and 1890. Literature and periodicals of the time chronicle the development of the use of flowers and decorations—widely greeted as symbols of resurrection and life—as part of the inventions of the tradition yet having no basis in religious or historical practice till that point. Schmidt described the initial commercialization of Easter in this manner:

> Beginning in the late 1870s, the number of goods for Easter—cards, toys, plants, flowers, confectionery, and other novelties—mushroomed at an astonishing rate. The commercial production of endless varieties of Easter eggs was but one example of this proliferation. "There are," the *New York Herald* marveled in 1881, "paper eggs, wooden eggs, satin and silk eggs, plush eggs, tin eggs, silver eggs, gilt eggs, gold eggs, glass and china eggs and sugar eggs." Priced from ten cents to more than a hundred dollars and ranging in size from the Lilliputian to the Brobdingnagian, Easter eggs had rolled out of the field of folk custom into the American market place. (219)

A greater complication arises if we look further back into the history of Easter which derives its place in the church as much from the Gospel accounts of the life of Jesus Christ as from the decree of the Council of Nicea under Constantine setting its time of observance. Indeed the term "Easter" is widely believed to have been borrowed from Anglo-Saxon or Babylonian pagan beliefs as are the iconic rabbits (bunnies, if you prefer) and eggs that may have represented fertility in a spring rite. Indeed, Easter as it is observed in modern Western society may well be a true reflection of the interplay of indigenous beliefs with Imperial influences as transmitted by dominant religious belief systems. In other words, Easter demonstrates the fluidity and mixability, if you will, of culture through the ages. Kovacs (2008, 26–27) noted that the term Easter appears only once in a single version of the modern Bible and was probably a mistranslation when it did appear. He is among those who connect the secular trappings of Easter with the following of the pagan goddess Ishtar (or Easter):

> It was not until hundreds of years after the crucifixion and resurrection of Jesus that the fertility customs associated with the pagan goddess Easter firmly mixed with Christianity. As Christianity spread, many new converts to the teachings of Jesus did not abandon their heathen customs. Some new Christians continued their egg decorating and their homage to the pagan "Easter Bunny."

The observations of Wolf (1982, 387) are relevant here, as he noted the extent to which groups use inherited cultural materials "to impart new evaluations or valences to them, to borrow forms more expressive of their interests, or to create wholly new forms to answer to changed circumstances." He suggests, further, that "'a culture' is thus better seen as a series of processes that construct, reconstruct, and dismantle cultural materials, in response to identifiable determinants."

CONTESTING THE EROSION ANALOGY

A bus in Kuwait (driven by an Indian expatriate) carries a destination sign at the front in English and Arabic that is not the name of a Kuwaiti town or district. Rather, it is the name of an international hotel chain. The bus is not a hotel bus but rather a Kuwait Public Transport Company bus. The hotel has become a landmark in the city and the name of the international hotel replaces the names of the local town. An international corporate venture symbolically replaces a traditional town name in a cultural appropriation of place and space. There is also a Canada Dry Street in Kuwait.

US tourists returning from vacations in Jamaica often mistakenly use the name of their hotel for the name of the town or village they stayed at. Many are convinced that they stayed at a town called Hedonism (the name of a hotel in Ocho Rios), for example. In the tourist experience, the brand name replaces the traditional name of the space.

In Trinidad, a squatter settlement in the central part of the island was once known as Datsunville. Japanese Datsun motor vehicles were shipped "completely knocked down" to plants on the island for assembly. The shipping boxes were sturdy enough to be salvaged as building materials for the squatters' shacks and all bore the Datsun brand on their surfaces (Boodan 2004). These and many similar examples suggest encroachment of the materials, symbols, practices, and ideas of global corporate enterprise onto cultural and traditional spaces, forms of what is popularly conceived of as cultural erosion.

The importance of the erosion metaphor has not been lost on scholars of media and culture. Varan (1998), for example, applied concepts from geology to explain the processes of cultural erosion with specific reference to the impact of television across cultures. He identified and explored "cultural abrasion," which he contended results from friction between the contrasting values of the audience and the foreign media; "cultural deflation," in which the most vulnerable audience members are affected; "cultural deposition" of foreign values and ideas; and "cultural saltation," where audiences respond to the perceived threat of foreign media influences. His frame of reference was the experiences of "cultures under threat" (58).

Another common theme in the erosion literature is the biodiversity metaphor for culture. In this view, the diversity of human cultures is likened to the diversity of species and imbued with the same importance and urgent concern for its loss. Lieber and Weisberg (2002, 281) characterized the biodiversity approach this way:

> Part of the richness of human culture is its variety, its trueness to its own cultural roots, but global popular culture dominated by American products and ideas destroys this diversity of cultural production. So there is fear and backlash against what is viewed as a leveling force, a sweeping homogeneity or Disneyfication of culture.

Rothkop (1997), however, argued that the erosion of cultural identity is highly unlikely in today's world, though he suggests that the trends observed as globalization today are the acceleration of a historical process in which different groups have become aware of each other and developed alliances leading to similarities. He also noted that culture is far from static, growing through reverence for particular privileged traditions and practices.

The notion that globalization automatically leads to erosion of culture, therefore, requires some interrogation. At the heart of this notion is the question of identity. Manuel Castells (1997), for example, argued that globalization and identity are conflicting trends. This sentiment is echoed by countless others who see the forces of globalization as essentially stripping away culture from those subject to its influences in favor of a homogenous and homogenizing set of values promoted by global corporate entities.

This view, while popular, belies a concept of culture as somehow pure of influences, traditional, and also incompatible with modern thought, expression, and artifacts. This view lacks the flexibility to account for the infinite variations of cultural makeup found among humanity today and in the past. We have mentioned before the notion of interculturality, in which all cultures can be seen to be dynamic and transient manifestations of all other cultures they have ever encountered. Any such conceptualization of culture will lead to the conclusion that the identity and erosion paradigms are the result of an overly insular and limited notion of culture.

In a strong denunciation of the old order of cultural analysis, Nobel laureate Mario Vargas Llosa (2000, para. 7) has argued that

> the arguments in favor of "cultural identity" and against globalization betray a stagnant attitude towards culture that is not borne out by historical fact. Do we know of any cultures that have remained unchanged through time? To find any of them one has to travel to the small primitive, magico-religious communities made up of people living in caves worshiping the gods of thunder or wild animals and who, due to their primitive condition, become progressively more vulnerable to exploitation and extermination. All others, particularly those with the right to call themselves modern or alive, have evolved into a barely recognizable image of what they were only two or three generations back. This is precisely the case of France, Spain or England where changes in the last half century have been so profound as to make it almost impossible that Proust, García Lorca or Virginia Woolf could have recognized the societies into which they were born and whose conditions they helped to renew.

Along with these rapid changes comes a web of cross-influences that include both internal and external forces on identity which necessarily include global corporate interests and globally mediated messages. As we noted in the lessons of the steel pan, culture (however defined) in our modern world owes a tremendous debt to the contributions of global and local corporate enterprises. A simple example of the vacuum cleaner is instructive in this regard. We encountered previously, the fact that when a British person cleans house, they are very likely to do some "Hoovering." This represents a contribution to the culture of both a word and word concept that comes directly from the branding of a commercial product. In this case there is a language contribution but this corporate innovation also changed the material practices of the people in the culture.

Whereas there is a vast literature of cultural loss which views the role of corporate and globalized cultural change as a one-sided process we might argue that it is more of a process of exchange, including additions and innovations to cultures. The processes of trade and commerce (widely decried as harbingers of cultural doom) have always played a major role in shaping what we now think of as culture. In the book *In Praise of Commercial Culture*, Tyler Cowen (2000) is supportive of the role of commerce in promoting culture—however, Cowen's work generally addresses the traditional and limited conception of culture as the product of artistic endeavor and various systems of artistic patronage. The largely unconscious everyday production of culture by all members of a society in their individual and group practice is a much more substantial area of concern. Curtin (1984, 1) argued in favor of seeing commerce as a facilitator of culture and also as a mechanism to allow the broadening of cultural horizons:

> Trade and exchange across cultural lines have played a crucial role in human history, being perhaps the most important external stimuli to change, leaving aside the unmeasurable [*sic*] and less-benign influence of military conquest. . . . No human group could invent by itself more than a small part of its cultural and technical heritage.

An example of the importance of such trading relationships and their connection with culture and interculturality is found in Southeast Asia where Federspiel (2001, 4) argued that

> Islam became acceptable to the Malay-Indonesian peoples only when it appeared in a form that was familiar to them. This seems to have happened when traders and their accompanying religious teachers from Gujerat and other cities in the Indian coastline became prominent in the trading activities that centered in Southeast Asia.

The Nabateans of Petra in what is today Jordan have been mentioned in previous chapters. Their power and influence rose out of their prowess as traders, and Graff (2003, 434) noted that that the city of Petra was the "entrepreneurial clearing house for the frankincense and myrrh of South Arabia." Their activities as traders were documented by various historical sources including Roman writers of the time. They have been called "one of the most important commercial bodies in the Middle East during the last few centuries BCE through the fourth century CE" (Freedman, Myers, and Beck 2000, 937) and their commercial successes are widely linked to their widespread borrowing of cultural, linguistic, and even architectural ideas reflected in the eclectic nature of the facades in the city of Petra. The Nabateans are an important example because not only do they demonstrate the relationship between commerce and culture, but they also were quite technically advanced for their time, suggesting that the effects of their trading activities went beyond material gain and linguistic borrowing, perhaps also into technical and scientific borrowing and exchange.

Curtin (1984) was particularly interested in the so-called trade diasporas—groups of merchants and traders who lived in foreign places or facilitated foreign trade, often becoming settlers themselves and inter-marrying with local populations. Yet, the existence of such diasporas would be possible only after many years of contacts between groups; which leads to the question of how such trading contracts might be initiated. One method involved what Curtin called "silent trade," described in the following terms:

> Traders from a distance are described as bringing their goods to an accustomed place of exchange in the countryside, away from towns or villages. They deposited the goods and went away. Local traders then appeared, deposited a quantity of their own goods and went away in their turn. When the first traders returned, they judged the value of the goods they found. If they thought an exchange was equitable, they took the new goods and left their own. (12)

From such beginnings, Curtin argued that, in the long run, "Western commercial culture became the common culture of commerce throughout the world in an era of multinational corporations" (3–4). While we may take issue with the characterization of commercial culture as uniquely Western (see the Nabateans above), it is not difficult to see how important trade and commerce are to the progress of culture—and I use the term "progress" quite deliberately as I wish to emphasize the progressive and cumulative nature of the phenomena we commonly refer to as culture.

A warning, however, should be heeded. It is that the interplay of cultural influences from trade or other experiences of material goods is not always as smooth or productive as in the example outlined above. It would be a material omission to ignore one glaring example of the effects of material goods from one culture—the cargo cult. The most common example of this phenomenon comes from Papua New Guinea where, since the late eighteenth century, natives fetishized foreign goods to such an extent that they developed religious associations with these items, sometimes building airstrips and mock aircraft to attract the goods from afar. Godsen (2004, 95) wrote that

> they [cargo cults] are easy to misinterpret as the desire for Western consumer goods, a form of naïve native greed. Instead, they are a much more profound search for the cosmological sources of those goods, an attempt to tackle the riddle of why Europeans had so many material things in comparison to Papua

New Guineans. The answer people gave was that Europeans had discovered access to spiritual sources of material wealth, or had wrested control of these sources from Papua New Guineans at some time in the past. . . . Cargo cults were a means of reconnecting people to their ancestors and the productive powers their ancestors helped control.

Despite some of the concerns that cargo cults may represent cultural distortion in the manner that Star Trek's "prime directive" sought to avoid, it is clear that the material goods of one culture can become a major force not only in the material practices of other cultures, but also in the worldview and even spiritual ideas of other cultures. Unintended consequences notwithstanding, it is from the perspective of trade and commerce as forces of cultural exchange that I wish to contest the erosion analogy and the notion of cultures being made extinct. When a species dies in nature, we may correctly call that extinction. When a language "dies" in culture it is often because it has been exchanged for another. When a particular way of being passes it is not exchanged for a void, but rather for an alternative, usually better way of being. So let us look again at some of the contentions about cultural erosion.

Thomas L. Friedman (2007, 404–405), in his important volume *The World Is Flat: A Brief History of the Twenty-First Century*, recounted his conversation with an Egyptian friend about perceived erosion of a particular Ramadan observance in Egypt:

> She had done a story . . . about the colorful lanterns called *fawanis*, each with a burning candle inside, that Egyptian schoolchildren traditionally carried around during Ramadan, a tradition dating back centuries to the Fatimid period in Egypt. Kids swing the lanterns and sing songs, and people give them candy or gifts, as in America on Halloween. For centuries, small, low-wage workshops in Cairo's older neighborhoods have manufactured these lanterns—until the last few years.
>
> That was when plastic Chinese-made Ramadan lanterns, each with a battery-powered light instead of a candle, began flooding the market, crippling the traditional Egyptian workshops. [She said], "They are invading our tradition—in an innovative way—and we are doing nothing about it. . . . These lanterns come out of our tradition, our soul, but [the Chinese versions] are more creative and advanced than the Egyptian ones." [She] said that when she asked Egyptians, "Do you know where these are made?" they would all answer no. Then they would turn the lanterns over and see that they came from China.

The same observance can also be found in the countries of the Arabian Gulf and is known in some places as *gergian*. In parts of the Gulf it is not so much the influx of foreign-made lanterns (no local ones are manufactured anymore anyway) that causes consternation but rather the dual-pronged concerns of children not following the traditions at all, or confusing the tradition with the Western Halloween tradition that they are much more likely to see portrayed on their television screens.

It is also important that Friedman uses Egypt as an example here since the very traditions that the Egyptian friend mourns are in fact relatively recent importations into Egyptian culture. Consider that records of Egyptian civilization and culture date back to before the third millennium BC (and some sources suggest that a civilization existed there as far back as the tenth millennium BC), the Arab Muslim presence starting in AD 639 is a relatively recent cultural addition. The integration of Islamic and Arab identities among Egyptians is a fascinating manifestation of the progression of culture.

While there are many ruins and physical artifacts, it is difficult to find any vestige of the cultural and religious practices of pre-Islamic Egypt beyond the elaborate spectacles staged for tourists. Some accounts suggest that there remains a festival held around Luxor involving a parade that harkened back to pre-Islamic times (possibly related to the Festival of *Opet Luxor*)—but despite the public nature of the event, locals are hesitant to discuss it— perhaps intimidated by the currents of Islamic fundamentalism still felt in Egyptian society.

So while Friedman's friend mourns the passing of her culture, she fails to acknowledge that her culture as she perceives it is only one stage in the progression of a cultural stream spanning millennia. Her notions of tradition and of culture are thus shortsighted, but no more so than other prevailing notions of tradition and culture.

OF VEILED TRUTHS AND MISREPRESENTED TRADITIONS

To stay with the Egyptians and the Middle East, one of the most visible icons of Middle Eastern culture, religions, and lifestyle is the veil. It may in fact be the most contentious piece of fabric in history (outside of certain national flags or tribal clothing). Veiling fits into something called *hijab,* which is far more extensive that the question of whether or not a woman wears a veil or headscarf. The concept and practice of the *hijab* extends into codes of behavior and rule of interaction for both sexes—but practice and culture generally focus on restrictions on women.

It is not uncommon in some areas of the Middle East to see young husbands wearing jeans and T-shirts with the names of Italian soccer stars accompany their wives who, draped in square yards of featureless black fabric, experience the outside world through a small slit in their *niqab* (the face covering associated with veiling). It is particularly because of this disparity that Mernissi (1992, 81) argued that this practice of *hijab* may be more of a throwback to ancient Arabian and Middle Eastern customs than adherence to religious precepts, asking: "Is it possible that the *hijab,* the attempt to veil women, that is claimed today to be basic to Muslim identity, is nothing but the expression of the persistence of the pre-Islamic mentality . . . that Islam was supposed to annihilate?" Hoodfar (2005, 409) traced these ancient practices even further in time and further afield geographically, writing that

> the practice of veiling and seclusion of women is pre-Islamic and originates in non-Arab Middle Eastern and Mediterranean societies. The first reference to veiling is an Assyrian legal text that dates from the thirteenth century BC, which restricted the practice to respectable women and forbade prostitutes from veiling. Historically, veiling, especially when accompanied by seclusion, was a sign of status and was practiced by the elite in the ancient Greco-Roman, pre-Islamic Iranian, and Byzantine empires.

Ahmed (1993, 5) contended that this practice of veiling arose not out of injunctions or religious tenets of Islam but rather from the practices of peoples and cultures encountered in Islamic expansion:

> The adoption of the veil by Muslim women occurred by a similar process of seamless assimilation of the mores of the conquered peoples. The veil was apparently in use in Sasanian society, and segregation of the sexes and use of the veil were heavily in evidence in the Christian Middle East and Mediterranean regions at the time of the rise of Islam. During Muhammad's lifetime and only toward the end at that, his wives were the only Muslim women required to veil. . . . After his death and following the Muslim conquest of the adjoining territories, where upper-class women veiled, the veil became a common-place item of clothing among Muslim upper-class women, by a process of assimilation that no one has yet ascertained in much detail.

Hoodfar (2005, 409) has been more direct in her assessment of the adoption process and makes the point that the practice of veiling was not a religious tenet set down by Islamic doctrine, writing that

> Muslims adopted the veil and seclusion from conquered peoples, and today it is widely recognized, by Muslims and non-Muslims as an Islamic phenomenon that is presumably sanctioned by the Qur'an. Contrary to this belief, veiling is nowhere specifically recommended or even discussed in the Qur'an.

Evaluation of the particular theological arguments and interpretations of scriptural references are beyond the scope of this present work. However, it is important to note that Hoodfar's statement, however bold, does not end the debate since there are Qur'anic verses that are interpreted (however loosely) as making such recommendations. In the context of the present argument, one might argue that the long-prevailing prescriptive norms for veiling have involved some level of retroconstruction. The extant and still referenced religious statements have been reinterpreted in line with current practice and then re-historized in keeping with such practices. Even the translations and interpretations of Qur'anic verses reflect this process. Ahmed (1993, 55–56) wrote on this point that

> veiling was apparently not introduced into Arabia by Muhammad but already existed among some classes, particularly in the towns, though it was probably more prevalent in the countries that the Arabs had contact with, such as Syria and Palestine. In those areas, as in Arabia, it was connected with social status, as was its use among Greeks, Romans, Jews, and Assyrians, all of whom practiced veiling to some degree. It is nowhere explicitly prescribed in the Quran; the only verses dealing with women's clothing, aside from those already quoted, instruct women to guard their private parts and throw a scarf over their bosoms. (Sura 24:31–32)

Ahmed (1993, 56) went on to explain that a set of rules pertaining to only a specific group of people may have been extended through reinterpretation and subsequently retroconstructed into cultural norms for all, saying that

> throughout Muhammad's lifetime veiling, like seclusion, was observed only by his wives. . . . The Muslim conquests of areas in which veiling was commonplace among the upper classes, the influx of wealth, the resultant raised status of Arabs, and Muhammad's wives being taken as models probably combined to bring about their general adoption.

The verses of the Qur'an are often difficult to interpret, even for native speakers of the Arabic language. It is therefore common practice in Islamic communities to depend on what is known as *tafsir* (exegesis or commentary) of the Qur'an for explanation of the meanings of particular verses. Hoodfar (2005, 409) implicated these processes of Quranic interpretation in the development of norms that have led to the practices of veiling and gender restrictions in Muslim societies:

> At the heart of the Qur'anic position on the question of the veil is the interpretation of two verses (Surah al-Nur, verses 30–31) that recommend women to cover their bosoms and jewelry; this has come to mean that women should cover themselves. Another verse recommends to the views of the Prophet to wrap their cloaks tightly around their bodies , so as to be recognized and not be bothered or molested in public (Surah al-Azhab, verse 59). Modern commentators have rationalized that since the behavior of the wives of the Prophet is to be emulated, then all women should adopt this form of dress. In any case, it was not until the reign of the Safavids (1501–1722) in Iran and the Ottoman Empire (1357–1924), which extended to most of the area that today is known as the Middle East and North Africa, that the veil emerged as a widespread symbol of status among the Muslim ruling class and urban elite.

Additionally, Ahmed (1993) noted the power of the chroniclers to refashion the tradition of the hijab as a natural component of traditional Islamic society, noting that we have no reactions of the wives of Muhammad whereas their views on many other matters were well known and reported.

Mernissi (1992, 85) argued that the unequal imposition of the practice of hijab upon women is ironic as the imposition of the concept in Islamic theology came as a barrier between two men—namely the Prophet Muhammad and a *sahaba* (companion of the prophet) named Anas Ibn Malik. It seems that these centuries of female oppression and restrictive cultural practices have their basis in the bad etiquette of a wedding guest. It was just following the marriage of the Prophet to one of his (many) wives when the wedding guests (Anas Ibn Malik was in charge of the guests) lingered too long after the feast. The Prophet eventually drew a curtain separating himself and his bride from Anas and the remaining guests and at that time the religious edict commonly known as the verse of the veil was revealed to the Prophet. Mernissi also quite competently attacks several oft-repeated openly misogynistic *hadith* or sayings of the Prophet, demonstrating that these popularly believed quotations are often tinged with political motivations on the part of the reporters of the sayings.

Armstrong (1999, 184), herself a former nun, compared the Muslim attitudes to women with Christian attitudes and concludes that while both are contrived by men, Islamic attitudes were also influenced by the cultures of the conquered, writing that

> unfortunately, as in Christianity, the religion was later hijacked by the men, who interpreted texts in a way that was negative for Muslim women. The Koran does not prescribe the veil for all women but only for Muhammad's wives, as a mark of their status. Once Islam had taken its place in the civilized world, however, Muslims adopted those customs of the Oikumene which relegated women to second class status. They adopted the customs of veiling women and secluding them in harems from Persia and Christian Byzantium, where women had long been marginalized in this way.

The roots of the veil in Muslim misogyny, cultural assimilation and retroconstructed religious authority demonstrate that the mass delusions perpetrated by modern media are not unique in their contributions to human culture. Here is a body of thought that vast seas of human beings (including the women who are oppressed by their tenets) hold to be true. These ideas have been spread over the centuries, fraudulently upheld by convenient religious interpretations and (partly through the agency of something called culture) are still entrenched in continuing generations of human societies. When Muslim women (including many who are not particularly devout), deluded by centuries of misinformation, religiously defend the veil as part of their essential identity, this also demonstrates the dangers of this thing called culture whether it parades as religion or not. Make no mistake, despite the growing body of work demonstrating that the idea of hijab is tremendously misconstrued and has been deliberately misrepresented over the centuries, the arguments find little purchase among many who are culturally identified (or self-identify) as Arab, Islamic, or Muslim.

Were the matter as simple and clear cut as this, we could leave it at this point. However, the implications of invented traditions and cultural manipulation run far deeper than whether or not Muslim women veil. The web of influences within which this debate falls spreads much farther since veiling arises a part of the modern movement toward what is characterized as conservative Islam, driven in large part by Saudi Arabian fundamentalist thinking known as Wahabism (or sometimes *Wahabi*ism) that we have encountered in previous chapters.

Wynbrandt (2004, 114) recounted the birth of the leader of the Wahabi movement to which much of the Islamic fundamentalism in today's world can be traced:

> In about 1703 an infant who would have as great an influence on the future of Arabia as any member of the House of Saud was born in Uyaina. Muhammad ibn Abd al-Wahab was the grandson of a respected theologian and the son of Abdullah ibn Muammar's *qadi*, or religious judge, who was dismissed by Kharfish in 1726. Abd al-Wahab could trace his lineage back 16 generations. A devoted and precocious student, he is said to have memorized the Quran by age 10. To complete his learning, in his teens he embarked on a grand tour, studying with leading clerics as he traveled to Mecca, Medina, and Basra. In this last city his reputation for wisdom and knowledge began to spread beyond the schools. Offended by the changes that had overtaken the Islamic community, he called for a return to the principles set down by Muhammad.

From the accounts of Wynbrandt (2004), Saikal (2003), and others, Abd al-Wahab was an extremist who proceeded to cut down trees in the town of Uyaina because he was outraged that the locals were venerating them. His extremism brought him into conflict with those around him. He was set upon by the locals in a town called Huraimila when he lived there. It turns out that he was morally offended by the conduct of some of the agricultural workers in the town. These same workers set upon him in his sleep intent on exacting some satisfaction. Luckily for Wahab, his neighbors scared off the mob and he was able to escape with his life. After he passed a sentence of stoning to death on a woman who admitted to adultery (we are not told what happened to the man), people in the region had had enough. DeLong-Bas (2007) asserted that Wahab's methods and practices were somewhat more studied and nuanced than many reports claim. However, we may draw other conclusions from evidence such as the fact that his own brother led a campaign of opposition to Wahab's teachings in the various communities and a price was eventually put on his head. Again he escaped death and was eventually banished to another region called Diriya in 1744. Niblock (2006, 26) argued that even if it is true that Wahab was somehow more studious, moderate, and flexible (as held by DeLong-Bas) than the above evidence and later developments bear out a conclusion that "the historical reality is that the more rigid interpretation of 'Abd Al-Wahab's thought has prevailed."

The implications of this otherwise bizarre and quaint parochial holy man's rantings would have been of little importance historically, except that he eventually got in with a powerful crowd. This Wahab eventually became friendly with members of the Saudi royal family of the time and rose to power and influence because of this association. It is to an eccentric closed-minded zealot such as this that we owe the current crop of Islamists, terrorists, and other fanatical Muslim groups of today. Their power and influence are direct results of the power of religion to warp culture and society and the implications of cultural innovations as purposive devices of social policy in whatever form.

DeLong-Bas (2007) made the argument that the area where Wahabism originally developed, the Najd, was not a place frequented by travelers and thus maintained its independence from foreign influences. From this she concludes and states categorically that Wahabism cannot be seen as a response to colonialism. However, that the birthplace of the movement was isolated cannot be taken as an indication that the spread of the movement was similarly isolated. Nor can the broader context of colonial influence in the region be somehow separated from internal currents of religious revival. While the movement may have started as the work of a single zealot, its development was not without the involvement of many others in many places and its spread was not in a vacuum from the surrounding political realities.

Thus despite the assertion of DeLong-Bas to the contrary, I argue that the spread of Wahabism can indeed be seen as an example of cultural reinvention or retroconstruction that took place under the pressure of colonial influences. In support of this view, writing in 1912, Toy (1912, 513) argued that

> in recent times contact with European thought has led many devout Moslems to what is really a reconstruction of Islam. The cruder elements of the Koran are discarded, its conception of Allah and its eschatology are purified, the character of Mohammed is idealized, and in general Islam is made into what is regarded as a perfect system of religious thought.

We have already encountered another such example of colonialism-fueled cultural (re)invention since Hoodfar (2005, 409) placed the practice of veiling squarely in this territory as well:

Significantly, it is only since the nineteenth century, after the veil was promoted by the colonials as a prominent symbol of Muslim societies, that Muslims have justified it in the name of Islam, and not by reference to cultural practices.

Hoodfar (2005, 411) also addressed the broader significance of this cultural change masquerading as religion in the context of colonial pressure, contending that

> it was in the late eighteenth and early nineteenth century that the West's overwhelming preoccupation with the veil in Muslim cultures emerged. Travel accounts and observations from commentators prior to this time show little interest in Muslim women or the veil. . . . Some pre-nineteenth-century accounts did report on oriental and Muslim women's lack of morality and shamelessness based on their revealing clothes and free mobility. . . . By the nineteenth century the focus of representation of the Muslim orient had changed from the male barbarian, constructed over centuries during the Crusades, to the "uncivilized" ignorant male who masculinity relies on the mistreatment of women, primarily as sex slaves. In this manner images of Muslim women were used as a major building block for the construction of the orient's new imagery, an imagery that has been intrinsically linked to the hegemony of Western imperialism.

Further, today, many Middle Eastern societies suffer from what Shayegan (1997) has described as a kind of "cultural schizophrenia" in which they readily consume Western media products, including music, television, films, and magazines, while simultaneously condemning the West for its lack of values and its various excesses. Is this too, the product of past colonialism? Or is it an indicator of modern globalization? Chances are that it is a combination of the two in a fluid mix of identities, ideas, and aspirations. In the face of a failed religious revival and its legacies of anti-Western rhetoric, we can find Arab youths gleefully embracing Western media messages and the attendant value and lifestyle implications. Several young people from diverse Middle Eastern countries such as Egypt, Lebanon, and Kuwait even indicated (unprompted) in interviews (for an unrelated research project of mine) that they found Western television and movies to be more "authentic" than Arab productions. To the consternation of the conservatives, Arab youth are not only watching foreign television shows on the satellite, they are also downloading them (along with even less traditionally acceptable content) on the Internet.

EAST AND WEST

Leaving the East behind, here is where the task becomes more difficult. Thus far we have examined the vagaries of cultural influences upon others. If such a thing as culture exists, consider now, how much more difficult it becomes to turn that critical eye upon our own cherished ideas and beliefs.

Mythologies do become shared, misplaced, and reconstructed. We just all tend to believe that our own mythologies are pure and thus the cultures upon which they are based, authentic. I referred in an earlier chapter to the error of citing the creation story of Adam and Eve as a Western creation myth. I must return to that notion now to examine the extent to which some of our cherished notions of Western thought and religious beliefs are not indeed Western at all.

Our now traditional associations of Christianity with Europe and (today) the United States, often create what seems to be a natural association between Christianity and the West (with no disrespect to my friends in the Eastern Orthodox Church). Godsen (2004, 111–112) argued, instead, that several Eastern influences played upon the development of Christian thought despite its claim to being Western, writing that

> all the early influences leading to the growth of Christianity were from the east. Zoroastrianism, which grew up in Iran after 1000 BC, was a major model for Christianity. Beliefs in life after death, good versus evil, a single beneficent god and the notion of a redeemer were all doctrinal elements derived from Zoroastrian beliefs. . . . The Sun Cult in Rome had many of the elements of monotheism, and the fact that the churches face east towards the rising sun, the idea of Sunday and the fact that 25 December was seen as the day on which the sun was born all derive from the influence of the sun cult on Christianity.

Much earlier, Robinson (1917) argued that both Isis-worship and Mithraism were also among the chief influences on the early Christian church. According to Robinson and other sources, in these earlier religious traditions we can find the concept of life after death, moral judgment, the idea of divine rulings or commandments, ritual initiation by submersion in water (baptism), ritual banquets featuring bread, water and wine, and resurrection. Scholars and critics alike have cited the Egyptian "Book of the dead," as the possible progenitor not just of the wording of the Judaic commandments and the derived Christian "Ten Commandments" but also of many of the basic ideas of death, judgment, and resurrection found in modern belief systems. McCown (1925, 363) argued that "the fact that the Hebrews borrowed from Egyptian literature can no longer be denied" adding that "the mass of evidence is cumulative in effect, and certain of the individual items are decisive." This is not, as many apologists claim, a modern revision of ancient truths, but rather a debate that has raged since the seventeenth century. Assmann (2005, 83) is among those who recognize a fairly long history of such analysis, arguing that

> the Egyptian idea of the judgment of the Dead removed final judgment regarding the success of a human life decisively away from worldly powers and interests and placed the norms of social existence on a transcendental basis. With this step, there began an evolution in the area of images of death and in that of mortuary rituals, one that quickly affected the entire culture and ultimately radiated out into the world beyond Egypt.

They trace the arguments for an Egyptian basis to particular Judeo/Christian ideas to the work of John Marsham who wrote the *Canon chronicus Aegyptiacus, Ebraicus, Graecus* around 1672. Among the ideas, Marsham traced the Ten Commandments to antecedents in ancient Egyptian writings and to the presence of the Hebrews in Egypt during ancient times. Assmann (2005, 86) also noted that "the concepts of a life to come and a reward or punishment in the next world are foreign to the Old Testament" a fact also observed since the seventeenth century. Thus they argue that the notions of resurrection and the afterlife owe more to Egypt than to Christian innovation, citing the notion of moral investment and its heavenly reward as a legacy of Egyptian culture.

Even a mundane (but curious) fact of modern life such as the prohibition of pork in Jewish (and Muslim) religious/cultural observance can be traced back to this Egyptian influence. Lobban (1994, 59) described the connection in the following terms:

> By the time of the Egyptian New Kingdom (16th century BC), there may already have been a formal taboo, at least for the nobility. . . . Pork was still widely eaten by poorer people. The historical reconstruction of the Jewish prophet Moses places him in the role of a high-ranking civil servant during the reign of Pharaoh Ramses II, thus exposing him to the upper-class food preferences and prohibitions. . . . Moses fled with his followers into the wilderness of the Sinai but saw no reason to abandon this already established taboo. As a marker of "civilized" social status and, later, of Jewish ethnicity, the strict observance of the taboo on swine flesh was given supernatural sanctions.

The same author also suggested that Muslims may have adopted the taboo in order to distinguish themselves from Christians, who had already adopted significant changes to the ancient Jewish dietary laws by the time of the advent of Islam in the seventh century. The suggestion is often made that the pork taboo was adopted by Muslims in part due to the close early relationship with the Jewish tribes at Yathrib (Medina). While this is reasonable, it does not explain why the Jewish prohibition on eating camels was not also adopted.

Even in relatively more modern times, such basic concepts as "heaven" and "hell" (that exist not only in religious discourse but also very much in the so-called popular culture) have undergone radical changes. Hilton (2007, 237) noted such changes in the Victorian era, writing that

> there was a famous incident in 1853 when Frederick Denison Maurice was dismissed from his professorship at King's College, London, for daring to suggest that there was no Hell, meaning no place where the damned were literally roasted and tormented and for eternity. Twenty, even ten years later he would have kept his job. By then it would have been widely accepted in Church of England circles that Hell was either a temporary reformatory . . . or else a state of nothingness.

Hilton (2007, 237) also traced a similar change in Victorian notions about heaven:

> Earlier it had been pictured in the same exaggerated way as Hell, as a place of jeweled pagodas and hallelujah choruses. But then, as the literal image of Hell receded so Heaven began to be domesticated, came to be seen in terms of a cozy fireside where saints would be surrounded by their long lost loved ones and by all *mod cons* and creature comforts.

There is no need to overemphasize these changes either, bearing in mind that the "earlier" images referred to here were not in fact the result of original church or gospel dictates but rather more likely the result of readings of Dante's *Divine Comedy* of the early fourteenth century and other literary or artistic works on the topics of heaven and hell such as Milton's *Paradise Lost* (1667). Our own popular image of a red devil with horns, hooves, and a pitchfork, for example, is a conflation of several different traditions and an image that has evolved quite out of sync with any guidance from mainstream religious texts or teachings. Many early European depictions of Satan were in fact blue.

That the vagaries of artistic fashion or politics can influence both religion and culture is sometimes hard to fathom, particularly for the religious-minded. Yet, the far-reaching consequences of historical, political, and commercial events have often created religious and cultural precedents with major and enduring consequences for later generations. Constantine's decision to call the 325 Council at Nicea, for example, had major implications for future generations—as did Constantine's victory at what is known as the battle of the Milvian Bridge in October of AD 312. The emperor's dreams before that battle played some part in his decision to allow Christianity in the empire in AD 313 and his own eventual conversion. Yet, both the battle and the council were (arguably) actions of political expediency rather than of religious or cultural importance.

Similarly, elaborate systems of defense have been created by Islamic scholars to argue against the influence of both Christian and Jewish (religious and cultural) traditions on the thinking and life of Muhammad and on the practices now considered so uniquely Islamic. Toy (1912), for example, wrote that

> local places of worship (mosques) were established, one day in the week was set apart for public worship, and the order of service in the mosque, consisting of prayer, reading from the sacred scriptures, and an address, was copied from that of the synagogues and the churches.

There is also clear evidence from the most authoritative biographical sources that Muhammad was in contact with and even endorsed by several Christian holy men early (one of them being the cousin of his wife Khadija) in his mission. The commercial importance of his caravan trading and the fact that it was a major factor in his exposure to ideas from Christianity and Judaism are jealously suppressed lest they lead to an acceptance of these influences. Tritton (1942, 837) argued that "it is only natural that Islam should show some influence of the older religions among which it grew up" and suggests that "new ideas came in with converts or through talk with men of other faiths." Judith Romney-Wegner (1982) argued as well that the Jewish presence at Yathrib (Medina) as well as an initial openness to Judaic traditions figured into a strong Talmudic influence on later Islamic jurisprudence. Schacht (1950, 10) earlier wrote that

> the far-reaching influence of Judaism and Christianity on Islamic cult and ritual, and that of Roman Byzantine and Persian Sassanian administration on Islamic political and fiscal institutions are matters of common knowledge. It is important for our purpose to realize that these foreign elements have been so thoroughly assimilated and Islamicized that, taken in their ordinary Islamic setting, they hardly seem to reveal a trace of their foreign origin.

But just like the West would rather forget that the traditions of the modern Christian west probably depended on the dreams of a megalomaniac emperor and the influences of sun-worshippers and ancient Pharaoh-worshipping Egyptians, the modern Islamic East would also like to forget their debt to pre-existing currents of religious and cultural thought. Von Grunebaum (2005) went a step farther, arguing that the overwhelming evidence of Christian and Judaic influences on Islamic religious thought are not in fact relevant to the question of originality since in religious thought generally, religious truth is conceived as preexisting, having only been re-discovered by prophets or others. This is certainly true of even modern Islamic thought that often styles Islam as the religion of Abraham and Jesus (Abbara 2008)—a claim that often, perhaps understandably, riles Jewish and Christian opponents.

In all of this mixing of religious and cultural traditions it is difficult to escape the pigeonholes of cultural discourse which make sharp distinctions between different groups and different modes of thought and history. That is, unless we step back from traditional lines of demarcation between such apparently diverse and divergent traditions. It is from a distance that, perhaps, we realize such seemingly mundane realities like the fact that Constantinople is situated in the country we call Turkey today—which is at once both Islamic and secular and whose cultural background is still a barrier to its entry to the European Union. When we consider this and other examples of how intertwined the histories of supposedly separate cultures are, we may begin to realize how fragile our notions of culture have been. However, it does not free us from the continuing interplay of culture, (personal and national) identity, and religion.

The relationships between religions and cultures are difficult to address without prejudice as most of us are conditioned into such prejudices. The separation of culture and religion is possible in theory but generally does not exist in practice. Consider, for example, Richard Kyle's characterization of early twentieth-century US Protestantism in his book *Evangelicalism: An Americanized Christianity* (2006, 55–56):

> Protestants believed that America (with Britain's help) was God's chosen vessel to Christianize and civilize the world. Evangelicals had their differences, but they saw themselves as part of a great crusade spreading the blessings of Christianity and civilization throughout the globe. Utterly convinced that America was a Christian civilization and of Anglo-Saxon cultural superiority, evangelicals believed victory—even global dominance—to be close at hand. To most evangelicals Christianization, Americanization, and civilization were one and the same. . . . Most evangelicals were oblivious as to how much their faith had become a religion of culture.

The cultural baggage of each religious tradition makes itself known in the historical unfolding of religious practice, which I would argue here, is little more than cultural practice imbibed with the sacrosanct trappings of some sort of divine worship. Discourses of religion and culture even up to modern times allow that a person may convert from one religion to another but not so easily from one culture to another. I would argue that this is a false distinction derived from a privileged notion of religion and a limited notion of culture. The mutual exclusivity of religious traditions, so heavily prized throughout recorded history is also something of an invention, the lines having been drawn by people who had an interest in developing their own hegemony over specific groups.

The mechanism for developing and preserving such hegemony has often included outright slander and alienation of the "other." What better form of xenophobic incitement than the notion that the "other" was not just socially different, but also spiritually evil and dangerous. For example, Hobson (2004, 107) described medieval Europe as a heterogenous grouping in need of a uniform identity, writing that:

> The only way to forge a single identity was to construct an external "other" against which a homogenous "self" could be constructed. . . . Islam was immediately condemned by the Christians as an idolatrous pagan religion (even though the two religions shared many vital similarities).

He goes on to suggest that the invention of this evil "other" required "considerable ingenuity" (108) given the commonalities in beliefs (e.g., iconoclasm and monotheism) and common religious ancestry in Judaic and Abrahamic roots. Yet, in the interest of political (if not religious) goals, this enemy was cast as an idolatrous and imminent threat.

In this and other instances throughout history, such "pagans" or "infidels" were to be avoided based on the threat of the danger or imminent attack, or even on the fear of social contamination (e.g., by intermarriage or interbreeding) and eternal damnation. From such contrived exclusivities, religious leaders have conspired to exact from their followers the allegiances needed to enact political ends whether that be the conquest of Jerusalem, the taking of Mecca, or the expansion of imperial vision in various corners of the globe. Case in point is our old friend Christopher Columbus whose letters to the King and Queen of Spain clearly indicate that his maritime mission was undertaken to help finance the re-conquest of Jerusalem by Christian forces (Zamora 1993; Hobson 2004).

Chapter Nine

Long Live Culture?

Jamaican icon Louise Bennett's (1966) poem "Colonization in Reverse" chronicled the waves of immigration to England by Jamaicans "Fe immigrate an populate De seat a de Empire" and suggests a bit of a turnabout or payback for the experience of imperialism. In *India under Colonial Rule, 1700–1885*, Douglas M. Peers (2006, 91) suggested that this process has continued over the years and included the influences of other major former colonies such as India, writing that

> it is estimated that restaurant—goers in Britain spend nearly £2 billion annual-ly in Indian restaurants, and that the amount of mango chutney sold in the United Kingdom tops £7 million. That it has come to this was interestingly foretold nearly two centuries ago when a contributor to the oriental herald, a magazine established in Britain for returning Anglo-Indians, wrote in September 1828, "from the excellence of the dishes that the Indian condiments are capable of producing, coupled with the cheapness with which a rice is now to be had in this country, we think it probably that at no distant period curry and rice will become one of the national dishes of England." Chip shops in Glasgow offering haggis pakoras, the cross-over success of bhangra music, and periodic bouts of imperial nostalgia as evidenced in the popularity of many merchant and ivory films attest to the grip that India continues to have on British culture.

Watson (2004, 157) suggested that even the spread of fast-food outlets and culture around the world has resulted in important social changes:

> Visits to McDonald's and KFC quickly became signal events for children who approach fast-food restaurants with a heady sense of empowerment. In this sense, therefore, American-style fast food has indeed had a global impact: it has changed the experience of childhood in many parts of the world.

The frequency and complexity of global, mediated, cultural exchange are this simple and also far more complex and are played out on (computer and television) screens daily:

> [The] British program, Pop Idol, became fabulously popular in the United States as American Idol and then was picked up all over the world. This format program was ideally suited to local cultures as every nation could choose contestants to perform local music in the local language. When the program was aired in Lebanon as Superstar, it included contestants from several Arab countries—making it a regional production. But when a Jordanian singer won the Beirut-based contest and the people celebrated her victory in the streets of Amman, the Islamic Action Front in Jordan accused the Jordanian government of promoting the singer and the contestant to "distract the masses" with non-sense. . . . Some local spokespeople commented that the popular program allowed the citizens to be distracted from the serious public issues in the country. When the program aired in India as Indian Idol, Abhijeet Sawant, the winner, was besieged by parents wanting him to accept marriage proposals on behalf of their daughters. An estimated 48 million Indians watched the final round. (Ogan 2007, 306)

These are not only mediated realities, but also lived ones. Sutton (1987), for example, spoke of the transnational sociocultural system among Caribbean migrants in New York who enjoy relatively continuous flows of information and ideas and commodities between their new home and their native countries. Such connections between the migrants and their regional homes are possible because of modern communication technologies. She suggests that they are transnational because unlike previous generations of immigrants, they maintain robust ties and strong identities associated with the homeland. Written in 1987, this analysis would not have included the impact of technologies such as Skype and others that allow immigrants virtual contact with their families back home.

Beyond interpersonal contacts, mass-media exchanges also contribute to this transnational identity. Caribbean music finds a ready market in many metropolitan centers of the United States and Canada in the form of CDs and music videos. More recently, Caribbean-based television stations have been popping up on metropolitan cable services. Additionally, several popular Caribbean comedy stage shows and television programs have been successfully marketed among diaspora communities in places such as New York.

Many Caribbean immigrants in the metropolitan centers and elsewhere regularly read online versions of newspapers from their home countries. The close proximity of the Caribbean to North America also means regular visits from family members. An interesting transnational consciousness is evident in such meetings. The immigrants are often surprised at the extent of their visitors' knowledge of mass-mediated information and events, even if these are just the current state of *American Idol* or the latest twist in *Desperate*

Housewives. The visitors are similarly surprised at their immigrant counter-parts' knowledge of events back in the home country including elections, crime, and even the juiciest scandals.

Similar experiences are reported among Turkish immigrants in European countries, particularly with the agency of satellite broadcasting that brings immediate coverage of home-country events to the diaspora communities (Robins and Aksoy 2006). There is an emerging body of scholarly work into these phenomena in which "new media technologies are making it possible to transcend the distances that have separated 'diasporic communities' around the world from their 'communities of origin'" and use the term "di-asporic media" to describe new media technologies that provide "new means to promote transnational bonding, and thereby sustain (ethnic, national or religious) identities and cultures at-a-distance" (86–87).

However, modern notions of identities can be surprisingly fluid as well. Quite apart from sustaining identities at a distance, multinational marketers and advertisers subscribe to a somewhat bizarre notion of global citizenship involving identity through consumption. Strizhakova, Coulter, and Prince (2008, 57) described how "the allure of the global brand becomes even more promising as developments in telecommunications and technologies bring the world together and break down traditional national borders as signals of cultural identification." They argue that participation in the global branding system facilitates involvement in a kind of global citizenship. As extreme as this may sound, the international marketers probably do have a point when they argue that the traditional notion of the nation-state has become less relevant in the context of selling to global audiences (Cayla and Arnould 2008). Piller (2001, 153), for example, argued that the concept of identity today is complicated by mediated construction of global consumer meanings, noting that

> contemporary social identities are hybrid and complex, and the media play a crucial role in their construction. A shift from political identities based on citizenship to economic ones based on participation in a global consumer market can be observed.

Conversely, Stevenson (1997, 44) echoed the same sentiment in terms of cultural citizenship in Western societies, relating such citizenship not primar-ily to participation in global brands (most of them Western anyway) but rather to consumption of the perceived exotic:

> People are increasingly becoming citizens through their ability to be able to purchase goods in a global market; hence citizenship becomes less about for-malized rights and duties and more about the consumption of exotic foods,

Hollywood cinema, Brit pop CDs and Australian wine. To be excluded from
these commercial goods is to be excluded from citizenship (that is full membership) in modern Western societies.

Complicating this perspective are more nuanced views like those of Peter
Jackson (1999) who argued that the much-maligned international marketing
of ideas and products is increasingly an agglomeration of globalized corporate efforts and local cultural influences in which companies such as McDonald's and Coca-Cola actively utilize local language and culture to contextualize their marketing in particular locations. He cited examples like the
shooting of a Coca-Cola ad in Spanish at Machu Picchu for the Peruvian
market. We could add McDonald's introduction of the McArabia wrap in
Middle-Eastern markets or several other examples to show that the global
forces of marketing and ideas are increasingly sophisticated. Cultural influences become less of a one-way street and more of an interconnected web—
particularly when local businesses and governments in search of foreign
investment are willing partners with foreign corporations to introduce, market, contextualize, and integrate the globally oriented material and commod-
ified cultural artifacts.

Hoffman (2002, 111) argued, on the other hand, that "globalization has
not profoundly challenged the enduring national nature of citizenship," adding that "economic life takes place on a global scale, but human identity
remains national." Yet we must note that even the question of national identity receives murky answers in a globalized environment as Ardizzoni (2005,
509) pointed out in describing the election (by popular vote) of Miss Italy in
1996:

> In September 1996, Italian public television broadcast the election of the first
> black Miss Italy in the country's history. Denny Mendez, the controversial
> beauty queen, was an 18-year-old of Dominican origins at the time of the
> election. Mendez was a naturalized Italian who had moved to Italy in the early
> 1990s when her mother married an Italian citizen.

Somewhat ironically, other Caribbean nations have had the converse of this
problem with their representation at international beauty pageants as both
Jamaica and Barbados have seen national outcries in the past when their
representatives to international pageants were (either perceived or actually)
of Caucasian descent (Edmondson 2003; López Springfield 1997).

Despite the obvious complications of such identity-challenging incidents,
arguments like Hoffman's above are joined by claims that native cultures are
being destroyed—Zahid (2007) claimed the figure stands at twenty-two thousand—and audiences brainwashed, as well as claims that audiences are savvy
and accept only what they want, maintaining their local cultures while engag-
ing with foreign influences. Somewhere in all of this are assumptions about

what constitutes culture and even claims that cultures are being eroded or homogenized into a globalized McSameness inflicted in part by the forces of global commerce and neo-colonialism.

Traditional notions of culture (whether perceived as being under dire threat or surprisingly resilient and persistent) are all suspiciously romantic. Watson (2004, 145) argued that the concept is one that has needed revision for some time, particularly since even people in the same social groups are found to vary tremendously in their ideas about the world; she wrote that the

> concept of culture has become one of the most controversial issues in modern social sciences. During most of the twentieth century, anthropologists defined culture as a shared set of beliefs, customs and ideas that held people together in recognizable, self-identified groups. Starting in the mid 1970s and culminating in the 1990s, however, scholars in many disciplines challenged the notion of cultural coherence as it became evident that members of close knit groups held radically different versions of their social worlds. Culture is no longer perceived as a preprogrammed mental library—a knowledge system inherited from ancestors. Contemporary anthropologists, sociologists, and media specialists treat culture (if they use the term at all) as a set of ideas, actions, and expectations that is constantly changing as people react to changing circumstances.

This constantly changing set of beliefs and attitudes, fuelled by ever increasing global information flows and interchange, renders specious our old and cherished notions of culture. That thing we once called culture may well be dead. Cameron and Gross-Stein (2000, S20) described the extent to which these global information flows may render traditional notions of national culture irrelevant:

> Globalization works to transcend and even, at times, to supersede national cultures. Its processes create a common cultural environment where everyone who is "connected" has access to the same messages, the same icons, and the same calligraphy, produced and disseminated through the tightly controlled transnational corporate networks of television and film. Many of these networks are currently headquartered in the United States and their products increasingly dominate global cultural markets. These products no more reflect the diversity of American culture than they do the diversity of others' cultures. For the first time, global cultural production is mass-produced.

SO WHAT?

If culture is dead, then the question is—so what? The value of culture has frequently been overemphasized to the detriment of humankind as a whole. Not only did the culturally enshrined notions of colonialism and *manifest destiny* destroy entire societies but they have created lasting chasms of development between groups and nations that work to no one's benefit.

Hanson (2007, 4) noted,

> It is important to recognize that culture works best to provide mechanical solidarity when it is closed: when its tenets are clear, unequivocal, and fixed, and when its adherents accept them as unquestionably true, support them ardently, and reject alternatives out of hand. Dissent, or even lukewarm acquiescence, weakens the consensus.

The transnational and transcultural scales of modern globalized and mediated culture, however, create problems with this formulation. The closed culture as described above has generally ceased to exist today with most people belonging to large communities with variously defined borders and subcultures. The dynamics of cultural maintenance have therefore been thrown into disarray on a scale hitherto unknown.

None of which is to necessarily claim that all cultures are equally open. Indeed, the modern Bedouin communities in Jahra, Kuwait are reputed even among Kuwaitis (perhaps unfairly) to be famously averse to the arrival of outsiders, though many of them do have satellite television and mobile phones. On the island of Dominica, up to a few years ago, locals claim (again, perhaps a little unfairly) that visitors to the native Carib reserve ran the risk of having their cars stoned. Again, lest one be lulled into the sense that these are only issues in developing countries, I would note that in 1988, while visiting New Jersey I watched what was said to be clandestine video of the inhabitants of the Ramapo Mountains who were reputedly also quite averse to visitors from outside (the video purported to show them chasing the videographer's car away from their land). Till this day, this community of about five thousand people (known as the Ramapo—or Ramapough—Mountain Indians or sometimes as the Ramapough Lenape Nation) exists in relative isolation with even their origins being a matter of some debate.

Outside of the exceptional cases of isolated communities, there is still a tendency in modern society to appeal to culture as an essentially positive force bordering on the sacrosanct. Indeed, Oloka-Onyango (2005) is among those who have argued for "cultural rights" (as a complement or analogue to "human rights"). The idea that something called culture is valuable is itself a cultural notion and has inherent dangers. For example, culture is at the root of much of the hatred and strife we encounter today. Old cultural ideas dating back thousands of years strangle expressions of human creativity and deny groups their otherwise well-established rights under the guise of religion and tradition. Modern twists of cultural ideas are responsible for conspicuous consumption and environmental degradation. Hanson (2007, 11) argued that "culture, originally well adapted to the small, homogenous communities that characterized the early conditions of human life, has become maladapted to the heterogeneous societies in which most human beings live today." Kearney (1995, 556) took this idea one step further, writing that "the conditions of transnationalism are causing anthropologists to reconsider the value of the culture concept."

Thus while it might be easy to blame corporations and their foot soldiers in advertising and marketing for the demise of culture, it might be a tad shortsighted to deny that culture itself is in need of revision. There are many reasons, but perhaps the starkest of all is the use of culture in the guise of tradition or religion as the motivation for some of history's most heinous acts. Grieg (2002, 225) argued, for example, that cultural differences, while enabling distinctions between groups and impeding mutual understanding, have also "provided the basis for some of the world's bloodiest conflicts." According to Rothkop (1997, 40),

> cultural differences are often sanctified by their links to the mystical roots of culture, be they spiritual or historical. Consequently, a threat to one's culture becomes a threat to one's God or one's ancestors and, therefore, to one's core identity. This inflammatory formula has been used to justify many of humanity's worst acts. . . . Religion-based conflicts occur between Christians and Muslims, Christians and Jews, Muslims and Jews, Hindus and Muslims, Sufis and Sunnis, Protestants and Catholics, and so forth. Cultural conflicts that spring from ethnic (and in some cases religious) differences include those between Chinese and Vietnamese, Chinese and Japanese, Chinese and Malays, Normans and Saxons, Slavs and Turks, Armenians and Azerbaijanis, Armenians and Turks, Turks and Greeks, Russians and Chechens, Serbs and Bosnians, Hutus and Tutsis, blacks and Afrikaners, blacks and whites, and Persians and Arabs.

We have previously discussed the inescapable interconnectedness of culture and religion both in terms of tradition and lived experiences. The need for revision that we identified with culture is equally relevant to its partner, religion. Evidence from ancient cultures suggests this very kind of relationship and the failure of one with the other. Cupitt (1997, 81), for example, argued that "a major religion is an object that resembles a whole civilization or cultural tradition, rather than a clear cut ideological system," adding that these very traditions are themselves permanently waning:

All our present major religious traditions are now coming to an end, just as the once very grand religions of ancient Mesopotamia, Egypt, and Greece came to an end in antiquity. As happened in the previous cases, we may expect that something of the great works of art will survive but virtually nothing of the doctrine. Most of Christian theology has already been lost, as we soon discover if we ask people to explain, for example, just how Christ's death has made atonement for our sins, or the difference between Calvinism and Arminianism, or the doctrine of the Trinity. These are—or were once—very grand and important matters, but people at large lost all knowledge of them generations ago, and it is not coming back.

Like many other concepts, culture is an academic creation. That is not to say that culture does not exist until analyzed, but rather, to contend that the analysis often creates that which it analyzes. Thus students of intercultural communication and adherents of Hofstede's cultural dimensions begin to look for power distances and male/female orientation when they visit or encounter a new culture. They fail to realize that, rather than being inherent parts of all cultures, these constructs themselves are culturally determined ways of interpreting others (Cayla and Arnould 2008). They may not in fact exist at all—despite our many measurements to prove the existence of the concepts we created ourselves.

The culture that we impose as a concept does not necessarily have anything to do with the lives of those living that culture. Consider the notion of aboriginal art. In many places around the world, tourists purchase artifacts from the cultures they visit. The attempt is usually to secure some item or image that bears the cultural stamp of the culture in which it originated. A "native" artist is then forced to paint or otherwise create a set of images or artifacts that conform to the expectations of the outsiders. If the native artist paints a Big Mac and a Coke, it then becomes not "cultural" enough to be saleable—even if the native artist just had a Big Mac and a Coke and just painted the picture of them right in his own village. Thus culture is what exists as the expectation of the observer and not as a lived experience.

Lieber and Weisberg (2002, 282) noted that this area of folk or indigenous culture is one of the domains where globalization is commonly cited as being particularly destructive but warn of several difficulties with this as a natural assumption. Pointing out that many of the critics are not themselves from these cultures, they argue that the assumptions of purity and authenticity are misplaced, arguing instead that "Folk art, rather than demonstrating purity, provides an excellent case study of the dynamics of assimilation and differentiation as it is usually a mixture of local production and aesthetics with outside influences." They cite two examples from Navajo culture. They point to the Navajo weavers' adoption of German aniline dyes in the nineteenth century creating what outsiders consider to be the typical look of (very prized) Navajo rugs. They also explain that the style of Navajo jewelry was adjusted to suit the preferences of tourists, traditional designs tending to be bulky to indicate power while tourist were more likely to choose more elegant lines. They argued that

> these are clear examples of cultural output influenced by foreign technology and tourist preferences. Among other things, we thus ought to view folk culture as more complex and more calculated than it is generally conceived. (283)

Widely flung examples of the speciousness of identity and authenticity abound. Larkin (2002, 739), for example, described *bandiri* music in Nigeria as not only a hybrid cultural form but also an active cultural reconstruction and appropriation of foreign forms:

> Once, while my Vespa was in a line waiting to be repaired, one of the assistants switched cassettes on an old tape player and started playing a *bandiri* tape. As he did so one of the customers started to hum along, recognizing the Indian film tune on which the song was based, but not knowing the words of this Hausa variation. *Bandiri* singers are *Hausa* musicians who take Indian film tunes and change the words to sing songs praising the prophet Mohammed.

Additionally, Larkin (2002, 750) noted that one of the common denominators facilitating this hybridization and borrowing is a common history of British colonialism that also accounts for the popularity of Indian films that present themes important to Indians and Nigerians that would not be found in Hollywood films:

> This was brought over to me in a discussion about the film *Maine Pyar Kiya* starring Salman Khan, a hit in Nigeria as elsewhere. My male friend identified hugely with the central tension of the films—Salman Khan's father forbidding his son permission to marry a poor girl and attempting to force him to marry the rich daughter of a business friend. The overt sentimentality was not seen in terms of fantasy but as something that emerges out of the historical experience of common people—an historical experience common to Nigeria and India: the power of elders over youth and the corruption of traditional relations by the pursuit of money.

Indian movies on Kuwait's state-owned local stations are not run to cater only to the many expatriate Indians who populate Kuwait in jobs ranging from bank managers to laborers. According to senior staff members at Kuwait TV—while the programming authorities are certain that Indian expatriates enjoy those movies, the Indian movies are run primarily to cater to the extremely strong following of such films among Arab Kuwaitis themselves.

Indian movies have also been extremely popular in Trinidad and Tobago which has a population of ethnic Indians descended from indentured laborers brought to the island by the British since the nineteenth century. These movies provide the basis for much of what passes for Indian culture among this diaspora many of whom are today at least four generations removed from the initial immigration. Manuel (1998, 22) described the influence of what we today call Bollywood movies on the local culture of the Indo-Trinidadian diaspora:

> The advent of commercial Hindi films to the Caribbean in the mid-1930s added a new dimension of Indian cultural presence in the diaspora. By the early 1940s Hindi cinema had become widely popular among Indo-Caribbeans, providing what many have perceived as a direct link to the cherished but otherwise remote homeland.

The primary broadcast showcase for local Indo-Trinidadian culture for many years was a television program called *Mastana Bahar*. Manuel (1998, 22–23) noted the influence of the imported Indian movies on local culture in less than complimentary terms:

> Aside from the decidedly amateurish quality of most such performances, questions have arisen as to whether all this activity constitutes local creativity or obsequious imitation of India's commercial entertainment culture. Critics have alleged that rather than promoting grassroots creation, Mastana Bahar has in fact served to stifle it with an inundation of film pop. Accordingly, local film singers are typically praised not for their originality, but as "the Voice of [film singer Mohammmad] Rafi," or as "a true imitator." And while the many teachers and semi-professional performers of film dance choreograph their own routines to songs of their choosing, the style is, with a very few exceptions, derived wholly from the jerky, calisthenic Bombay studio idiom rather than from, for example, the graceful, local chutney style, which evolved organically from *Bhojpuri* folk dance.

There was in fact a significant local component to the show that Manuel misses—though a lack of empirical data precludes a fruitful outcome to debating that issue here. More germane is Manuel's implicit condescension to the commercial imported cultural form and his obeisance to the "organically" evolved form(s). The implication here is that the imported and commercial are somehow lesser quantities than the "organically" evolved. Yet this organically evolved form bears just as little relevance to the lived existence of the practitioners as the imported and commercial. In fact, the audience for *Mastana Bahar* would have far greater recognition of acts borrowed from Bollywood films than obscure ancestral forms of song or dance. But wait—there's more, the so-called chutney forms themselves are not as "pure" as we might imagine—heavily influenced as they are by borrowed African rhythms from the local African diaspora. Young Indo-Trinidadians often find little relevance either in the imported or evolved traditions of their homeland—opting often enough for alternative influences in music and dance, and their own eclectic identities in everyday life with these so-called cultural influences relegated to secondary influences and, perhaps, providing a sense of emotional security.

The notion of culture as a kind of security is not exactly a far-fetched idea. Inglis (2004, 161), for example, contended that the practical uses of culture do involve a kind of personal security related to identity and even ethnicity:

> We cannot do without culture and we cannot do with it. It is an indispensable moral weapon with which to invent and mark off such precious values as identity and ethnicity. . . . It was never easy to escape self-righteousness in cultural commentary, not other such sins of egocentric commission as condescension, straight and inverted snobbery, rhetorical vulgarity, and discourtesy amounting to cruelty. Culture as a so very contested concept is the more prone to prompt such zones of being, those where identity, both willed and given, draws strength from custom and ceremony.

Similarly, Cupitt (1997) was also acutely aware of the emotional and identity dimensions of culture. He interrogates the religion-as-culture relationship as well as the practice of literal interpretations of spiritual doctrine. He pointedly suggested that the process of globalization creates the conditions for divesting ourselves of previously "necessary" and inevitably parochial notions:

> We cleave to, and we are chauvinistic about, our own particular body of supernatural beliefs and stories because *its distinctiveness is our identity*. It communicates, in coded form but very effectively nonetheless, our own distinctive vision of the world and form of life. Because in the past it was generally felt to be essential to the maintenance of one's ethnic cultural tradition for all this material to be passed on without change and thoroughly assimilated by everyone, it was commonly taught and understood realistically—as if describing a really existing invisible supernatural world above. But today the globalization of our scientific theory, our technologies, and our communications has suddenly democratized naturalism everywhere. (94, italics in original).

Further concerns about the decreasing relevance of culture in its various forms, are arguments about what even constitutes culture anymore. Morley (2006, 36–37) argued that concerns about erosion (couched, for example, as cultural imperialism) raise fundamental questions about what constitutes not just authentic culture but even what constitutes culture itself:

> The basic cultural imperialism thesis also seems to lead fairly directly to policies of cultural protectionism—designed to defend indigenous cultures against their corruption, "pollution" or destruction by foreign elements. Evidently, the problem here is how one is to define what constitutes the original,

indigenous, culturally pure forms that are to be defended, without falling into
an essentialist position. How far back in history do you have to go to find the
pure elements to be defended?

He further argued that the premise of "pure, authentic, cultural spaces" (37)
is itself fundamentally flawed, describing it as a fantasy based "on the inaccurate presumption that cultural mixing is a new and recent phenomenon."
He argued instead that "all cultures (if to different degrees) have routinely
absorbed and indigenised elements from other sources, throughout history."
We have seen evidence to support this contention in previous chapters with
groups as diverse in type and time as the ancient Nabateans, the colonial
Hindus, and the modern Caribbean diasporic immigrant. Inadequacies in
addressing this complex diversity and interconnectedness of cultures may be
due to the fact that we have too long searched for simplistic truisms; it may
be due to a tradition of classification inherited from European pre-science. In
our modern cultural analyses we have still tended to lean toward categorical
contrasts and generalizations that have precluded a broader view of culture as
a global phenomenon.

It may be, however, that we can only now adopt this view because the
global environment is becoming the primary referent of cultural analysis.
Lester Thurow (1988, 19) contended that the slow transmission of culture
from one generation to another has been replaced by modern media influences that expose generations to traditions not experiences by their ancestors,
arguing that this presents a global culture to new generations based not on
tradition but on commerce; he argued that

> for the first time in history, the cultures of the past are going to be challenged
> by what is not just a global culture but an economic one. Modern culture is
> what sells and not what is transmitted from the past. . . . With individuals
> increasingly having direct satellite links with the world's culture and being
> less and less dependent upon links that are, or can be, nationally controlled,
> national cultures will for the first time have to compete with a global culture.
> Some national cultures will undoubtedly survive this global competition, but
> others will not.

With this in mind, the prevailing popular sentiment in many developing
nations (as we have noted before) is a fear of the influence of the culture of
metropolitan nations embodied in so much modern globalized transnational
media. However, the distinction between global media and local media is not
necessarily an easy one anymore. Many Middle Eastern broadcasters, for
example, disseminate their television signals to their own local populations
via satellite. These signals then automatically become part of the regional
viewing menu as they are both readily available to all their neighbors and
linguistically accessible as well. Additionally, several of the services are then

picked up for rebroadcast via satellite to North American and European satellite bouquets. In this way, what is perceived to be "local culture" is broadcast via electronic media but also regionalized and internationalized through media. Not all of the content is "traditional." Mixed in with the odd traditional show are many popular music programs, game shows, and commercially sponsored sporting events.

Foreshadowing this commercialization and electronic dissemination of culture, Theodor W. Adorno (1975, 2007) argued that the so-called culture industry was already so dominant in the middle of the twentieth century that to ignore its influence and its power would be naive. Despite such warnings, the wide spread of culture as a commodity and commercialization as a fact of cultural life means that the distinctions between culture and business are no longer possible and probably no longer useful. Any "culture," both in expressed and implicit forms, and on micro and macro scales, has become so intertwined with commercial forces and the global forces of both media and capital that to attempt a meaningful separation would be pointless.

The very notion of culture itself has become progressively less relevant and less useful, prompting us to examine the baggage that it has created—often to the detriment of societies. Hanson (2007, 12), for example, argued that

> culture has become an obstacle to the productive communication and interaction that it originally enabled. For it again to become a positive aspect of social life, people must free themselves from being so exclusively and irrevocably saturated with their own cultural premises that they are existentially threatened by alternatives.

Even the everyday and childhood cherished traditions so important to many can be less about culture than about histories of exploitation and domination. Jamaicans and Trinidadians, for example, tout their cherished dishes with ingredients such as ackee and saltfish (traditionally salted cod) or pickled mackerel. They often claim these as culturally their own—forgetting that these dishes emerged from the provisions of slave ships and colonial cargo. They forget that ackees, far from being native to Jamaica, were imported and cultivated by the British to feed the colonies. They forget that breadfruit, similarly imported, was food only for pigs and slaves until modern reinventions decided to utilize this food crop and even tout it as a cultural tradition.

In these acceptances are the bases for an inability to interrogate the assumptions of culture and its formation. The entrenchment of these items and their loaded significance becomes visible only when the bases of their popularity are questioned. In the late 1980s, the Jamaican government realized that colonial era subsidies on saltfish were too expensive to maintain and dropped them. The price of saltfish skyrocketed and there was a huge outcry because common folk could no longer afford to prepare the "national dish." It was at this time when some people began to ask why this was the national dish and what this meant in terms of the island's history of slavery and colonialism. Nor was this the first time that colonial (or otherwise received) traditions passing as culture was questioned in the region. Wilk (1999) recounted that the debate about what constituted food traditions and local food culture became part of Belize's independence debate in 1964.

More than being simply a perceptual or political obstacle, culture has also proven to be a dangerous and sometimes lethal concept with Rothkop (1997, 41) characterizing culture as a frequent accomplice to genocide:

> One need only look at the 20th century's genocides. In each one, leaders used culture to fuel the passions of their armies and other minions and to justify their actions among their people. One million Armenians; tens of millions of Russians; 10 million Jews, Gypsies, and homosexuals; 3 million Cambodians; and hundreds of thousands of Bosnians, Rwandans, and Timorese all were the victims of "culture"—whether it was ethnic, religious, ideological, tribal, or nationalistic in its origins. To be sure, they fell victim to other agendas as well. But the provocative elements of culture were to these accompanying agendas as Joseph Goebbels was to Adolf Hitler—an enabler and perhaps the most insidious accomplice.

Though this might be seen by some as an overstatement (it is certainly a strong statement), the point is a valid one and needs to be made, especially in the face of the sanctification (and often, sanctimoniousness) of both the concept of culture and most academic notions of cultural analysis.

In popular discourse, the dangers and the allure of this simplistic approach to culture can be seen in the popularity of Huntington's (1996) *The Clash of Civilizations* and its emphasis on cultural and religious differences as primary bases of discontent and discord. Barkey (2005, 6) argued that Huntington's thesis "struck a dark cord of popular simplicity, dividing the world into essentialized categories and reinforcing the pathological status of the 'other.'" She calls it an "inherently perilous document" whose approach "erects impervious boundaries between different cultures elevated to the status of civilizations."

Barkey (2005) further argued that the approach found in work such as Huntington's critique reflects an inaccurate picture of the development of culture and identity. Here I would add that much of so-called cultural analysis suffers the same deficiencies, espousing a narrow and traditional view of culture that seeks to create or rely on the very same fissures and comfortable distinctions that fuelled colonialism and institutionalizes "other-ness." Mikhail Epstein (2009, 328) argued, instead, for what he terms a "transcultural" perspective in which the traditional strictures of culture are transcended; he wrote that the transcultural perspective opens a possibility for globalization not as homogenization but, rather, as further differentiation of cultures and their "dissemination" into transcultural individuals, liberating themselves from their dependence from their native cultures. The global society can be viewed as the space of diversity of free individuals rather than that of fixed groups and cultures. It is an alternative to the clash of civilizations and a hope for lasting peace.

The traditional discourse of culture and even the discourse of erosion/homogenization are, then, not only passé but also incompatible with the realities of modern globalized information exchange. In the modern globalized environment, no matter how far to the periphery one might be, the influences of other cultures in both their mediated and material forms cannot be far away. Whether it is the Indian expatriate laborer buying a German candy bar in a supermarket in Kuwait, or an Egyptian child with Ramadan lanterns made in China, or an American office worker using a computer with components from Japan and Korea, or a Trinidadian watching a DVD copy of a Nigerian sitcom, we are all connected in this globalized environment.

In material and intellectual terms, our separate cultures are slowly becoming less evident and our assumptions about them becoming less sustainable. What becomes clearer in their place is not that individual cultures are being eroded or have died, but rather, that they were primarily a fiction in the first place, borne out of the complex interplay of political and economic forces that delineated the relationships among nations and which emphasized regional and visible differences in human existence over the common needs, aspirations, and experiences of humankind. Anabelle Srebreny (2005, 443) put it well, saying that "the problem is the assumption of 'culture' as an exclusive club with sealed boundaries within which only some people are full members, rather than as fluid and pliable depending on people's choices and lived contexts."

The broadest conceptual notions of globalization cause us to raise such heretical questions about culture. As Szeman (2003, 92) put it, "globalization has produced the conditions that might permit us to rethink culture in a larger historical frame, a process that would allow us to see that the concept of culture has always been other than what it claimed to be."

With the ability to experience the other and with the ability of modern business to globalize communications and commerce, the sentimental links to tradition and culture have not only begun to fade, but have also begun to show their age and weakness. A new sense of being and a new sense of belonging are possible through globalization as never before. Continuing inequities in information technology access may still prevent us from confidently claiming that we live in a global village, but for how much longer? Our tribes are being made redundant and our villages are being drawn into the world of markets and brands and shared understandings that transcend our borders. There is little to suggest that this process will be reversed or stopped.

While we may be tempted to think of these changes as happening in the abstract and external to our own selves, there is growing evidence that we are all (to varying degrees) personally affected. This means that the changes we see in the concept of culture and its execution may not only be reflected in what we see on television, but also by what we encounter in our own lives and, as Hermans and DiMaggio (2007, 35) argued, in our very selves:

> The increasing interconnectedness of nations and cultures does not only lead to an increasing contact between different cultural groups but also to an increasing contact between cultures within the individual person. Different cultures come together and meet each other within the self of one and the same individual.

They suggested that this leads to "novel and multiple identities" to which many of us can already relate, such as someone "educated in a French school system but working for a Chinese company" or "English-speaking employees living in India but giving technical training courses via the Internet to adolescents in the United States." They argue, further, that simultaneous possession of these multiple identities leads to a "dialogical self," one in which there is (or has to be) a continuing dialog among the several cultural identities.

Thus, today—more than ever, it is possible to hold multiple identities in an environment where we can transcend the traditional boundaries of space and time and also overcome the imposed boundaries of culture, religion, and tradition. All of this opens a new world of possibilities—an era where global citizenship becomes closer than we have dared to dream in the past, a time where peace can be fostered rather than imaginary differences foisted, an age where treasured but false traditions give way to enlightenment and scientific progress without the trammels of superstition and prejudice. All of this and more results from the impact of global communications, the spread of global commerce, and the globalization of culture.

Chapter Ten

The Future of Culture

Culture is dead; long live culture. As we look beyond traditional notions of culture, it becomes necessary to examine, even if only briefly, some of the extant (and still quite alive) patterns of thought and behavior that surround us and others in various forms, whether we choose to call them culture or not. More specifically, we need to look at how global issues may evolve to impact global culture(s). Beyond the narrow parochialisms and axioms of past analysis, we need to look to the usefulness of global perspectives on global issues in the emerging global environment. One of these issues most closely bound to the emerging global scope of reference is that of energy. The relationship between energy and culture has been one of the important underexplored developments of mankind's recent history and will possibly be one of the most important issues for the near future.

In March of 2009, TATA Motors of India launched their Nano motor vehicle for sale in their home market of India. The vehicle was priced at about US$2,000 and weighed less than 1,500 pounds. Not surprisingly, this stripped-down automobile (with a single wiper and no airbags) will not be reaching US showrooms any time soon. Rather than being a globalized phenomenon, the product itself specifically reflects the economic reality of its own home country, priced as it is, to be accessible to the average Indian consumer and to meet that consumer's needs. Part of that cultural environment also includes limited access to resources (both monetary and petroleum-based), at least by comparison to the United States.

The Fossil Fuel Revolution

Moan, Smith, and McCurtain (2007) identified the Industrial Revolution of the mid-nineteenth century in Europe as the point at which Western culture made the switch from biomass, water, and other renewable sources of power to fossil fuels. It is not unreasonable to characterize the Industrial Revolution as a fossil fuel revolution that has been accompanied over subsequent decades with the evolution of particular cultural attitudes to power consumption, a notion also examined in great detail by Earley (1997) in his work *Transforming Human Culture*. Earley questioned the propositions of White ([1943] 1987) who suggested that energy use is a predictor and measure of social development. White stated his general law of cultural development as follows:

> Culture develops when the amount of energy harnessed by man per capita per year is increased; or as the efficiency of the technological means of putting this energy to work is increased; or, as both factors are simultaneously increased. (239)

In his analysis of culture and energy, White did not distinguish between fossil fuels and solar power, taking the position that the energy in fossil fuels is in fact a result of past solar energy. White concluded that civilization would never have progressed much beyond the level of the classical age without harnessing fuel as demonstrated in the Industrial Revolution:

> The invention of the steam engine, and of all subsequent engines which derive power from fuels, inaugurated a new era in culture history. When man learned to harness energy in the form of fuel he opened the door of a vast treasure house of energy. Fuels and engines tremendously increased the amount of energy under man's control and at his disposal for culture-building. (245)

Earley (1997, 65) argued, on the other hand, that while measuring social evolution in terms of energy use and efficiency may have been a useful approach in the past, the situation is now changing so that "the successful societies of the future will minimize energy throughput."

Other than in times of high oil prices, there is a tendency in modern—particularly Western—cultures to treat fossil fuel sources as inexhaustible. This idea becomes caught up in many of the manifestations of modern life and Western culture in which we have come to take for granted such luxuries as automobile transportation, air travel, and domestic electricity. Our everyday lives, and our cultural expectations of a normal day are based on energy assumptions that have developed over the years and become normalized over generations but which have also evolved with an illusion of constant supplies of energy. While the illusion rings true in times of plentiful resources, the future of culture may have much more to do with energy adaptation than we have hitherto experienced in modern times.

Energy, Resources, and Culture

As we have examined previously, cultures (however conceived) developed partly as relationships with the natural environment, energy being a part of that relationship. At the same time, we might also argue that culture can be seen as oppositional relationships with the environment. That is to say, that culture can be (and has been) perceived as ways of overcoming the environment rather than co-existing with it. To the point of the fossil fuel revolution and to the extent that various groups are involved in carbon-based fossil fuel consumption, all cultures worldwide have become part of a revolution (focused on overcoming the natural environment) that can only be limited in its life span.

Wilk (2002, 110) made the point that there are cultural variations, even among industrialized countries, in conventions and practices related to the consumption of energy:

> People in the United States tend to believe that a comfortable house is kept heated in winter and cooled in the summer, so there is a relatively constant temperature. . . . Swedes for example, find American homes terribly overheated, overcooled and under-ventilated. Until very recently, houses in Japan were not heated in winter at all. Japanese people heated the space under a sunken dinner table and trapped the heat with a cloth around the edge of the table. This was not a hardship—people were genuinely more comfortable this way—and in Japan there is still widespread resistance to domestic space heating and cooling. Even in the United States it took more than thirty years to convince Americans that air conditioning was not going to cause disease.

Following on many years of industrial development and the globalization of industrial commercial cultural norms, and given continuing patterns of energy demand growth, we may see energy deficits become a global reality, absent significant technological and cultural change that can take us to more efficient use of energy from renewable sources and reductions of energy and resource consumption overall. The globalization of overconsumption may well lead to a globalization of cultural change toward sustainability. Indeed, Georgescu-Roegen (1993) in his list of recommendations for change toward energy sustainability listed several overtly cultural measures. His cultural recommendations at the macro level focused on re-directing resources from war to survival. At a more personal level, he advocated reducing demand for items of extravagance so that markets cease to exist for them, and he advocated getting rid of fashion, including the idea that new items are to be acquired for the sake of being new when old ones can continue to serve the purpose. He also advocated manufacturers creating more durable items (which would reduce the need for additional production). While these are (for some) laudable aims, Georgescu-Roegen did not suggest how they might be achieved. It is somewhat telling that his quote decrying fashion dates to the year 1750. The point to be made here, however, is that culture is an integral part of the use of resources in general and energy in particular.

In some instances, the sheer magnitude of the wasteful extravagance of cultural products draws attention to their (often overlooked) impact. The vast resources expended on the creation of fantasies and fictions in today's industrialized West may provide an example of the kinds of changes that may eventually be necessary to create the conditions of sustainability. The expenditure of millions of dollars of resources on works of filmic fiction has become a cultural norm in the West with little thought to the ironies (obscenities?) of their production and distribution (e.g., that their budgets often dwarf the health or education budgets of some small nations). While there is significant economic activity around these huge film projects, there is little questioning of the ultimate value of these expenditures. Future generations may well condemn us for the wasteful extravagance of such ventures, particularly when the shortsighted culture of corporate gain has passed into a more sensible approach to sustainability.

Sustainability

If culture, in its traditional sense, is dead (or simply globalized out of relevance), then the need for cultural change of a much more vast and sweeping kind becomes apparent in terms of the energy and resource equations. Our future may well involve cultural changes that will see a return to our dependence on and symbiosis with the natural environment. Without depleting reserves of fossil fuel and the development of fossil burning technologies, our modern industrialized cultures run the risk of collapse in the long run absent significant changes in technology or culture. More realistically speaking, we are likely to see the evolution of technologies and lived practices that seek to make fossil fuel consumption more efficient. However, this is a delaying tactic at best—often shortsighted in its collateral costs—such as the use of natural gas resources instead of coal—a switch that decreases cost and emissions in the short run, but which may also reduce the impetus for technological and cultural change to deal with the finite supply of either fuel.

The globalization of culture may provide the opportunity for re-thinking so many of the axioms of our culturally entrenched practices in terms of global imperatives. While we have in 2008 and 2009 seen how much of the financial world and the global food supply depend on global forces and interdependencies, we have yet to recognize other factors such as the global energy and environmental imperatives that may emerge. It is here that we may find our most pressing imperatives for globalization on a cultural dimension, spelling not only the death of culture, but also its rebirth, as a set of strategies unifying and synchronizing humankind with our planet. At the same time, this also suggests another important lesson, which is that the present form of globalization is not the necessary form. The casting of unbridled markets and unrestrained corporate expansion as the necessary and inevitable outcomes of the globalization process is not a perspective that will last forever, no more so than the paradigms of the past such as conquest, crusades, and colonization. Global interdependencies, so linked today with the expansion of business and markets, may yet give way to relationships based more on the welfare of the planet and its many people than on the profit motives of a few.

EVEN NATIONS

Environmental sustainability may not be the only outcome of the globalization of culture. Rising awareness of the strictures of culture and the historical baggage of geopolitics with which it is often tinged, also leads one to reconsider some of the other foundational organizations of modern human society. Karim (2006, 267–268), for example, reconsidered the nation-state as a function of imagination, writing that

> ideas of the nation-state have involved the coalescence of ethnicity and territory to imply the existence of an ancestral homeland belonging to a particular people having kinship ties that are reflected in a common language and culture. But this idea has been consistently problematic. Nations in reality have not been containers of "pure ethnicities."

It is not that one would expect nation-states to suddenly disappear, entrenched as they have been as the basic model of the international system for so many years. We can expect, however, shifts in the conceptual boundaries of nation-states as there have ever been, and attempts to follow more rational models of organization alongside state structures—the European Union being one such example. We can also expect a more rational approach to the idea of the nation-state as the result of the vagaries of history and political choices rather than the birthright inheritance of ancient generations.

As globalization advances and culture recedes, both the natural environment and the political realities come into sharper focus. The globalization of culture prompts us to reconsider both our physical and political environments with greater rationality than we have in the past. What awaits is not the hopelessness of cultural imperialism or the blandness of homogenization, but freedom from the trammels of superstition, guilt, and fear that have paraded as culture these many decades. Awareness of the dynamic and sometimes capricious ebb and flow of cultural ideas and an appreciation of these as global process not just now but also in the past, is a liberating undertaking. A worldview either free of, or even just aware of, the limitations of old ideas about culture would allow us to truly experience and benefit from the emerging global realities in which both commerce and civilization may be advanced. Yet ignorance, xenophobia, and good old-fashioned self-interest are probably not going anywhere soon and the challenges faced by humanity are probably not going to simply disappear. So as "kumbayah" as all this sounds, there remains the need for analysis and interrogation of our assumptions about the world we live in, and oversight of the dominant social forces including multinational corporations and the various roles of global media.

Afterword

On Tuesday, January 20, 2009, approaching five o'clock, I wrote some portions of this work while sitting in a hotel room in Salmiyah, Kuwait, watching *BBC World*'s coverage of the inauguration of Barack Obama in Washington, DC. The commentators discussed the significance of the president elect's use of his middle name "Hussein" and how this might play with the rest of the world. They also discussed the fact that his father was from Kenya and there was coverage of reactions in the Kenyan village where his father was born and in the rest of that country. "Parties across Kenya on Inauguration Day" proclaimed the announcer to pictures of reveling Kenyans.

No one could escape the historic importance of that moment for the United States. The legacies of slavery and segregation notwithstanding, that moment demonstrated that modern society has the ability to shake off the shackles of culture and tradition when they are the source of injustice and wrong. When we become nostalgic for tradition and clamor for the culture of the past, we are well reminded that human progress has moved us all over the world to an improved cultural outlook (and that the good old days were not always all that good).

The international coverage of this event and its broad impact on people around the world also pointed to the impossibility of containing culture to its own context. Billions of people around the world watched those events and made their own meanings—but also built this historical moment into their own histories. This is what both global media and global culture have brought us to. It is not necessarily a bad thing.

This is admittedly a special case as the implications of the US presidency are inherently important because of the geopolitical and economic influence of the United States, but the immediacy of the event and the communing of the international audience in this event are demonstrative of how culture has evolved and communicating (especially in its sense of communing or coming together) is bringing the world closer together.

Bibliography

Abbara, Rashid. 2008. "Muslims Get on the Bus: Florida Muslims Are Putting Ads on City Buses to Promote Tolerance and Teach Their Neighbours about Islam." *Guardian*, December 18. http://www.guardian.co.uk/commentisfree/cifamerica/2008/dec/18/florida-islamic-awareness-bus-ads.

Adams, Kathleen M. 1997. "Ethnic Tourism and the Renegotiation of Tradition in Tana Toraja (Sulawesi, Indonesia)." *Ethnology* 36: 390–420.

Adorno, Theodor W. 1941. "On Popular Music." *Studies in Philosophy and Social Sciences* 9: 17–18.

———. 1975. "Culture Industry Reconsidered." Translated by Anson G. Rabinbach. *New German Critique* 6: 12–19.

———. 2007. *The Culture Industry: Selected Essays on Mass Culture*. New York: Routledge.

Adorno, Theodor W., and Max Horkheimer. 1972. *Dialectic of Enlightenment*. New York: Herder and Herder.

Ahmed, Leila. 1993. *Women and Gender in Islam: Historical Roots of a Modern Debate*. New Haven, CT: Yale University Press.

Al Faruqi, Isma'il R. 1963. "A Comparison of the Islamic and Christian Approaches to Hebrew Scripture." *Journal of Bible and Religion* 31: 283–93.

Amin, S., and David Luckin. 1996. "The Challenge of Globalization." *Review of International Political Economy* 3: 216–59.

Ang, Ien. 1985. *Watching Dallas*. London: Methuen.

Ardizzoni, Michela. 2005. "Redrawing the Boundaries of Italianness: Televised Identities in the Age of Globalisation." *Social Identities* 11: 509–30.

Armstrong, Karen. 1999. *A History of God from Abraham to the Present: The 4000-Year Quest for God*. London: Vintage, Random House.

Arondekar, Anjali, R. 2000. "A Perverse Empire: Victorian Sexuality and the Indian Colony." PhD diss., University of Pennsylvania.

Asher, Catherine B., and Cynthia Talbot. 2006. *India before Europe*. Cambridge: Cambridge University Press.

Assmann, Jan. 2005. *Death and Salvation in Ancient Egypt*. Translated by David Lorton. Ithaca, NY: Cornell University Press.

Augustine of Hippo. 426 (1972). *The City of God*. Translated by Henry Bettenson. Harmondsworth, England: Penguin.

Bainbridge, Jason, and Craig Norris. 2008. "Madman in the House: Understanding Media Merchandising, the Implications for Convergence and New Knowledge Economies." Paper presented at "Sustaining Culture," annual conference of the Cultural Studies Association of Australia, Adelaide, Australia, December.

Bakan, Joel. 2004. *The Corporation: The Pathological Pursuit of Profit and Power*. New York: Free Press.

Barkey, Karen. 2005. "Islam and Toleration: Studying the Ottoman Imperial Model." *International Journal of Politics, Culture, and Society* 19: 5–19.

BBCNews.com. 2007. "Halliburton Plans Move to Dubai." *BBC News*, March 11. http://news.bbc.co.uk/2/hi/6440365.stm.

Bendix, Regina. 1989. "Tourism and Cultural Displays Inventing Traditions for Whom?" *Journal of American Folklore* 102: 131–46.

Benelli, Dana. 2002. Hollywood and the Travelogue. *Visual Anthropology* 15: 3–16.

Bennett, Louise. 1966. "Colonization in Reverse." http://louisebennett.com/newsdetails.asp?NewsID=8.

Berkey, Jonathan P. 2003. *The Formation of Islam: Religion and Society in the Near East*. Cambridge: Cambridge University Press.

Bettig, Ronald V. 1996. *Copyrighting Culture: The Political Economy of Intellectual Property*. Boulder, CO: Westview.

Bhagwati, Jagdish. 2004. *In Defense of Globalization. A Council on Foreign Relations Book*. New York: Oxford University Press.

Bhatia, Nandi. 2003. "Fashioning Women in Colonial India." *Fashion Theory: The Journal of Dress, Body, and Culture* 7: 327–44.

Bloch, R. Howard. 1992. *Medieval Misogyny and the Invention of Western Romantic Love*. Chicago: University of Chicago Press.

Bobbitt, Philip C. 2003. *The Shield of Achilles War, Peace, and the Course of History*. New York: Anchor / Random House.

Bonsu, Samuel K. 2009. "Colonial Images in Global Times: Consumer Interpretations of Africa and Africans in Advertising." *Consumption, Markets, and Culture* 12: 1–25.

Boodan, Adrian. 2004. "Death and Disease in Enterprise." *Trinidad Guardian Newspaper*, January 18. http://legacy.guardian.co.tt/archives/2004-01-18/news4.html.

Bordwell, David, Janet Staiger, and Kristin Thompson. 1985. *The Classical Hollywood Cinema: Film Style and Mode of Production to 1960*. New York: Columbia University Press.

Bowman, Wayne. 2009. "Call for Soca Ban: Angry Jamaicans Target T&T as Rude Reggae-Dancehall Songs Taken Off Airwaves." *Trinidad Express Newspaper*, February 11. http://www.trinidadexpress.com/index.pl/article_news?id=161437890.

Branden, Nathaniel. 2008. *The Psychology of Romantic Love: Romantic Love in an Antiromantic Age*. New York: Jeremy P. Tarcher.

Brecht, Martin. 1985. *Martin Luther*. Translated by James L. Schaaf. Philadelphia: Fortress Press.

Brown, Dan. 2003. *The Da Vinci Code*. Garden City, NY: Doubleday.

Bullough, Vern L. 1977. "Sex Education in Medieval Christianity." *Journal of Sex Research* 13: 185–96.

Cairncross, Frances. 1997. *The Death of Distance: How the Communications Revolution Will Change Our Lives*. Boston: Harvard Business School Press.

Cameron, David, and Janice Gross-Stein. 2000. "Globalization, Culture and Society: The State as Place amidst Shifting Spaces." *Canadian Public Policy / Analyse de Politiques* 26: S15–S34.

Campbell, Mary B. 1999. *Wonder and Science: Imagining Worlds in Early Modern Europe*. Ithaca, NY: Cornell University Press.

Carlsson, Ulla. 2003. "Information Society: Visions and Governance. The Rise and Fall of NWICO—and Then? From a Vision of International Regulation to a Reality of Multilevel Governance." Paper presented at EURICOM Colloquium, Venice, Italy, May.

Carver, Ronald P. 1973. "Effect of Increasing the Rate of Speech Presentation upon Comprehension." *Journal of Educational Psychology* 65: 118–26.

Castells, Manuel. 1997. *The Information Age: Economy, Society and Culture*. Vol. 2. Oxford: Blackwell.

Cayla, Julien, and Eric Arnould. 2008. "A Cultural Approach to Branding in the Global Marketplace." *Journal of International Marketing* 16: 86–112.

Chamberlain, Mary. 2006. *Family Love in the Diaspora: Migration and the Anglo-Caribbean Experience (Memory and Narrative)*. New Brunswick, NJ: Transaction.

Chambers, Erve. 2000. *Native Tours: The Anthropology of Travel and Tourism*. Long Grove, IL: Waveland Press.

Chandrasekaran, Rajiv. 2001. "Cambodian Village Wired to Future: Satellite Internet Link Transforming Economy and Culture." *Washington Post Foreign Service*, May 13, A01.

Chaplin, Charles, dir. 1936. *Modern Times.* Motion picture.

Cheal, David J. 1988. *The Gift Economy*. New York: Routledge.

Chidester, David. 2000. *Christianity: A Global History*. New York: HarperCollins.

Child Workers in Asia Foundation. 1997. Child Camel Jockeys in the Gulf States. *CWA Newsletter* 13: 1. http://www.cwa.tnet.co.th/Publications/Newsletters/vol13_2-3/v13_2-3_cameljockeys.html.

Chitnis, Ketan S., Avinash Thombre, Everett M. Rogers, Arvind Singhal, and Amy Sengupta. 2006. "(Dis)Similar readings: Indian and American Audiences' Interpretation of *Friends*." *International Communication Gazette* 68: 131–45.

"Christmas Is Tradition." 1954. *Science News-Letter* 66: 378–79.

Clairmont, Frederic. 2000. "The Global Corporation: Road to Serfdom." *Economic and Political Weekly*, January 8.

Clark, Elizabeth A. 2000. "Vitiated Seeds and Holy Vessels: Augustine's Manichean Past." In *Images of the Feminine in Gnosticism,* edited by Karen L. King, 367–401. London: Continuum International.

Clarke, John. 1991. *New Times and Old Enemies: Essays on Cultural Studies and America*. London: HarperCollins.

Clinard, Marshall B. 1990. *Corporate Corruption: The Abuse of Power*. New York: Praeger.

Cohen, Abner. 1993. *Masquerade Politics: Explorations in the Structure of Urban Cultural Movements*. Oxford: Berg.

Cowen, Tyler. 2000. *In Praise of Commercial Culture*. Cambridge, MA: Harvard University Press.

Cox, Harvey. 1999. "The Market as God." *The Atlantic Monthly* 283: 18–23.

Crane, Jonathan H., and Carlos F. Balerdi. 2008. *Ackee Growing in the Florida Home Landscape*. Gainesville, FL: Institute of Food and Agricultural Sciences.

Croteau, David, and William Hoynes. 2003. *Media Society: Industries, Images and Audiences*. Thousand Oaks, CA: Pine Forge Press.

Cupitt, Don. 1997. *After God: The Future of Religion*. Jackson, TN: Basic Books.

Curtin, Philip D. 1984. *Cross-cultural Trade in World History*. Cambridge: Cambridge University Press.

Davis, Stanley M. 1984. *Managing Corporate Culture*. Cambridge, MA: Ballinger.

de las Casas, Bartoleme. 1552 (1992). *The Devastation of the Indies: A Brief Account*. Translated by Herma Briffault. Baltimore: Johns Hopkins University Press. Originally published as *Brevisima relacion de la destruccion de las Indias*, Seville, Spain.

Deeks, John. 1993. *Business and the Culture of the Enterprise Society*. Westport, CT: Quorum Books.

DeLong-Bas, Natana. J. 2007. *Wahhabi Islam: From Revival and Reform to Global Jihad*. London: I. B. Tauris.

Denike, Margaret. 2003. "The Devil's Insatiable Sex: A Genealogy of Evil Incarnate." *Hypatia* 18: 10–43.

Dershowitz, Alan M. 2007. *Blasphemy: How the Religious Right Is Hijacking the Declaration of Independence*. New York: Wiley.

Desmond, Jane C. 1999. *Staging Tourism: Bodies on Display from Waikiki to Sea World*. Chicago: University of Chicago Press.

Doniger, Wendy. 2009. "India, Valentine's Day and Gender Violence." *Ekklesia: A New Way of Thinking*, February 13. http://www.ekklesia.co.uk/node/8649.

Doty, William G. 2004. *Myth: A Handbook*. Westport, CT: Greenwood Press.

Drahos, Peter, and John Braithwaite. 2002. *Information Feudalism: Who Owns the Knowledge Economy?* New York: Earthscan.

Drucker, Peter F. 1999. "Beyond the Information Revolution." *Atlantic Monthly* 284: 47–57 .

Earley, Jay. 1997. *Transforming Human Culture: Social Evolution and the Planetary Crisis.* Albany, New York: State University of New York Press.

Edmondson, Belinda. 2003. "Public Spectacles: Caribbean Women and the Politics of Public Performance." *Small Axe* 13: 1–16.

Eickelman, Dale F. 2003. "Communication and Control in the Middle East: Publication and Its Discontents." In *New Media in the Muslim World: The Emerging Public Sphere*, 2nd ed., edited by Dale F. Eickleman and Jon W. Anderson, 33–44. Bloomington, IN: Indiana University Press.

Elasmar, Michael G., and John E. Hunter. 2003. "A Meta-analysis of Crossborder Effect Studies." In *The Impact of International Television: A Paradigm Shift*, edited by Michael Elasmar, 133–55. Mahwah, NJ: Erlbaum.

Epstein, Mikhail. 2009. "Transculture: A Broad Way between Globalism and Multiculturalism." *American Journal of Economics and Sociology* 68: 327–51.

Farley, Margaret A. 1976. "Sources of Sexual Inequality in the History of Christian Thought." *Journal of Religion* 56: 162–76.

Federspiel, Howard M. 2001. *Islam and Ideology in the Emerging Indonesian State: The Persatuan Islam (Persis), 1923 to 1957.* Leiden, Netherlands: Brill.

Feng, Jiayun. 2008. "Constructing Hyper-masculinities, Conquering Multiculturalism: A Narrative Criticism of *Infernal Affairs* and *The Departed*." Paper presented at the annual meeting of the National Communication Association's 94th annual convention, San Diego, CA, November. http://www.allacademic.com/meta/p245320_index.html.

Ferro, Marc. 2005. *The Use and Abuse of History or How the Past Is Taught to Children.* Rev. ed. Translated by Norman Stone and Andres Brown. New York: Routledge.

Fine, Gary A. 1985. "The Goliath Effect: Corporate Dominance and Mercantile Legends." *Journal of American Folklore* 98: 63–84.

Fisher, Glen. 1997. *Mindsets: The Role of Culture and Perception in International Relations.* Yarmouth, ME: Intercultural Press.

Frank, Thomas. 2000. "The Rise of Market Populism: America's New Secular Religion." *The Nation*, October 12. http://www.thenation.com/article/rise-market-populism.

Frazer, James G. 1916. "Ancient Stories of a Great Flood." *Journal of the Royal Anthropological Institute of Great Britain and Ireland* 46: 231–83.

Freedman, David N., Allen C. Myers, and Astrid B. Beck. 2000. *Eerdmans Dictionary of the Bible.* Grand Rapids, MI: Eerdmans.

Friedman, Thomas L. 2007. *The World Is Flat: A Brief History of the Twenty-First Century.* New York: Picador / Farrar, Straus and Giroux.

Gamson, Joshua. 1994. *Claims to Fame: Celebrity in Contemporary America.* Berkeley: University of California Press.

Gathercole, Sandra. 1987. "Changing Channels: Canadian Television Needs to Switch to a New Format." In *Contemporary Canadian Politics: Readings and Notes*, edited by Robert J. Jackson, Doreen Jackson, and Nicolas Baxter-Moore, 79–86. Scarborough, ON: Prentice-Hall Canada.

Gay, Derek. 2000. "Steel Drums to Steelpans." In *Proceedings of the International Conference on the Science and Technology of the Steelpan*, edited by Anthony Achong, 11–22. Port-of-Spain, Trinidad: ICSTS.

Geertz, Clifford. 1973. "Thick Description: Toward an Interpretive Theory of Culture." In *The Interpretation of Cultures: Selected Essays*, edited by Clifford Geertz, 3–30. New York: Basic Books.

Georgescu-Roegen, Nicholas. 1993. "Selections from 'Energy and Economic Myths.'" In *Valuing the Earth: Economics, Ecology, Ethics*, edited by Herman E. Daly and Kenneth N. Townsend, 89–112. Cambridge, MA: Massachusetts Institute of Technology.

Gibbon, Edward. 1776 (2003). *History of the Decline and Fall of the Roman Empire.* Edited by Hans-Friedrich Mueller. New York: Modern Library.

Giles, David. 2000. *Illusions of Immortality: A Psychology of Fame and Celebrity.* Basingstoke, England: Palgrave Macmillan.

Giroux, Henry A. 2000. *Impure Acts: The Practical Politics of Cultural Studies.* New York: Routledge.

———. 2004. "Beyond Belief: Religious Fundamentalism and Cultural Politics in the Age of George W. Bush." *Cultural Studies–Critical Methodologies* 4: 415–25.

Glyn-Jones, Anne. 1996. *Holding Up a Mirror.* 2nd ed. Exeter, England: Imprint Academic.

Godsen, Chris. 2004. *Archaeology and Colonialism: Cultural Contact from 5000 BC to the Present.* Cambridge: Cambridge University Press.

Gordon, Avery. 1995. "The Work of Corporate Culture: Diversity Management." *Social Text* 44: 3–30.

Goswami, Surabhi. 2010. "Indian Diaspora's Use of Social Networking Sites for Identity Construction and Community Building: The Case of Indians in London (IIL) Community on Orkut." Master's thesis, Roskilde University.

Graff, David F. 2003. "Nabateans." In *Near Eastern Archaeology*, edited by Suzanne Richard, 434–39. Winona Lake, IN: Eisenbrauns.

Green, Cecelia. 1998. "The Asian Connection: The U.S.-Caribbean Apparel Circuit and a New Model of Industrial Relations." *Latin American Research Review* 33: 7–47.

Grieg, J. Michael. 2002. "The End of Geography? Globalization, Communications, and Culture in the International System." *Journal of Conflict Resolution* 46: 225–43.

Halavais, Alexander. 2000. "National Borders on the World Wide Web." *New Media and Society* 2: 7–28.

Hall, Edward T. 1959. *The Silent Language.* New York: Doubleday.

———. 1966. *The Hidden Dimension.* New York: Doubleday.

———. 1976. *Beyond Culture.* New York: Doubleday.

Hall, Stuart. 1997. *Representation: Cultural Representations and Signifying Practices.* London: Sage.

Hamelink, Cees T. 1983. *Cultural Autonomy in Global Communications.* New York: Longman.

Handler, Richard. 1986. "Authenticity." *Anthropology Today* 2: 2–4.

Hannerz, Ulf. 1992. *Cultural Complexity: Studies in the Social Organization of Meaning.* New York: Columbia University Press.

Hanson, F. Allan. 2007. *The Trouble with Culture: How Computers Are Calming the Culture Wars.* Albany, NY: State University of New York Press.

Harrison, Simon. 1999. "Cultural Boundaries." *Anthropology Today* 15: 10–13.

Hatchen, William H. 1999. *The World News Prism: Changing Media of International Communication.* 5th ed. Ames: Iowa University Press.

Hefner, Robert W. 1998. "Multiple Modernities: Christianity, Islam, and Hinduism in a Globalizing Age." *Annual Review of Anthropology* 27: 83–104.

Herman, Edward S., and Robert W. McChesney. 1998. *The Global Media: The New Missionaries of Corporate Capitalism.* London: Cassell.

Hermans, Hubert J., and Giancarlo DiMaggio. 2007. "Self, Identity, and Globalization in Times of Uncertainty: A Dialogical Approach." *Review of General Psychology* 11: 31–61.

Hertz, Noreena. 2001. *The Silent Takeover: Global Capitalism and the Death of Democracy.* New York: Harper-Collins.

Hilton, Boyd. 2007. "Religion, Doctrine and Public Policy." In *The Victorian Studies Reader*, edited by Kelly Boyd and Roham McWilliam, 235–43. London: Routledge.

Hobsbawm, Eric J., and Terence O. Ranger, eds. 1992. *The Invention of Tradition.* 10th ed. Cambridge: Cambridge University Press.

Hobson, John M. 2004. *The Eastern Origins of Western Civilization.* Cambridge: Cambridge University Press.

Hoffmann, Stanley. 2002. "Clash of Globalizations." *Foreign Affairs* 81: 104–15.

Hofstede, Geert. 1980. *Culture's Consequences: International Differences in Work-Related Values.* Newbury Park, CA: Sage.

———. 1986. "Cultural Differences in Teaching and Learning." *International Journal of Intercultural Relations* 10: 301–20.

———. 1998. "Masculinty/Femininity as a National Characteristic." In *Masculinity and Femininity: The Taboo Dimension of National Cultures*, edited by G. Hofstede and W. A. Arrindell, 3–28. Newbury Park, CA: Sage.

Hofstede, Geert, and Michael H. Bond. 1984. "Hofstede's Cultural Dimensions: An Independent Validation Using Rokeach's Value Survey." *Journal of Cross Cultural Psychology* 15: 417–33.

Hoodfar, Homa. 2005. "The Veil in the Minds and on Our Heads: Veiling Practices and Muslim Women." In *Magic, Witchcraft, and Religion: An Anthropological Study of the Supernatural*, 6th ed., edited by Arthur C. Lehmann, James E. Myers, and Pamela A. Moro, 407–22. New York: McGraw-Hill.

Horst, Heather A. 2010. "Keeping the Link: ICTs and Jamaican Migration." In *Diasporas in the New Media Age: Identity, Politics and Community*, edited by Andoni Alonso and Pedro J. Oiarzabal, 136–50. Reno: University of Nevada Press.

Huntington, Samuel P. 1996. *The Clash of Civilizations and the Remaking of World Order*. New York: Simon & Schuster.

Huxley, Aldus. 1932 (1998). *Brave New World*. London: Chatto & Windus. Reprint, New York: Harper Perennial Modern Classics.

Inglis, Fred. 2004. *Culture*. Cambridge: Polity Press.

Innis, Harold A. 1950 (2007). *Empire and Communications*. Oxford: Oxford University Press. Reprint, Lanham, MD: Rowman & Littlefield.

Irving, W. 1828. *History of the Life of Christopher Columbus*. New York: Carvill.

Jackson, Peter. 1999. "Commodity Cultures: The Traffic in Things." *Transactions of the Institute of British Geographers*, n.s., 24: 95–108.

Jenkins, Henry. 2004. "Pop Cosmopolitanism: Mapping Cultural Flows in an Age of Media Convergence." In *Globalization: Culture and Education in the New Millennium*, edited by Marcelo M. Suárez-Orozco and Desirée B. Qin-Hillard, 114–40. Berkeley: University of California Press.

Jenkins, Philip. 2008. "The Christian Revolution." In *The Globalization Reader*, 3rd ed., edited by Frank J. Lechner and John Boli, 379–86. Malden, MA: Blackwell.

Jones, Eric L. 2006. *Cultures Merging: A Historical and Economic Critique of Culture*. Princeton, NJ: Princeton University Press.

Kapur, Jyotsna. 2009. "An 'Arranged Love' Marriage: India's Neoliberal Turn and the Bollywood Wedding Culture Industry." *Communication, Culture, and Critique* 2: 221–33.

Karim, Karim H. 2006. "Nation and Diaspora: Rethinking Multiculturalism in a Transnational Context." *International Journal of Media and Cultural Politics* 2: 267–82.

Karsh, Efraim. 2007. *Islamic Imperialism*. New Haven, CT: Yale University Press.

Kearney, Michael. 1995. "The Local and the Global: The Anthropology of Globalization and Transnationalism." *Annual Review of Anthropology* 24: 547–65.

Kellner, Douglas. 1995. *Media Culture: Cultural Studies, Identity, and Politics between the Modern and the Postmodern*. New York: Routledge.

Khalaf, Sulayman. 2000. "Poetics and Politics of Newly Invented Traditions in the Gulf: Camel Racing in the United Arab Emirates." *Ethnology* 39: 243–61.

King, Paul E., and Ralph R. Behnke. 1989. "The Effect of Time-Compressed Speech on Comprehensive, Interpretive, and Short-Term Listening." *Human Communication Research* 15: 428–43.

———. 2000. "Effects of Communication Load, Affect, and Anxiety on the Performance of Information Processing Tasks." *Communication Quarterly* 48: 74–84.

King, Richard. 1999. "Orientalism and the Modern Myth of 'Hinduism.'" *Numen* 46: 146–85.

Kingston, Anne. 2005. *The Meaning of Wife: A Provocative Look at Women and Marriage in the Twenty-First Century*. New York: Farrar, Straus and Giroux.

Kitty, Alexandra. 2005. *Don't Believe It! How Lies Become News*. New York: Disinformation Company.

Kovacs, Joe. 2008. *Shocked by the Bible: The Most Astonishing Facts You've Never Been Told*. Nashville, TN: Thomas Nelson.

Kraidy, Marwan M. 2005. *Hybridity, or the Cultural Logic of Globalization*. Philadelphia: Temple University Press.

———. 2009. "Reality Television, Gender, and Authenticity in Saudi Arabia." *Journal of Communication* 59: 345–66.

Kristeva, Julia. 1986. "Word, Dialogue, and the Novel." In *The Kristeva Reader*, edited by Toril Moi, 35–61. New York: Columbia University Press.

Kuhn, Thomas S. 1962. *The Structure of Scientific Revolutions*. Chicago: University of Chicago Press.

Kyle, Richard G. 2006. *Evangelicalism: An Americanized Christianity*. Edison, NJ: Transaction.

Lacher, Hannes. 2006. *Beyond Globalization: Capitalism, Territoriality and the International Relations of Modernity*. London: Routledge.

Lambert, Frank. 2003. *The Founding Fathers and the Place of Religion in America*. Princeton, NJ: Princeton University Press.

Lane, Jan-Erik. 2006. *Globalization and Politics: Promises and Dangers*. Surrey, England: Ashgate.

Larkin, Brian. 2002. "La musique bandiri, globalisation et expérience urbaine au Nigeria [Bandiri Music, Globalization and Urban Experience in Nigeria]." *Cahiers d'Études Africaines* 42: 739–62.

———. 2008. "Itineraries of Indian Cinema: African Videos, Bollywood, and Global Media." In *The Anthropology of Globalization: A Reader*, 2nd ed., edited by Jonathan X. Inda and Renato Rosaldo, 334–51. Malden, MA: Blackwell.

Leeds-Hurwitz, Wendy. 1990. "Notes in the History of Intercultural Communication: The Foreign Service Institute and the Mandate for Intercultural Training." *Quarterly Journal of Speech* 76: 262–81.

Levine, Phillipa. 2007. *The British Empire: Sunrise to Sunset*. Essex, England: Pearson Longman UK.

Levitt, Theodore. 1983. "The Globalization of Markets." *Harvard Business Review* 61: 92–102.

Lieber, Robert J., and Ruth E. Weisberg. 2002. "Globalization, Culture, and Identities in Crisis." *International Journal of Politics, Culture, and Society* 16: 273–96.

Liebes, Tamar, and Elihu Katz. 1993. *The Export of Meaning: Cross-cultural Readings of Dallas*. 2nd ed. Malden, MA: Polity Press.

Lindholm, Charles. 2008. *Culture and Authenticity*. Malden, MA: Blackwell.

Lobban, Richard A. 1994. "Pigs and Their Prohibition." *International Journal of Middle East Studies* 26: 57–75.

Lopez, Barry. 1990. *The Rediscovery of North America*. Lexington: University Press of Kentucky.

López Springfield, Consuelo. 1997. *Daughters of Caliban: Caribbean Women in the Twentieth Century*. Bloomington: Indiana University Press.

Lorenzen, David N. 1999. "Who Invented Hinduism?" *Comparative Studies in Society and History* 41: 630–59.

Lucas, George, dir. 1971 (2004). *THX 1138*. Burbank, CA: Warner Home Video. DVD.

Lundsten, L., and M. Stocchetti. 2004. "The War against Iraq." In *US and the Others: Global Media Images on "the War on Terror,"* edited by S. A. Nohrstedt and R. Ottosen, 87–108. Göteborg, Sweden: Nordicom.

Luton, Daraine. 2009, February 10. "Dancehall Under Attack—Broadcasting Commission Sticks to Ban on Vulgar Lyrics." http://www.jamaica-gleaner.com: http://www.jamaica-gleaner.com/gleaner/20090210/lead/lead2.html.

Madanat, Hala N., Ralph B. Brown, and Stephen R. Hawks. 2007. "The Impact of Body Mass Index and Western Advertising and Media on Eating Style, Body Image and Nutrition Transition among Jordanian Women." *Public Health Nutrition* 10: 1039–46.

Mainsah, Henry. 2009. "Cameroonians in Oslo, Diaspora, and Uses of the Media." *Nordicom Review* 30: 83–94.

Malinowski, Bronislaw. 1922. *Argonauts of the Western Pacific: An Account of Native Enterprise and Adventure in the Archipelagoes of Melanesian New Guinea*. London: Routledge.

———. 1926. *Crime and Custom in Savage Society*. New York: Harcourt, Brace.

———. 1929. *The Sexual Life of Savages in North-Western Melanesia*. New York: Halcyon House.

———. 1935. *Coral Gardens and Their Magic*. New York: American Book Co.

Manuel, Peter. 1998. "Music, Identity, and Images of India in the Indo-Caribbean Diaspora." *Asian Music* 29: 17–35.

Marcus, Alan. 2006. "Nanook of the North as Primal Drama." *Visual Anthropology* 19: 201–22.

Marcuse, Herbert. 2002. *One-Dimensional Man: Studies in the Ideology of Advanced Industrial Society.* London: Routledge Classics.

Marín, José. 2008. "Globalization, Education and Cultural Diversity." In *Educational Theories and Practices from the Majority World,* edited by Pierre R Dasen and Abdeljalil Akkari, 346–66. New Delhi: Sage.

Marsden, Magnus. 2007. "Love and Elopement in Northern Pakistan." *Journal of the Royal Anthropological Institute,* n.s., 13: 91–108.

Marshall, David. 1997. *Celebrity and Power.* Minneapolis: University of Minnesota Press.

Martin-Barbero, Jesus. 2000. "Transformations in the Map: Identities and Culture Industries." Translated by Janer Zilkia. *Latin American Perspectives* 27: 27–48.

Martinez, Mark A. 2009. *The Myth of the Free Market: The Role of the State in a Capitalist Economy.* Sterling, VA: Kumarian Press.

Mattelart, Armand. 1979. *Multinational Corporations and the Control of Culture: The Ideological Apparatuses of Imperialism.* Translated by Michael Chanan. Sussex, England: Harvester Press.

Mayr-Harting, Henry. 2002. "The West: The Age of Conversion (700–1050)." In *The Oxford History of Christianity,* edited by John McManners, 101–30. Oxford: Oxford University Press.

McCown, Chester C. 1925. "Hebrew and Egyptian Apocalyptic Literature." *Harvard Theological Review,* 18: 357–411.

McDaniel, Jay. 1997. "The Sacred Whole: An Ecumenical Protestant Approach." In *The Greening of Faith: God, the Environment, and the Good Life,* edited by John Edward Carroll, Paul T. Brockelman, and Mary Westfall, 105–23. Hanover, NH: University Press of New England.

McFarland, Sofia. 2001. "Catholic Church Funds Philippine Web Access." *Wall Street Journal,* March 12, A:19D.

McKay, John P., Bennett D. Hill, and John Buckler. 2006. *A History of Western Society.* 8th ed. Boston: Houghton Mifflin.

McLaughlin, Neil. 1999. "Origin Myths in the Social Sciences: Fromm, the Frankfurt School and the Emergence of Critical Theory." *Canadian Journal of Sociology* 24: 109–39.

McLuhan, Marshall, and Quentin Fiore. 1967. *The Medium Is the Massage.* New York: Bantam.

McPhail, Thomas. 1981. *Electronic Colonialism: The Future of International Broadcasting and Communication.* Newbury Park, CA: Sage.

McSweeny, Brendan. 2002. "Hofstede's Model of National Cultural Differences and Their Consequences: A Triumph of Faith, a Failure of Analysis." *Human Relations* 55: 89–118.

Menninger, David. 1985. "Political Science and the Corporation." *PS: Political Science and Politics* 18: 206–12.

Mernissi, Fatima. 1992. *The Veil and the Male Elite: A Feminist Interpretation of Women's Rights in Islam.* Translated by Mary Jo Lakeland. New York: Basic Books.

Merriman, John. 2004. *A History of Modern Europe.* 2nd ed. Vol. 1. New York: Norton.

Meyer, Birgit, and Peter Geschiere. 1999. *Globalization and Identity: Dialectics of Flow and Closure.* Oxford: Blackwell.

Mitter, Partha. 2001. *Indian Art.* Oxford: Oxford University Press.

Moan, Jaina L., and Zachary A. Smith. 2007. *Energy Use Worldwide: A Reference Handbook.* Santa Barbara, CA: ABC-CLIO.

Mohammed, Shaheed N., and Avinash Thombre. 2003. "A Model of (Mis)Information in the Information Age: The Case of Severe Acute Respiratory Syndrome (SARS) and the Internet." Paper presented at the National Communication Association Convention, Miami Beach, FL, November.

Moore, Jerry D. 2004. *Visions of Culture: An Introduction to Anthropological Theories and Theorists.* 2nd ed. Walnut Creek, CA: AltaMira Press.

Moore, Robert I. 1990. *The Formation of a Persecuting Society: Power and Deviance in Western Europe, 950–1250*. Boston: Blackwell.

Morley, David. 2006. "Globalisation and Cultural Imperialism Reconsidered: Old Questions in New Guises." In *Media and Cultural Theory*, edited by James Curran and David Morley, 30–43. New York: Routledge.

Morley, David, and Kevin Robins. 1995. *Spaces of Identity: Global Media, Electronic Landscapes and Cultural Boundaries*. London: Routledge.

Morris, Desmond. 2005. "Communicating: Desmond Morris on Cross-cultural Communication." http://www.forbes.com/2005/10/19/morris-desmond-cross-culture-comm05-cx_lr_1024morriscross.html.

MothersDayCentral.com. n.d. "Mother's Day History." http://www.mothersdaycentral.com/about-mothersday/history/.

Munro, Dana C. 1895. *Urban and the Crusaders*. Vol. 1, no. 2, of *Translations and Reprints from the Original Sources of European History*. Philadelphia: University of Pennsylvania Press.

Nagel, D. Brendan. 2006. *The Ancient World: A Social and Cultural History*. Upper Saddle River, NJ: Pearson Prentice Hall.

Nelson, Robert H. 2003. "What Is 'Economic Theology'?" Speech delivered to the Second Abraham Kuyper Consultation "Theology and Economic Life: Exploring Hidden Links," Princeton Theological Seminary, Princeton, New Jersey, March 22.

New Orleans Police Department. 1997. "Internet Subscribers." http://www.mardigrasday.com/police.html.

Niblock, Tim. 2006. *Saudi Arabia: Power, Legitimacy and Survival*. London: Routledge.

Nietzsche, Friedrich W. 2006. *The Use and Abuse of History*. New York: Cosimo.

O'Barr, William M. 1994. *Culture and the Ad: Exploring Otherness in the World of Advertising*. Boulder, CO: Westview.

Oberg, Kalervo. 1960. "Culture Shock: Adjustments to New Cultural Environments." *Practical Anthropology* 7: 177–82.

Ogan, Christine L. 2007. "Communication and Culture." In *Global Communication*, 2nd ed., edited by Yahya R. Kamalipour, 293–318. Belmont, CA: Thomson Wadsworth.

Ohmae, Kenichi. 1995. *The Borderless World: Power and Strategy in the Interlinked Economy*. London: Fontana.

Oloka-Onyango, Joseph. 2005. "Who's Watching 'Big Brother'? Globalization and the Protection of Cultural Rights in Present Day Africa." *Human Rights Quarterly* 27: 1245–73.

Olson, Scott R. 1999. *Hollywood Planet: Global Media and the Competitive Advantage of Narrative Transparency*. Mahwah, NJ: Erlbaum.

Orwell, George. 1949. *Nineteen Eighty-Four*. London: Secker and Warburg.

Palmer, Allen. 2007. "Following the Historical Paths of Global Communication." In *Global Communication*, 2nd ed., edited by Yahya R. Kamalipour, 1–21. Belmont, CA: Thomson Wadsworth.

Pandey, Ram Niwas, Pitambar Chettri, Ramesh Raj Kunwar, and Govinda Ghimire. 1995. *Case Study on the Effects of Tourism on Culture and the Environment: Nepal Chitwan-Saurah and Pokhara-Ghandruk. Bangkok*. Thailand: UNESCO Principal Regional Office for Asia and the Pacific.

Patterson, Steve. 2006. "Patterns of Prejudice." *Source* 40: 142–58.

Peers, Douglas M. 2006. *India under Colonial Rule, 1700–1885*. Seminar Studies in History. Essex, England: Pearson Longman.

Perelman, Michael. 2003. *The Perverse Economy: The Impact of Markets on People and the Environment*. New York: Palgrave Macmillan.

Peterson, Mark A. 2004. *Anthropology and Mass Communication: Myth and Media in the New Millenium*. Oxford: Berghahn Books.

Piller, Ingrid. 2001. "Identity Constructions in Multilingual Advertising." *Language in Society* 30: 153–86.

Plunkett, John. 2003. *Queen Victoria: First Media Monarch*. Oxford: Oxford University Press.

Potter, David M. 1954. *People of Plenty: Economic Abundance and the American Character*. Chicago: University of Chicago Press.

Puri, Shalini. 2004. *The Caribbean Postcolonial: Social Equality, Post-nationalism, and Cultural Hybridity.* London: Palgrave Macmillan.

Rampal, Kuldip R. 2001. "Cultural Bane or Sociological Boon? Impact of Satellite Television on Urban Youth in India." In *Media, Sex, Violence, and Drugs in the Global Village*, edited by Yahya R. Kamalipour and Kuldip R. Rampal, 115–52. Lanham, MD: Rowman & Littlefield.

Rantanen, Terhi. 2005. *The Media and Globalization.* Thousand Oaks, CA: Sage.

Reid, Jennifer I. 2004. *Religion and Global Culture: New Terrain in the Study of Religion and the Work of Charles H. Long.* Lanham, MD: Lexington Books.

Representation and the Media (Featuring Stuart Hall). Directed by Sut Jhally. Northampton, MA: Media Education Foundation. Videocassette.

Robins, Kevin, and Asu Aksoy. 2006. "Thinking Experiences: Transnational Media and Migrants' Minds." In *Media and Cultural Theory*, edited by James Curran and David Morley, 86–99. Oxon, England: Routledge.

Robinson, Charles H. 1917. *The Conversion of Europe.* New York: Longmans, Green.

Rogers, Everett M, William B. Hart, and Yoshitaka Miike. 2002. "Edward T. Hall and the History of Intercultural Communication: The United States and Japan." *Keio Communication Review* 24: 3–26.

Romney-Wegner, Judith. 1982. "Islamic and Talmudic Jurisprudence: The Four Roots of Islamic Law and Their Talmudic Counterparts." *American Journal of Legal History* 26: 25–71.

Rook, Dennis W. 1985. "The Ritual Dimension of Consumer Behavior." *Journal of Consumer Research* 12: 251–64.

Rosenberg, Howard, and Charles Feldman. 2008. *No Time to Think: The Menace of Media Speed and the 24-Hour News Cycle.* New York: Continuum.

Rothenbuhler, Eric W. 2005. "The Church of the Cult of the Individual." In *Media Anthropology*, edited by Eric W. Rothenbuhler and Mihai Coman, 91–100. Thousand Oaks, CA: Sage.

Rothkop, David. 1997. "In Praise of Cultural Imperialism? Effects of Globalization on Culture." *Foreign Policy* 107: 38–53.

Roy, Olivier. 2008. "Globalized Islam: The Search for a New Ummah." In *The Globalization Reader*, 3rd ed., edited by Frank J. Lechne and John Boli, 364–69. Malden, MA: Blackwell.

Rubin, Barnett R. 2002. *Blood on the Doorstep: The Politics of Preventive Action.* Washington, DC: Brookings Institution.

Rupke, Heidi N., and Grant Blank. 2009. "'Country Roads' to Globalization: Sociological Models for Understanding American Popular Music in China." *Journal of Popular Culture* 42: 126–46.

Sadowsky, George. 1996. "The Internet Society and Developing Countries." *OnTheInternet*, November/December, 23–29. http://www.isoc.org/oti/articles/1196/sadowsky.html.

Saikal, Amin. 2003. *Islam and the West: Conflict or Cooperation?* New York: Palgrave Macmillan.

Sandon, Emma. 2000. "Projecting Africa: Two British Travel Films of the 1920s." In *Cultural Encounters: Representing "Otherness,"* edited by Elizabeth Hallam and Brian V. Street, 108–47. London: Routledge.

Scarre, Chris, and Brian M. Fagan. 2003. *Ancient Civilizations.* 2nd ed. Upper Saddle River, NJ: Prentice Hall.

Schacht, Joseph. 1950. "Foreign Elements in Ancient Islamic Law." *Journal of Comparative Legislation and International Law,* 3rd ser., 32: 9–17.

Schiller, Herbert, I. 1976. *Communications and Cultural Domination.* Armonk, NY: Sharpe.

Schmidt, Leigh E. 1997. *Consumer Rites: The Buying and Selling of American Holidays.* Princeton, NJ: Princeton University Press.

Schultze, Quentin J. 1991. *Televangelism and American Culture: The Business of Popular Religion.* Eugene, OR: Wipf and Stock.

Scott, Bruce R. 2001. "The Great Divide in the Global Village." *Foreign Affairs* 80: 160–77.

Scrase, Timothy J. 2002. "Television, the Middle Classes and the Transformation of Cultural Identities in West Bengal, India." *International Communication Gazette* 64: 323–42.

Seabrook, Jeremy. 1996. *The Myth of the Market: Promises and Illusions.* Montreal, ON: Black Rose Books.

Seeger, Pete. 1958. "The Steel Drum: A New Folk Instrument." *Journal of American Folklore* 71: 52–57.

Shayegan, Daryush. 1997. *Cultural Schizophrenia: Islamic Societies Confronting the West.* Translated by John Howe. Syracuse, NY: Syracuse University Press.

Sherrow, Victoria. 2006. *Encyclopedia of Hair: A Cultural History.* Westport, CT: Greenwood.

Sigel, Lisa Z. 2000. "Filth in the Wrong People's Hands: Postcards and the Expansion of Pornography in Britain and the Atlantic World, 1880–1914." *Journal of Social History* 33: 859–96.

Singh, Jyotsna. G. 1996. *Colonial Narratives, Cultural Dialogues: Discoveries of India in the Language of Colonialism.* New York: Routledge.

Singhal, Arvind, Everett M. Rogers, and M. Mahajan. 1999. "The Gods Are Drinking Milk! Word-of-Mouth Diffusion of a Major News Event in India." *Asian Journal of Communication* 9: 86–107.

Smart, Barry. 2003. *Economy, Culture and Society.* Buckingham, England: Open University Press.

Smith, Adam. 1776. *An Inquiry into the Nature and Causes of the Wealth of Nations.* London: W. Strahan and T. Cadell.

Smith, Alex D. 1999. "The Gem Trail: Diamonds—From Angolan Mine to Third Finger Left Hand." *The Independent,* February 13. http://www.independent.co.uk/life-style/the-gem-trail-diamonds--from-angolan-mine-to-third-finger-left-hand-1070530.html.

snopes.com. 2006. "Bread and Media Circuses." *Urban Legends Reference Pages.* http://www.snopes.com/photos/gruesome/crushboy.asp.

Sollors, Werner. 1987. *Beyond Ethnicity: Consent and Descent in American Culture.* New York: Oxford University Press.

Sreberny, Anabelle. 2005. "'Not Only, but Also': Mixedness and Media." *Journal of Ethnic and Migration Studies* 31: 443–59.

"St. Croix to Welcome First Ship of the Season." 2008. http://www.caribbean-on-line.com/travel-news/cruise-news/st-croix-to-welcome-first-ship-of-the-season.html.

Standage, Tom. 1998. *The Victorian Internet: The Remarkable Story of the Telegraph and the Nineteenth Century's On-line Pioneers.* New York: Walker.

Stannard, David E. 1992. *American Holocaust; Columbus and the Conquest of the New World.* New York: Oxford University Press.

Stearns, Peter N. 2001. *Consumerism in World History: The Global Transformation of Desire.* Oxon, England: Routledge.

Stevenson, Nick. 1997. "Globalization, National Cultures and Cultural Citizenship." *Sociological Quarterly* 38: 41–66.

Strangelove, Michael. 2005. *The Empire of the Mind: Digital Piracy and the Anti-capitalist Movement.* Toronto, ON: University of Toronto Press.

Straubhaar, Joseph D. 2008. "Global, Hybrid or Multiple? Cultural Identities in the Age of Satellite TV and the Internet." *Nordicom Review* 29: 11–30.

Strizhakova, Yuliya, Robin A. Coulter, and Linda L. Prince. 2008. "Branded Products as a Passport to Global Citizenship: Perspectives from Developed and Developing Countries." *Journal of International Marketing* 16: 57–85.

Sullivan, Clayton. 2006. *Rescuing Sex from the Christians.* London: Continuum.

Sutton, Constance, R. 1987. "The Caribbeanization of New York City and the Emergence of a Transnational Socio-cultural System." In *Caribbean Life in New York City: Socio-cultural Dimensions,* edited by Constance R. Sutton and Elsa M. Chaney, 15–30. New York: Center for Migration Studies.

Szeman, Imre. 2003. "Culture and Globalization, or, the Humanities in Ruins." *CR: The New Centennial Review* 3: 91–115.

Tambe, Ashwini. 2000. "Review: Colluding Patriarchies. The Colonial Reform of Sexual Relations in India." *Feminist Studies* 26: 586–600.

Tan, Alexis S., Gerdean Tan, and Todd Gibson. 2003. "Socialization Effects of American Television on International Audiences." In *The Impact of International Television: A Paradigm Shift*, edited by Michael G. Elasmar, 29–38. Mawah, NJ: Earlbaum.

Tannahill, Reay. 1980. *Sex in History*. Briarcliff Manor, NY: Stein & Day.

Tessler, Mark. 2002. "Islam and Democracy in the Middle East: The Impact of Religious Orientations on Attitudes toward Democracy in Four Arab Countries." *Comparative Politics* 34: 337–54.

Thompson, John B. 1990. *Ideology in Mass Communication: Critical Social Theory in the Era of Mass Communication*. Stanford, CA: Stanford University Press.

Thurow, Lester. 1988. "The Information-Communications Revolution and the Global Economy." In *The Information Revolution and the Arab World: Its Impact on State and Society*, by the Emirates Center for Strategic Studies and Research, 11–35. London: British Academic Press.

Tomlinson, John. 1999. *Globalization and Culture*. Chicago: University of Chicago Press.

Toy, Crawford H. 1912. "Mohammed and the Islam of the Koran." *Harvard Theological Review* 5: 474–514.

Tritton, Arthur S. 1942. "Foreign Influences on Muslim Theology." *Bulletin of the School of Oriental and African Studies* 10: 837–42.

Trouillot, M.-R. 2003. *Global Transformations: Anthropology and the Modern World*. New York: Palgrave Macmillan.

Tylor, E. B. 1871 (1903). *Primitive Culture: Researches into the Development of Mythology Philosophy, Religion, Language, Art and Custom*. London: John Murray.

US Department of Agriculture. 2003. "A Review of US Trade Restrictions and Grain Exports." http://www.fas.usda.gov/grain/circular/1997/97–09/feature/trd_rstr.htm.

US Department of State; Bureau of Democracy, Human Rights, and Labor. 2008. "US State Department International Religious Freedom Report, 2008." http://kuwait.usembassy.gov/policy-news/irfr.html.

US Food and Drug Administration; Office of Regulatory Administration. 2007. "Import Alert IA2111—IA #21–11, 7/3/00." http://www.fda.gov/ora/fiars/ora_import_ia2111.html.

Varan, Duane. 1998. "The Cultural Erosion Metaphor and the Transcultural Impact of Media Systems." *Journal of Communication* 48: 58–85.

Vargas Llosa, Mario. 2000. "Local Cultures and Globalization." http://www.trilateral.org/annmtgs/trialog/trlgtxts/t54/var.htm.

Von Grunebaum, Gustave E. 2005. *Classical Islam: A History, 600 A.D. to 1285 A.D.* New Brunswick, NJ: Transaction.

Wagner, Roy. 1981. *The Invention of Culture*. 2nd ed. rev. Chicago: University of Chicago Press.

Wang, Wei-Ching. 2008. "A Critical Interrogation of Culture Globalisation and Hybridity: Considering Chinese Martial Arts Films as an Example." *Journal of International Communication* 14: 46–64.

Watson, James L. 2004. "Globalization in Asia: Anthropological Perspectives." In *Globalization: Culture and Education in the New Millennium*, edited by Marcelo M. Suárez-Orozco and Desirée B. Qin-Hillard, 141–72. Berkeley: University of California Press.

———. 2008. "McDonalds in Hong Kong." In *The Globalization Reader*, 3rd ed., edited by Frank J. Lechner and John Boli, 126–34. Malden, MA: Blackwell.

Webster, Frank. 2001. *Culture and Politics in the Information Age: A New Politics?* Florence, KY: Routledge.

Weems, Mason L. 1806 (2009). "A History of the Life and Death, Virtues and Exploits of General George Washington." http://xroads.virginia.edu/~cap/gw/chap2.html.

Weigle, Marta. 1989. "From Desert to Disney World: The Santa Fe Railway and the Fred Harvey Company Display the Indian Southwest." *Journal of Anthropological Research* 45: 115–37.

Wheeler, Deborah. 2000. "New Media, Globalization and Kuwaiti National Identity." *Middle East Journal* 54: 432–44.

———. 2001. "The Internet and Public Culture in Kuwait." *International Communication Gazette* 63: 187–201.

———. 2006. "The Internet and Youth Subculture in Kuwait." *Journal of Computer-Mediated Communication* 8. http://jcmc.indiana.edu/vol8/issue2/wheeler.html.

White, Leslie A. 1943 (1987). "Energy and the Evolution of Culture." In *Perspectives in Cultural Anthropology*, edited by Herbert A. Applebaum, 236–54. Albany: State University of New York Press. Originally published in *American Anthropologist*, n.s., 45.

Wilk, Richard R. 1999. "'Real Belizean Food': Building Local Identity in the Transnational Caribbean." *American Anthropologist*, n.s., 101: 244–55.

———. 2002. "Culture and Energy Consumption." In *Energy: Science, Policy, and the Pursuit of Sustainability*, edited by Robert D. Bent, Lloyd Orr, and Randall Baker, 109–30. Washington, DC: Island Press.

Willetts, David. 1994. "The Market." In *Ideas That Shape Politics*, by Michael Foley, 46–53. Manchester, England: Manchester University Press.

Winkelman, Michael. 1994. "Cultural Shock and Adaptation." *Journal of Counseling and Development* 73: 121–26.

Winseck, Dwyane R., and Robert M. Pike. 2007. *Communication and Empire: Media, Markets, and Globalization, 1860–1930*. Durham, NC: Duke University Press.

Wolf, Eric. 1982. *Europe and the People without History*. Berkeley: University of California Press.

Wood, Frances. 2002. *The Silk Road: Two Thousand Years in the Heart of Asia*. Berkeley: University of California Press.

Woolf, Greg. 1997. "Beyond Romans and Natives." *World Archaeology* 28: 339–50.

Wright-Wexman, Virginia. 1993. *Creating the Couple: Love, Marriage, and Hollywood Performance*. Princeton, NJ: Princeton University Press.

Wynbrandt, James. 2004. *A Brief History of Saudi Arabia*. New York: Facts on File.

Ye'or, Bat. 1985. *The Dhimmi: Jews and Christians under Islam*. Madison, NJ: Fairleigh Dickinson University Press.

Zahid, Dilara. 2007. "Impact of Cultural Globalization on the Upper Class Youth in Dhaka City: A Sample Study." *Bangladesh e-Journal of Sociology* 4: 1–10.

Zamora, Margarita. 1993. *Reading Columbus*. Berkeley: University of California Press.

Index

Adorno, Theodor W., 20, 81, 161
advertising, 20, 22, 23, 36, 41, 49, 58, 62,
    68–69, 84, 86, 125, 126, 155; industry,
    49; multinational, 56
Africa, 3, 19, 28, 29, 30, 36, 73, 95, 97,
    117, 158; north, 30, 138; south, 26
anthropology, 4, 12–14, 58
Augustine of Hippo, 49, 119–121

Barbados, 21, 90, 152
BBC, 25, 33, 44, 88, 115, 171
Bedouin, 93, 154
Bible, 47, 127, 128, 130; Gutenberg, 106;
    Luther's German, 106
Boas, Franz, 12, 13
Bové, José, 25
Britain, 17, 78, 88, 103, 132, 145, 149;
    Victorian, 33, 78

cargo cults, 134–135
Caribbean, 21, 26–27, 38–39, 52, 64, 68,
    90, 95, 98, 103, 152; Hindi films in,
    158; migrants, 150, 160; music, 150;
    Pirates of the, 76
Christ, Jesus, 8, 16, 28–29, 70, 71, 116,
    121, 128, 130, 146, 120
Christianity, 29, 31, 32, 46, 50, 70, 101,
    104, 117, 119, 119–122, 129–130, 137,
    139, 143–144, 145–148, 155–156;
    Christian nation, 47; church, 70–71,
    119–121

Christmas, 49, 125, 128–129
CNN, 44, 115
colonization, 26, 33, 34, 36, 37, 38, 53, 70,
    118, 122, 141–142, 149, 154, 161, 162,
    169; British, 33, 35–36, 90, 118, 119,
    157; European, 32, 54, 105; impact on
    India, 34–35; neo-colonialism, 152
Columbus, Christopher, 32, 108–109, 148
commoditization, 81, 82, 94, 96
communication, 33, 37, 44, 50, 56, 58, 63,
    64, 67, 75, 89, 112, 113, 114; culture
    and, 7, 20, 150; global, 21, 55, 88, 114,
    159, 163, 164; intercultural, 4, 13, 37,
    58, 156; interpersonal, 37; mass, 20, 32,
    33, 34, 36, 88; policies, 38, 39;
    revolution, 73; technologies, 44, 78, 88,
    89, 106–107, 108, 150;
    telecommunications, 90, 149
corporations, 22, 45, 46, 49–50, 52, 53,
    54–55, 56–59, 64, 67, 69, 72, 81, 84,
    86, 101, 102, 114, 152, 155; media, 90;
    multinational, 45, 52, 53, 55, 97, 104,
    134, 169
crusades, 45, 71, 72, 78, 142, 147, 169
culture, 1–4, 7–10, 13–15; authenticity,
    96–98, 110, 117, 123, 156–157;
    corporate, 49, 51, 52, 57–58, 62, 64, 82,
    85, 101, 104; counterculture, 101–104;
    cultural adjustment, 15; cultural
    erosion, 69, 93, 131–136; cultural
    imperialism, 37, 39–42, 55, 159, 169;

About the Author

Dr. Shaheed Nick Mohammed was born in Trinidad and Tobago, a small island nation in the Southern Caribbean. He is associate professor of communication at Pennsylvania State University, Altoona. He holds a PhD in communication with an emphasis in intercultural communication from the University of New Mexico in Albuquerque. He has the distinction of being the first graduate of that program in 1998. At the University of New Mexico he worked with the late Everett M. Rogers (a key figure in the development of the field of communications in the United States and worldwide) and with intercultural notables like John Condon. He also had seminars with one of the founding fathers of intercultural communication, Edward T. Hall. He has lived and worked in many countries and has an abiding interest in the roles of media and communication in the lives of people around the world. He has published numerous articles and book chapters in the fields of culture, communication, and health.

CPSIA information can be obtained at www.ICGtesting.com
Printed in the USA
269308BV00002B/1/P